DATE DUE FOR RETURN

ORGANISATION FOR ECONOMIC CO-OPERATION AND DEVELOPMENT

ORGANISATION FOR ECONOMIC CO-OPERATION AND DEVELOPMENT

Pursuant to Article 1 of the Convention signed in Paris on 14th December 1960, and which came into force on 30th September 1961, the Organisation for Economic Co-operation and Development (OECD) shall promote policies designed:

- to achieve the highest sustainable economic growth and employment and a rising standard of living in Member countries, while maintaining financial stability, and thus to contribute to the development of the world economy;
- to contribute to sound economic expansion in Member as well as non-member countries in the process of economic development; and
- to contribute to the expansion of world trade on a multilateral, non-discriminatory basis in accordance with international obligations.

The original Member countries of the OECD are Austria, Belgium, Canada, Denmark, France, Germany, Greece, Iceland, Ireland, Italy, Luxembourg, the Netherlands, Norway, Portugal, Spain, Sweden, Switzerland, Turkey, the United Kingdom and the United States. The following countries became Members subsequently through accession at the dates indicated hereafter: Japan (28th April 1964), Finland (28th January 1969), Australia (7th June 1971) and New Zealand (29th May 1973). The Commission of the European Communities takes part in the work of the OECD (Article 13 of the OECD Convention).

Publié en français sous le titre :
LES FEMMES ET LE CHANGEMENT STRUCTUREL
NOUVELLES PERSPECTIVES

FOREWORD

Sweeping structural changes are taking place today in all the OECD countries, in terms of both the economy and society as a whole. Rapid advances in technology, increasing competition, and the development of new behaviour patterns and attitudes can all stimulate economic growth and social progress, provided that systems and individuals have the capacity to adapt.

The OECD has been entrusted with the task of studying the structural reforms implemented in its Member countries. In 1990 the Secretary-General appointed a Group of Experts to examine the interrelations between the process of structural adjustment and the integration of women into the economy, and to suggest priorities for future action. The members of the Group were Ms. Sumiko Iwao, Ms. Joyce Miller, Ms. Maria de Lourdes Pintasilgo, Ms. Liisa Rantalaiho, Mr. Francis Blanchard and Mr. Günther Schmid, M. Francis Blanchard chaired the Group, whose report is presented in the first part of this publication.

At the same time, the Secretariat prepared a report analysing the impact of employment restructuring on women during the 1980s. Three consultants – Ms. Friederike Maier, Ms. Susan Christopherson and Mr. Günther Schmid – and the OECD Working Party on the Role of Women in the Economy contributed to the report. The increasing presence of women in the labour force, the expansion of part-time work, the development of a service economy and the slowdown in public sector growth are factors that warrant the reappraisal of equal opportunity policies contained in the second part of this volume. Françoise Coré (Directorate for Education, Employment, Labour and Social Affairs) edited the final text of the report, which is published on the responsibility of the Secretary-General of the OECD.

TABLE OF CONTENTS

Part One

SHAPING STRUCTURAL CHANGE: THE ROLE OF WOMEN
Report by a High-level Group of Experts to the Secretary-General

Part Two

WOMEN AND EMPLOYMENT RESTRUCTURING
Report by the Secretariat

Chapter 1

OVERVIEW

Chapter 2

PATTERNS OF LABOUR MARKET PARTICIPATION

Chapter 3

PART-TIME EMPLOYMENT

Chapter 4
THE SERVICE SECTOR: A LABOUR MARKET FOR WOMEN

Chapter 5
WOMEN IN THE PUBLIC SECTOR

Chapter 6

EQUAL OPPORTUNITIES POLICIES ON THE LABOUR MARKET IN THE 1980s

Part One

SHAPING STRUCTURAL CHANGE: THE ROLE OF WOMEN

Report by a High-level Group of Experts to the Secretary-General

PREFACE

OECD countries will be faced in the 1990s with the multiple challenges of increasing globalisation and rapid technological advance and, in some countries, profound demographic changes. These require that economies and societies be both adaptable and dynamic. Structural adjustment and structural policies will need to ensure that the pattern of growth is a sustainable one, on economic and also, most importantly, on social grounds.

Despite considerable economic progress in OECD countries, a number of societal issues remain matters of concern. This applies particularly to the persistent inequality of opportunities for women. Inability to progress faster in this area also jeopardises progress in other areas, because it represents a failure to benefit generally and fully from the enormous contribution that women can make to economic growth and social improvement. Major rigidities in the socio-economic system need to be addressed. It is hence for these reasons that a high-level Group of Experts was invited to examine the interrelations between the process of structural adjustment and the integration of women in the economy in the 1990s.

M. Francis Blanchard, Special Advisor to the Secretary General of the United Nations and former Director General of the International Labour Organisation chaired the Group. His depth and breadth of experience, as well as his personal qualities, proved to be invaluable. The other members of the Group also brought to bear their diverse experience in labour relations, international affairs, the academic world and that of public policy, together with a rich knowledge of the changing economic and social role of women. The members served in their individual capacities: their report commits neither the organisations to which they belong nor OECD governments.

The report makes an important contribution to addressing a complex and much debated issue from a new perspective. It is noteworthy, given the diverse cultural and intellectual backgrounds represented, that the report was unanimously agreed. The report establishes clearly that the obstacles inhibiting fuller participation by women in the economy are structural in nature. Importantly, the directions for action that are indicated would bring forward progress that, in most cases, would accrue not only to women but more widely to the functioning of the whole socio-economic system.

The report is brought to the particular attention of OECD Member governments, for it promises to be a valuable input to the OECD's continuing work on structural adjustment. It is also directly relevant to making operational the New Framework for Labour Market Policies. The OECD Working Party on the Role of Women in the Economy has a special interest in the work of the Group, which builds on their past efforts; the report will undoubtedly stimulate their future deliberations. Indeed, I am confident that the report will stimulate discussion in many groups – including in business and in the trade unions, as well as in the media, community organisations, and women's groups.

Jean-Claude Paye
Secretary-General of the OECD

LETTER OF TRANSMITTAL

Dear Mr. Paye,

Last year you invited me to chair a High-Level Group of Experts with the challenging task of examining the interrelations between the process of structural adjustment and the integration of women into OECD economies in the 1990s. It is with great pleasure that I submit to you the report of that Group.

The Group decided that it was important to focus on structural issues with medium- to long-term implications. It is my personal belief that we are heading towards a different society, a new society. The report is based on the Group's strong conviction that effective structural adjustment, including the social transformation needed to achieve economic growth and social cohesion in the 1990s and beyond, depends upon empowering women to play a greater role in shaping structural change. That role implies increased participation in both employment and decision-making structures. The report indicates the changes needed to achieve that goal. Undoubtedly the task is not easy. It will require major efforts and a strong commitment.

Women's experiences are a mirror to the future. Women experience first hand the extent to which the current institutional framework – including labour market structures and the social infrastructure – has failed to keep pace with the changing technological, economic, social and political realities. In adjusting their own lives – to juggle labour market participation with family and other responsibilities – they give us insight into where future social and economic adjustment is needed. Women are well placed and have a definite interest in furthering the process of change – change that will also enhance men's choices and benefit society as a whole.

The report is in several sections. Each is headed with a ''statement'' – which defines an objective – and concludes with a set of related ''directions for action''. Together the statements and directions for action provide an overall policy response to the problem the Group has examined. A multiplicity of different players – from governments, unions, employers, international organisations and the media, to women's groups, community organisations and individual men and women – are involved in turning that response into reality.

The report carries our unanimous approval. The Experts' diverse outstanding professional experience and cultural backgrounds proved an invaluable asset in deliberating on a complex and far-reaching theme. Preparation of the report itself inspired our understanding of co-operative decision-making, and illustrates the richness and innovation that stems from drawing together a variety of different perspectives in the pursuit of a common goal.

The analytical report on women and employment restructuring prepared by the Secretariat provided us with useful background information. We would like to express our appreciation to the Secretariat team for their invaluable and unfailing support.

Francis Blanchard
President
Group of Experts on Women
and Structural Change in the 1990s

Geneva, November 1991

MEMBERS OF THE GROUP*

Francis BLANCHARD (Chairman)
Sumiko IWAO
Joyce MILLER
Maria de Lourdes PINTASILGO
Liisa RANTALAIHO
Günther SCHMID

SECRETARIAT

Françoise CORÉ
Sally WASHINGTON

---

* *Francis Blanchard* is former Director-General of the International Labour Organisation. *Sumiko Iwao* is Professor of Social Psychology, Keio University, Japan. *Joyce Miller* is Vice-President of the Amalgamated Clothing and Textile Workers Union, United States. *Maria de Lourdes Pintasilgo* is former Prime Minister, Portugal. *Liisa Rantalaiho* is Professor of Sociology and Psychology of work, University of Tampere, Finland. *Günther Schmid* is Professor of Political Economics, Free University of Berlin, Germany.

AN ACTIVE SOCIETY SHAPING STRUCTURAL CHANGE

An "active society"

An "active society" has been defined by this Group as their vision for the future and a guiding principle for structural reform. An active society is one characterised by opportunity and choice, cohesion and solidarity. It is responsive to changing social and economic needs and enables its members to influence the direction of change.

Enhancing "activity" goes beyond attempts to achieve full employment or increased labour force participation. It means taking bold steps to encourage economic and social participation by recognising the multiple areas of activity – market and non-market – that individuals are engaged in, and acknowledging the growing interdependence between those areas of activity.

Establishing an active society requires a long-term commitment. The future starts today. Societies create in the present the structures within which they will operate tomorrow.

Women as economic actors

Realising an active society demands a new perspective on women as economic actors. This report argues that the smooth functioning of OECD societies and their supporting economies in the 1990s and beyond depends on recognising women as principal economic actors and enabling them to realise their untapped potential. It challenges the traditional assumption that equity and efficiency are mutually exclusive outcomes that have to be traded off against each other. Women are not a problem for the economy. On the contrary, the solution to economic problems depends on enhancing women's economic role. Women are a key resource that is currently under-utilised, both quantitatively and qualitatively. The report stresses, however, that meeting the twin goals of equity and efficiency requires significant changes to the "system". Those changes represent a major structural adjustment challenge.

Structural adjustment

This report describes structural change as a global and dynamic process which profoundly modifies economies and societies. Economic, technical, social, political changes interact; the outcome of these interactions is what defines structural change. The various aspects of change are interdependent and cannot be considered in isolation.

The OECD approach to structural adjustment has developed over time. An initial focus on economic management has evolved to include social transformation as an integral element of the adjustment process. The communique of the 1991 OECD Council Meeting at Ministerial Level devoted a specific section to the "social field". This Group's report contributes to a broad definition and approach to structural adjustment. Structural change is not a predetermined development to which individuals have to adapt passively. It can be shaped according to societies' priorities. Social innovation – building new institutions and establishing rules of the game – is the process through which society both accommodates new constraints and possibilities emerging from technical and economic change, and responds to the changing needs of its members.

Effective structural adjustment depends upon all individuals, both women and men, playing an active role in shaping structural change. Women's opportunities to influence the adjustment process have so far been minimal and their share in the benefits brought by structural change limited. Empowering women to become active agents shaping structural change requires a redefinition of the inter-relationships between the social, economic and political factors that currently inhibit women's participation and life choices. It means applying a new perspective to the causes of inequality.

The need for a systemic approach

In the 1970s and 1980s, "women's issues" were largely defined in terms of discrimination. The key concern was the elimination of direct discrimination. Legislation was seen as the most appropriate tool for "protecting" women's interests and ensuring legal equality. Equal opportunity programmes designed to remove barriers and to "open the door" to labour market participation were introduced to complement anti-discrimination legislation.

Although a necessary condition for achieving gender equality, the limited impact of anti-discrimination and equal opportunity measures points to the systemic nature of gender-based inequalities, and the need for a systemic solution. That solution lies in applying an integrated approach to institutional change aimed at addressing the contradictions and tensions generated at the interface between the household, the community and employment structures. Clearly, the rewards of change will not accrue exclusively to women. Men's life choices will also be enhanced and society as a whole will benefit from such an integrated policy strategy.

The report identifies key areas where those tensions might be tackled. Compatibility between family responsibilities and labour market participation and shared roles between men and women are central issues for structural adjustment. They have been given high prominence by the Group. Occupational segregation and flexibility in employment have been identified as two other priority areas influencing women's role in structural adjustment. They need to be addressed in the context of efforts to achieve compatibility between family and employment and shared gender roles. Furthermore, valuing diversity in society and enabling women to take greater responsibility for decision-making will accelerate desired progress. The important role of international co-operation in the light of increased globalisation is also underlined.

Seizing opportunities for change

The climate of structural change affecting OECD economies and societies provides a favourable context in which to tackle age old problems and their modern manifestations.

Structural change offers a foot in the door – it opens up opportunities for further change which can be seized and built on. However, change also carries associated risks which need to be acknowledged and dealt with. Opportunities to enhance both economic efficiency and gender equity in the 1990s have to take into account the multiple influences of the structural forces at play and specific circumstances in each country. There is significant diversity amongst OECD countries, in terms of both the economic integration of women and industrial, labour market, social and political structures. This report does not dwell on the differences between countries; the nature of the problems and the objectives to be pursued are strikingly similar everywhere. Factors such as demographic and technological change, and the growing internationalisation and tertiarisation of OECD economies, are treated as contextual variables.

FAMILY AND EMPLOYMENT: UPDATING THE GENDER CONTRACT

More women – and also more men – are facing dual and often conflicting labour market and family responsibilities. *Ensuring the compatibility of employment and family commitments within individual lives* **is a major challenge emerging from the process of structural change.** *Shared family and employment roles* **will increase the potential labour force, promote a better utilisation of human capital, enhance gender equality, and improve quality of life.**

The "social contract" and gender

Life is organised around an implicit "social contract". Its two components, the gender contract and the employment contract define the current division of family and labour market roles. Within the gender contract women assume the bulk of family care and domestic functions, while men are ascribed primary responsibility for the family's economic or financial well-being. The employment contract reinforces this division of labour by defining as its norm, the sole breadwinner in continuous full-time lifelong employment.

The social contract conflicts with the new reality of men's and women's lives. Dual earner and single adult families are increasingly common while households with full time homemakers have declined dramatically. Female labour market participation has multiplied in response to women's high employment aspirations, the economic needs of families and demands from the economy for more labour. Most women are now forced to juggle household and family demands with involvement in paid work structures designed to fit male employment patterns. Men miss out on the emotional rewards of the care and development of children because they are similarly constrained by the gender-based division of household and employment responsibilities.

The need for adjustment policies

Despite the obvious need for a redistribution of household and caring tasks – to match the reallocation of employment responsibilities – the gender contract remains relatively static. Women have had to adjust their own lives to cope with conflicting employment and family roles. Those with financial resources employ someone else to fulfil part of their family responsibilities. Others delay or forego having children. Demographic trends mean that many women are confronted with increasing pressure to care for elderly relatives. Both the care of children and adult dependants puts constraints on women's labour market participation and career progression.

Specific features of taxation and social policies act as impediments to shared family and employment responsibilities. In spite of other efforts to encourage women's labour market participation, policies based on the sole breadwinner two-adult family – such as joint-income testing for social security benefits and dependent spouse allowances – have disincentive effects on women's employment and men's ability to play a greater role in family care.

Peripheral adjustments to the employment contract – such as part-time work – have in most cases done little to modify employment norms or gender roles. Because women often "choose" part-time work for family reasons, employment is seen as their secondary or peripheral activity. Most women working part-time do not experience a corresponding reduction in their domestic obligations. Evidence for some countries suggests that women working full-time are more able to transfer some domestic responsibilities to other family members. Ironically, the "double burden" may then be more pronounced for women working part-time. In its present context, part-time work may entrench the traditional gender-based division of market and non-market activities.

Compromise strategies are not solutions; they only deal with the symptoms of problems. The real cause – the traditional gender-based division of market and non-market activities and the incompatibility of employment and family responsibilities – remains intact. Failure to address those conflicts has high costs – increased stress for individuals, particularly women; possible declining quality of care for dependants; increased family breakdowns; as well as reduced productivity, increased absenteeism and staff turnover amongst workers facing competing family responsibilities.

Fundamental adjustment is required to resolve the current contradictions generated by the social contract. This means enhancing compatibility between domestic and employment responsibilities both on a daily basis and across the lifecycle, and developing a new institutional and social framework that reflects the changing labour force profile, and supports equal choices for men and women to combine employment with family responsibilities.

Flexibility in working time

Men as well as women are increasingly unwilling to sacrifice family time and quality of life for a job that places unreasonable demands on their time. A reassessment of the time commitments demanded of workers is needed. Rigid adherence to the full-time employment model inhibits the development of a new "worker profile" and blocks attempts at a new distribution of household and employment responsibilities. The inability or unwillingness to work long hours should not be seen as indicative of a worker's lack of commitment to employment.

Vertical career mobility is associated with pressure to work longer than regular hours. In most OECD countries, the working life span is now compressed into a relatively short period due to increased time spent in education and earlier retirement. The critical time for career advancement typically coincides with the period when children are young and the demands of family care are greatest. Women's domestic responsibilities create enormous obstacles to their ability to compete on the labour market. The "mommy track" describes the extent to which women with family responsibilities are slotted into separate and less lucrative career tracks. The same workplace commitments similarly distance men from sharing the rewards of household and caring functions.

New employment models need to be implemented which allow men and women to combine a career with family commitments while maintaining their quality of life. Schemes that allow workers to work reduced or flexible hours without changing jobs would enable men and women to remain in employment, and maintain their career progression, while assuming responsibility for family care. Flexibility in working time might take a number of other forms; intermediate part-time work with the option to return to full-time hours, flexitime, job-sharing, or the ability to "capitalise" time over the working week. Maintenance of seniority and work-related benefits are crucial factors in the success of any of these options. An overall reduction in working time might also have positive impacts on men's and women's ability to combine family and employment responsibilities.

Total "working time" for an individual includes the time spent in paid work and time spent fulfilling domestic commitments. In practice, flexibility in working time usually means women adjusting their domestic schedules to take on part-time employment. Real compatibility between family and employment responsibilities depends on enhanced flexibility in both working hours and in the organisation of household and caring tasks, supported by an adapted social infrastructure.

Career breaks

Continuous linear career progression is becoming less common as both men and women take breaks from employment at various points throughout their working lives. Time spent outside the paid workforce – whether for family care, travel, education or community and civic activities – should be viewed as opportunities for skills development and personal enrichment rather than periods of "inactivity". The interpersonal and organisational skills acquired in family care and child development have definite labour market value. Career breaks should not jeopardise an individual's future employment opportunities. On the contrary, when they are short and for a specific purpose, they should enhance career prospects.

Women now take relatively short breaks out of the labour market and their career attachment is increasingly strong. In spite of that, institutional arrangements and social attitudes remain tied to the past when family formation typically signalled long-term or permanent withdrawal from employment. The result is that women commonly have difficulty returning to employment that matches the level they enjoyed prior to taking leave. Career interruptions – however short – can still have long-term negative effects on earnings and income security.

Maternity leave is crucial for women workers, as are parental leave provisions for both male and female employees. However, when parental leave is only available to women, or chiefly used by women, it may also be used to justify employer discrimination against female employees. Schemes that include incentives for men to take family leave would encourage a more equal division of household and family tasks. Incorporating some form of earnings replacement, and maintaining superannuation payments and employment protection, increases the viability of parental leave for both parents.

Mechanisms for maintaining skills during prolonged leave or updating skills on re-entry to employment would help to counteract the current costs associated with career interruption. Employers providing reinsertion training and competence bridges can ensure the maintenance of a skilled and flexible workforce. Maintaining links with employees on leave has other advantages, such as having access to a supply of skilled workers who can be called on to meet short-term demands for additional staff.

Social infrastructures

Catering to the needs of families and workers depends on a range of social and personal services. Women still shoulder the bulk of child and dependant care as well as domestic tasks. Alternatives for providing these services would free women to compete on the labour market. Collective responsibility for social support networks must be recognised on a par with the accepted social responsibility for the supply and mainte-nance of transportation, communication and utility networks.

Experience in some countries suggests a high correlation between women's labour market participation and the public provision of family services. Other models may prove to be just as successful. These could include provision by private institutions operating on a market basis, community based co-operation, or some innovative mix of funders and providers. In all cases governments have an important role to play, especially in setting the ground rules, encouraging initiatives from various actors and facilitating the condi-tions under which they operate. The accessibility, comprehensiveness and quality of services depends on a co-ordinated approach.

Employers are discovering the multiple benefits to be gained from helping employees to meet their family obligations – especially the care of children and elderly relatives. Large enterprises have the resources to provide workplace creches, to sponsor school holiday programmes, mobile nursing care, or include childcare payments in remuneration packages. Small or medium-size enterprises can engage in joint ventures. All of these initiatives could be enhanced by state support or co-ordination. The pay-offs for employers range from reductions in absenteeism, decreased staff turnover and savings on associated recruitment costs, to an enhanced corporate reputation.

Services providing for the care and education of children require special considera-tion. It is generally agreed that access to employment for parents with very young children depends on the availability of comprehensive childcare services. There is a growing and equally important need for school holiday and after school care. School schedules have a profound impact on the nature and extent of women's labour market participation. When schools close at lunchtime on the assumption that a mid-day meal is provided for children at home, when the school day finishes in the early afternoon, or when schools close mid-week, parents are forced to find alternative care arrangements or to modify their own working hours.

Holiday and out-of-school programmes would also address growing concerns about the extent to which children are left either unattended or inadequately cared for in the gap between school hours and the end of the working day, or during holiday periods. Existing educational resources, including school buildings, libraries and other materials can be put to better use in the context of these programmes.

Demands from the growing number of elderly for care and services will also need to be urgently addressed – especially given the pressures on state-funded income support for senior citizens. Care of the very old or the very frail can require greater time commitments over a longer period than care of children – and typically involves increasing, rather than decreasing, levels of dependency. Enhancing opportunities for older people to maintain their social participation is an added consideration.

Other elements of the general social infrastructure – including transport services, the proximity of housing to the workplace, housing that fits diverse family types, and convenience of shop opening hours and services – also require revision in the light of changing family structures, and women's increasing labour market participation. Establishing "family friendly" urban environments is a key factor in combating increasing conflict and social disintegration in urban settings.

The social construction of gender

Women cannot fully respond to or play a major part in shaping structural change unless men's life patterns are also modified. Encouraging men and women to organise their lives differently by changing the structures in which they operate is likely to facilitate behavioural and attitudinal change.

Young people need to be well equipped for their future employment and family responsibilities. That will require further adjustments to the structures that mediate the social construction of gender. Attempts to remove gender bias from education have tended to concentrate on widening girls' employment horizons. Preparing boys for their future responsibilities as parents and partners is equally important.

[handwritten: Mod: is the Women's liberations something which goes across free market capitalism? Ct<p]

Directions for Action

Eliminate the sole breadwinner two-adult family as the primary norm for the range of taxation and social security policies.

Encourage men to take advantage of the opportunities to increase their participation in family care.

Develop systems that enable workers to make temporary exits from employment, or to modify their working hours, without sacrificing their career development prospects.

Seek innovative ways of providing essential household and caring services, and adjust the social infrastructure, to support women's increasing labour market participation, and diversity in family types.

Utilise the media and other forms of information dissemination to promote public acceptance of men and women as equal partners sharing family and employment responsibilities.

Conveying the universal benefits of shared family and employment responsibilities will develop community awareness and public acceptance of the revised gender contract. The media is a powerful tool for promoting positive images of shared gender roles and the new reality of household and family life. Information campaigns sponsored by government or private sector institutions can give specific visibility to certain aspects of change – such as the rewards available to men through playing a greater role in childcare and development.

OCCUPATIONAL SEGREGATION: ENHANCING CHOICE AND UPGRADING OCCUPATIONS

Occupational structures and the skills content of many jobs are undergoing profound changes. This creates opportunities for reducing occupational segregation and pay discrimination which are sources of labour market rigidity and gender inequality. *Broadening occupational choice and upgrading occupations will facilitate the development and efficient allocation of human resources and promote more equitable rewards.*

The gender segregation of occupations

The vast majority of workers are employed in occupations where their own gender predominates. The gender segregation of occupations persists in all OECD countries, despite dramatic increases in women's level of education, labour force participation, and attachment to employment.

Gender segregation creates a major labour market rigidity. It inhibits the smooth reallocation of workers from surplus to deficit sectors, thereby contributing to unemployment, short-term skills mismatches and longer-term skills gaps. The optimal use and development of the potential pool of human resources is subsequently constrained. Where the numbers of skilled young people entering the labour market are declining, the pressure to respond to changing labour market demands will impact mainly on the adult labour force. Adjustment will be limited by the degree of current segregation in the adult labour force.

Gender segregation is also a source of labour market inequalities. Different values and remuneration are attached to men's and women's jobs. Most female-dominated occupations are characterised by low status, poor remuneration and limited potential for skills acquisition, promotion or training. Some women's jobs are "economic ghettos" where low pay and benefits are the expected rewards even after long tenure. Women's aspirations are blocked and their talents are wasted because their choice of occupation is limited to a sub-set of options.

There are growing contradictions between the characteristics of women's jobs and those of their female incumbents. New generations of women are well educated and have continuous labour force attachment, yet many are still employed in either "unskilled" occupations – such as sales or personal services – or in skilled "female" occupations which offer relatively limited prospects for career advancement – such as nursing or teaching. Even in "mixed" occupations, women cluster at the lower levels or perform tasks that are consistent with traditional female roles.

The changing composition of occupations

Occupational structures and the content of many jobs are undergoing profound changes. New technologies, changing demand, innovative methods of production and work organisation, and modern decision-making structures all contribute to the redefinition of jobs and a new occupational composition of employment. In many cases occupational definitions and classifications are being revised. The redefinition of skills and the relative value of different types of skills is central to this exercise. This dynamic process offers a real opportunity to dismantle current gender-based occupational segregation.

To maintain a competitive edge in the 1990s, OECD economies will have to rely on their comparative advantage, that is their capacity for innovation and high quality production of goods and services. A highly qualified, functionally flexible and mobile workforce is therefore essential. Investment in skills upgrading is crucial. As an under-utilised labour market resource, women are an obvious target for upskilling. The demand for skilled labour will improve women's earnings capacity.

Despite the promising longer-term outlook, the immediate future is less rosy. Significant job losses are the inevitable outcome of economic restructuring in most OECD countries. This affects mainly unskilled workers, many of whom are older women with limited basic education and few transferable skills. Another critical concern is the exceptionally low status of some traditional female occupations. Some of these occupations – especially in the personal and social services – will continue to be growing employment sectors. Improvements in the status and conditions of these occupations are unlikely while the effects of past discrimination continue to distort market signals.

The current climate of structural change offers an ideal opportunity to challenge the inefficiencies and inequities mediated by the gender segregation of the workforce. Broadening women's occupational choice, upgrading female occupations, reducing organisational hierarchies and introducing more mobility in women's professional lives are directions through which the most detrimental effects of gender-based occupational segregation can be eliminated.

Enhancing occupational choice

Women's occupational choices are currently constrained. This impacts on their labour market and economic status as well as on their working and living conditions. Lifelong learning offers opportunities to enhance women's occupational choice. Initiatives related to initial education and further education and training need to be refocused to promote lifelong learning.

Initial education

Initial education is a major determinant of future occupational orientation. Gender inequalities in initial education now relate more to the type than the quantity of education received. In many countries girls surpass boys in their participation and performance in general education, yet their occupational choice remains relatively limited, mainly because general education tends to lack career orientation. Boys' initial education is more likely to be employment-oriented. Where girls do receive vocational training at the initial level, they are channelled into a narrow range of traditionally female occupations.

Broadening girls' occupational horizons depends on making the content and transmission of technical subjects more attractive and relevant. Skilled occupations require at least some understanding of basic technologies. Many girls tend to reject scientific subjects and therefore fail to acquire the prerequisites for specialised training. Girls are often discouraged from technical subjects by gender-biased teaching methods and curricula. Technical occupations also have to resolve an image problem if they want to attract more women. Research on the computer science field suggests that even though girls are highly attracted to computer technologies, many overlook a professional career in an area which they perceive to be male-dominated. There is considerable scope for occupations and industries to forge links with educational institutions to promote potential career opportunities. Attracting girls to scientific and technical fields is essential for avoiding critical skills gaps anticipated for the future.

Labour market recognition of the skills acquired through general education would also help to alleviate a growing "skills mismatch". While general education falls somewhat short in providing students with technical skills, it does instil a range of abilities – abstract thinking, problem-solving, interpersonal communication – that have an increasing value in the workplace. A report prepared for OECD Ministers of Education (*High Quality Education and Training for All*, 1992) states that "modern work processes imply the fostering of a broad range of human capabilities including the creative, co-operative, informed, versatile, analytical and open-minded." General education develops these skills and competencies which most girls therefore acquire. In contrast, purely vocationally-oriented initial education – which mainly boys receive – may be deficient in some of the key skills required in the modern workplace.

In the future, initial education will focus on providing a solid foundation for lifelong learning and developing an individual propensity and capacity for further learning. Initial education should equip all young people with a broad base of generic skills – literacy, numeracy, and interpersonal skills – all of which will be recognised as important labour market assets. In that context initial education would no longer determine or restrict occupational choices in different ways for girls and boys. It would also extend the opportunities to continuously redefine initial choice by developing an ability to participate in further education and training.

Further education and training

A general skills upgrading of the adult labour force is part of the process of modernisation being undertaken in OECD economies. Enabling women to take advantage of further education and training programmes will be a key factor in avoiding potential skills gaps. Women should be encouraged to train for occupations in growth areas which offer employment prospects and good earnings capacities.

Currently, women are less likely than men to benefit from further education and training programmes. Fiscal and political constraints mean that public training programmes usually give priority to acute short-term needs – typically unemployment. Women tend to miss out on public training opportunities because they are under-represented in unemployment registers and among unemployment benefit recipients.

Women are also more likely to miss out on enterprise training. Enterprises generally offer training on the basis of seniority and qualifications. Unskilled workers or workers in non-standard employment – many of whom are women – are often ineligible for enterprise training programmes. Employers' perceptions of the likelihood that the worker once trained will remain with the firm is also important. Despite women's increasing labour force attachment, the expected returns on investment in training female workers are still perceived to be lower than the returns on training male workers. Women's employment tends to be concentrated in small enterprises which lack the resources for comprehensive human resource development.

Stimulating enterprise training for women means promoting its potential benefits to employers. Employers who select trainees from part of the available pool are not making the best use of the human resources at their disposal. As the demand for skilled labour increases, their competitive position is likely to suffer. The expected returns on training are manifold. Providing training is an essential factor in maintaining a skilled and functionally flexible workforce. Human resource development and internal promotions enhance staff stability and employee attachment to the firm, which should be weighed against the costs and risks associated with external recruitment. Efficient investment in training depends on the rejection of outdated assumptions. The assumption that women are more likely than men to quit their jobs may create a vicious circle wherein women who are denied access to training and promotion are encouraged to leave.

The introduction of some form of "training entitlement" could ensure a more even spread of further education and training opportunities. Training entitlements are consistent with lifelong learning. It can be argued that each individual has a right to a certain amount of education and training across the lifecycle. This would enable those who received little initial education or vocational training – often middle-aged and older women – to have a "second chance" or to "catch up" at some later point. It would also be instrumental in side-stepping rigid eligibility criteria that have hitherto excluded women from opportunities for further learning. Entitlement models already exist in some OECD countries.

Developing innovative training models that fit women's daily schedules and life-cycle patterns will facilitate their participation in training programmes. Locally-based training initiatives are more accessible to women whose geographical mobility and time flexibility is limited by domestic and family responsibilities. Training options such as part-time courses, community-based initiatives, correspondence courses or distance learning should be developed. Modular training – training courses broken into self-contained and individually assessed training modules – offers more flexibility in the timing of skills development. Including childcare in the design of training courses greatly enhances their viability for women with young children.

Training has to cater to a broad range of needs. Some women lack initial education – including literacy skills – and require basic entry level qualifications. Women rejoining the labour market after a period of leave may require "bridging" courses – to update their skills and to rebuild their self-confidence. Women following the growing trend towards changing occupations at various points across the lifecycle require extensive training to acquire the skills needed in the new occupation.

Modern labour markets demand functionally flexible workers with skills that can be applied across industries rather than those that are firm- or even industry-specific. There is a growing need to increase the transferable skill level of the working population. It is imperative that all training is appropriately accredited to allow the transfer of skills and qualifications within and across industries. When women receive enterprise training, it is more likely to be informal on-the-job training rather than formal in-house or employer-supported external training. Informal on-the-job training is important for skills acquisition but those skills are rarely recognised or marketable outside the firm. Formal training is more likely to provide portable skills that have a positive impact on future earnings. Skills and competencies are also gained informally through socialisation and household management. Improving the transparency of skills is necessary to increase efficiency in the allocation of labour.

Breaking the cycle of under-investment in female training will require the development of a more comprehensive co-ordinated training environment. While individual employers could be pressed to provide specific job-skill training, an increase in investment in general training demands a more collective effort. Unions are involved in identifying training needs for different categories of workers. Governments will need to act as a catalyst by promoting co-operation – between enterprises, between industries, between industry and training providers, and between the social partners – to set standards, to plan future skills needs and to negotiate how these needs might be met. A collective approach to the provision of training means sharing both the costs and the rewards, and recognising the relative ability of individuals to pay for their own skills development. Women should be able to share in the rewards without having to bear costs that are beyond their means.

Directions for Action

Initiate positive action measures to promote a wider range of occupational choice for girls and women.

Ensure that initial education is devoid of gender bias and equips young people with a broad base of skills which develop adaptability and a propensity for lifelong learning.

Ensure that further education and training produce transferable skills that match employment prospects and improve women's earnings capacity.

Increase women's participation in further education and training through entitlements and innovative models of training.

Create incentives for enterprises – including small enterprises – to develop investment in human resource development.

Upgrading female occupations and building career paths

Workers in all areas are being asked to adapt to changing technologies and work processes. In some occupations these changes have resulted in modifications to existing job classifications, the development of new career paths and, as a result, improved remuneration. There is considerable scope to upgrade traditional female occupations in this way. Upgrading female occupations involves revaluing and enriching the skills content of those occupations and enhancing internal and external mobility. Reorganising work, in particular by changing rigid hierarchical structures, offers additional prospects for improving women's advancement in employment.

Upgrading skilled occupations may prove less difficult than upgrading unskilled occupations. Stiff competition for skilled personnel will force skilled female occupations to offer better conditions, improved remuneration and enhanced career development. Already some countries are facing a shortage of nurses or teachers. In the longer term, improved conditions will have an effect on gender segregation. Men will be more likely to enter occupations offering skills recognition and career advancement.

Updating job classifications

Many of the skills actually required in female occupations are not reflected in current occupational definitions or job descriptions. Informally acquired skills – "tacit" skills – tend to be ignored even when they are essential for the task at hand. These skills are undervalued because they are seen as "natural" female competencies, or because they mirror domestic tasks that women perform outside the workplace for free. The development of some of these competencies – particularly people-oriented skills – are an important component of specific training programmes, such as management training.

The introduction of new technologies has significantly increased or modified the skills requirements of many female occupations. For example, nurses have had to adjust to rapidly changing medical technologies, while new information technologies have totally transformed secretaries' tasks. However, in most cases the higher skill level involved is not recognised and the status of those occupations remains unchanged.

Reassessing the skills content of feminised occupations is part of the process of seeking acknowledgement for both the previously unrecognised skills and the new skill requirements of these occupations. Traditional job evaluation techniques tend to be gender-biased in that they value manual and technical skills typically held by men and undervalue organisational and social skills held by women. Methods identifying the full range of competencies actually required to perform a job – informally acquired skills as well as those gained through formal certification – give impetus to raising the relative value of feminised occupations to their true level. Job evaluations based on such methods demonstrate that many of the skills involved in "female" occupations are also applicable to other occupations. This would make it possible to include female occupations in "dynamic" occupational classifications allowing for a high degree of mobility.

Compared to male occupations, traditional female occupations are broadly defined and offer flatter career paths. To some extent women appear concentrated in a narrow range of occupations precisely because the definitions of those occupations are so broad. For example, "secretary" covers a multiplicity of different tasks, functions and levels of seniority. Mobility within the occupation can be high, but intra-occupational vertical mobility is severely constrained. Disaggregating broad occupational categories would reveal paths for career progression within occupations. Female occupations are also "closed" occupations, with few possibilities for inter-occupational mobility. Identifying specific levels at which links could be established with other occupational categories would be easier if female occupations were less broadly defined.

Opening up new career paths will enhance intra- and inter-occupational mobility. This is a crucial factor in ensuring the reallocation of workers between sectors in response to changes in demand for skills. The development of career paths will increase women's incentives to invest in their own training. Workers are more likely to seek training if they anticipate concrete rewards for their efforts.

Reorganising work

New forms of work organisation – that involve more participatory decision-making structures and a greater emphasis on team work and co-operation – are being introduced in some enterprises in response to changes in production and marketing methods and the dissemination of new technologies.

A co-operative integrated workplace is more "woman-friendly" than the traditional work environment based on individual competition and hierarchical structures. This applies to women in both skilled and unskilled occupations. Women tend to progress faster in modern dynamically organised firms than in those firms where traditional industrial hierarchies prevail. For example, there are cases where women's production teams – based on the sharing of skills and knowledge, and provision of peer support – have helped to overcome some of the barriers associated with women's entry to and isolation in non-traditional occupations.

Modifications in workplace organisation could assist in upskilling female occupations. This may prove particularly useful for enriching the skills content of occupations currently defined as "unskilled". Introducing variety and diversity into women's work would serve to increase the skills content of unskilled female occupations and enhance women's functional and occupational mobility.

Pay equity

Comparable worth or pay equity assessments carried out in selected OECD countries have revealed the extent to which feminised occupations are underpaid. Industries employing underpaid women are subsidised by the low wages paid to those workers. The consistent undervaluation of women's work distorts market signals, and results in a misallocation of workers, low productivity, and subsequent losses to economic growth.

Pay inequities are often so entrenched that they are unlikely to disappear without policies directed at earnings parity. Pay equity policies can reinforce the effects of other efforts to increase women's earnings capacity. A variety of "equal pay for work of equal value" schemes have been introduced in OECD countries. Many have not been in place long enough to judge their full impact. Some countries also address the problem in the context of their wage policy, in particular policies on minimum wages or low wages. National monitoring and international comparisons of attempts to reduce the "earnings gap" are needed to assess the relative efficacy of the various approaches.

Directions for Action

Revalue the unacknowledged skills content of "female" occupations.

Enrich the skills content of "female" occupations and construct new paths of career progression.

EMPLOYMENT FLEXIBILITY: MEETING THE NEEDS OF WORKERS

Employment flexibility and diversity is a growing reality generated by structural change. Flexible employment and mainstream employment should form a continuous spectrum of opportunities. *Developing new forms of flexibility and enhancing equity and mobility between the diverse forms of employment will reduce the risk of workers being marginalised on the periphery of the labour market.*

The demand for flexibility

Structural change drives a general demand for employment flexibility. Employment flexibility can accommodate the needs and preferences of an increasingly diversified labour force. It also greatly enhances the ability of enterprises to adjust to the changing economic environment. Flexibility takes many forms. It applies mainly to working-time, work organisation and employment contracts.

The concurrence between employers' and workers' demands for flexibility is not total. Preferences and needs diverge concerning the types and areas of flexibility. While it is recognised that flexibility in working-time arrangements and innovative or flexible forms of work organisation have positive effects on both productivity and employee satisfaction, the direction flexibility has taken in OECD countries is predominantly in the development of non-standard forms of employment.

Employment flexibility in principle has the potential to meet the needs of women workers. However, in practice not all types of employment flexibility are equally favourable. New forms of employment which have developed as a form of labour market flexibility in OECD countries over the past ten years offer significant opportunities but also present many drawbacks.

The development of non-standard forms of employment

"Non-standard" forms of employment – part-time work, sub-contracting, temporary and casual employment, home-work, short-term employment, and self-employment – are a growing reality in OECD countries. In a number of OECD countries this development has been facilitated or encouraged by public policy: relaxation of regulations applying to non-standard contracts, incentives for employers to create non-standard forms of employment, and incentives for the unemployed to accept such contracts.

Women appear in all non-standard employment categories. They form the vast majority of part-time workers, many are employed in small sub-contracting enterprises and they account for the largest share of the increase in self-employment. Non-standard forms of employment expand employment opportunities for women because they provide alternatives to the traditional standard employment model which – as noted above – typically restricts women's employment options. On the other hand, job and income security and conditions of employment are usually inferior in non-standard employment and there is a real risk of marginalisation on the labour market.

31

Flexibility versus security

Non-standard or flexible employment is increasingly referred to as the "unprotected sector". These forms of employment often fall outside the boundaries of existing protective labour regulations, and are usually excluded from provisions negotiated collectively or granted at the discretion of employers. Flexible employment usually means lower wages and lower security, thus undermining the theoretical assumption that there is a trade-off between wages and security.

Part-time work serves as a useful illustration of the reality of flexible employment as it affects women. More than three-quarters of part-time workers are female, and an increasing proportion of women in OECD countries are employed on a part-time basis. Part-time work not only involves shorter than normal hours; it is also usually associated with lower status. Part-time workers generally encounter less favourable conditions of employment across a whole range of benefits: paid leave (including maternity leave), access to training, pensions and in-kind benefits. Part-time workers tend to be considered peripheral and therefore dispensable, and their dismissal is easier and less expensive. Entitlement criteria to social security benefits designed by reference to "standard" employment often exclude part-time workers; in any case, the level of benefit is quite inadequate when it is earnings-related.

Employment in sub-contractor enterprises is another example of non-standard employment offering inferior protection and benefits. Many services which typically employ women (such as cleaning or food preparation) are sub-contracted by large public and private enterprises. Sub-contractors are usually small enterprises. They therefore meet with the usual size-related limitations on the provision of benefits and services, worker representation and leave opportunities (such as training or parental leave). Wages paid by sub-contractors tend to be less than those paid by core enterprises. Mobility between peripheral sub-contractor enterprises and core contracting enterprises is limited. Working for an intermediary or a sub-contractor rarely gives access to the internal labour market of the contracting enterprise.

Terms and conditions in non-standard contracts are often individually negotiated. The ability to bargain with an employer requires a high degree of self-promotion and assertiveness – characteristics that in the past have not been encouraged in women. Women often find themselves in situations where they have to trade off wages or other benefits for the time flexibility they need to meet their competing family responsibilities. When collective agreements apply, these elements are non-negotiable at an individual level. Unless steps are taken to equip workers with the tools of negotiation, non-standard employment may increase worker vulnerability and exacerbate the unequal power relationships between employers and individual workers.

Equality legislation has a limited impact on non-standard forms of employment. It is usually designed by reference to standard employment and its implementation depends on traditional industrial relations structures. In the case of pay equity legislation, for example, job evaluation techniques used in comparable worth assessments may be less appropriate in the case of flexible contracts involving equally flexible job descriptions. Moreover, because workers in flexible forms of employment are less likely to be organised, this reduces the opportunities to make collective pay equity claims.

Flexible employment and choice

Flexibility and enhanced choice develop in parallel. Employment ₁. increases opportunities for women, while non-standard forms of employment suc. part-time work and self-employment allow women to circumvent some of the mosᵗ stringent barriers they face in standard employment. However, there is scope to further exploit and improve these employment options.

Part-time employment

The experience of part-time workers reveals the limits and contradictions embodied in this type of employment. The advantage of part-time work is that it makes employment compatible with involvement in other areas of activity. For women with young children, part-time work is often the only employment option. However, this does not mean that part-time work always allows for regular family life. Workers with part-time jobs rarely have control over the hours they work and they often work atypical schedules – evenings, nights, weekends.

Part-time employment opportunities are relatively limited. Seeking part-time work usually means finding a part-time job. Only a few countries grant workers a statutory right to work reduced hours in their normal job (though in many countries a substantial number of full-time workers report a desire to work shorter hours). Part-time jobs are only available in a very limited range of occupations, often unskilled occupations offering low-status positions. Switching to part-time work therefore usually involves a change of job and even occupation. This change in occupation may result in career interruption. Because non-standard forms of employment increasingly constitute a separate segment of the labour market, the possibilities for a part-time worker to transfer back to full-time stable employment are limited. Career interruption mainly affects women. The fewer men who work part-time are typically older men or students, so part-time work does not interfere with their career development. While most women still cite the decision to work part-time to be a voluntary one, many are not aware of the effects that decision will have on their future labour market status.

The development of part-time employment may reduce full-time employment opportunities for women. Whole sectors of activity – typically feminised service activities – are now organised entirely on the basis of part-time work. An increasing proportion of those working part-time claim it to be involuntary – referring to the lack of full-time jobs. Flexible employment in that context restricts rather than enlarges choice. Most part-time jobs pay less than subsistence wages. The number of workers – or households – combining two part-time jobs is therefore increasing.

Self-employment

Self-employment has the potential to enhance women's work choices. It provides opportunities to combine family and employment, by giving greater control over working time. Many self-employed work from home or set up their workplace in close proximity. Self-employment offers an escape from discrimination in the workplace – including the ''glass ceiling'', the invisible barrier preventing women from reaching the top echelons of management – and enables women to impose their own values on their work environment. However, self-employment is not immune from the lack of income security attached to other forms of flexible employment – especially in terms of access to social protection. Small businesses are typically vulnerable to economic fluctuations and often require considerable support at the initial setting-up stage. Self-employed women face other specific forms of discrimination which may undermine their access to venture capital, business advice and other forms of support.

Enhanced flexibility – meeting the needs of workers

Flexibility in employment is no longer a peripheral or temporary phenomenon. The challenge for structural adjustment is to enhance flexibility in the context of standard employment and to improve security and equality between standard and non-standard employment. Flexible employment options and mainstream employment experience will then form a continuous spectrum of opportunities and choices across an individual's working life.

Developing better forms of flexibility

Innovative options are required for improving flexibility in the context of main-stream employment. Flexibility as a mere cost-containment strategy or flexibility that increases employment precariousness is counter-productive. The willingness of workers to accept structural change, to allow themselves to be assigned to new jobs, or to acquire new skills, increases with job security. According to an OECD report by a high-level group of experts on labour market flexibility, a more flexible management of working hours "at the enterprise level... can lead to acceptable combinations of better capacity utilisation and greater control by individuals over their time" (*Labour Market Flexibility*, 1986). Allowing workers more freedom to rearrange their working time would broaden the range of jobs performed on a part-time basis, including skilled jobs and management positions. The possibility to capitalise time over the working week, or even over longer periods, would also allow a much greater compatibility between employment and other activities.

New work models based on flexibility in how tasks are organised are of considerable interest to women. They release rigid working time and presence constraints, and provide scope for women to create a supportive culture in their working environment. As noted in the previous section, this is particularly valuable within a male-dominated organisation and as a means of increasing women's involvement in non-traditional occupations or industries.

° New technologies, especially in telecommunications, multiply opportunities for flex-ibility in the place of work. Workers can work from home, linked to the workplace by computer modem. Working at home allows additional flexibility in terms of when tasks are carried out. Effective support and liaison systems are needed to guard against social problems – including isolation – often experienced by employees working outside the formal workplace. Home-workers in unskilled occupations are the most vulnerable. Home-based self-employed workers may need specific support, such as access to net-works or service pools.

Improving the conditions of non-standard employment

The aforementioned report on labour market flexibility identified and criticised the inferior conditions accorded to workers in non-standard employment: "There is no reason why conditions of work should be worse for those not permanently employed". The report also noted that non-standard employment should not necessarily constitute a separate segment of the labour force: "It should not be assumed that there is no movement of peripheral workers to the solid core. For many peripheral employment may be no more than a short transition to core employment." Increased efforts are required to counter the trend towards marginalisation of workers in non-standard employment. Parity in terms of the conditions applying to workers in standard and non-standard employment, and mobility between the two types of employment, will reduce segmentation and the risk of marginalisation.

Despite progress in some countries, the benefits and protection granted to workers with non-standard contracts are still generally inferior to those granted to workers in standard employment. Measures such as leave entitlements, pensions, and access to training have to be made more widely available to workers in non-standard employment.

Advocacy for workers on non-standard contracts will help to improve conditions. Issues related to non-standard employment need to be put on the industrial bargaining agenda. Worker representatives have traditionally fought for the retention of conditions attached to standard employment. To continue to be effective, the industrial relations system needs to reflect the growing diversity in employment.

As conditions improve in non-standard employment, and flexibility is enhanced in the context of standard employment, the invisible barriers that prevent mobility between the two are also likely to fall away. Specific measures can accelerate the opening of internal labour markets to workers in non-standard employment – such as giving those workers priority in recruitment to regular jobs.

Income and social protection measures (discussed in the following section) will also need to adjust to new employment patterns. Increased portability of benefits and entitlements would facilitate individual mobility between different forms of employment and between different types of activities.

Directions for Action

Seek innovative options for enhancing flexibility in the context of mainstream employment.

Set conditions of employment on the same basis for all employees and promote equitable treatment for those in non-standard employment.

Improve advocacy for workers in non-standard employment in collective negotiations.

Enhance choice and mobility between non-standard and standard employment.

VALUING DIVERSITY

Changing social, demographic and employment patterns result in an increasingly heterogeneous society and a growing incidence of lifestyle changes across individual lifecycles. Diversity is an asset in a culturally varied and competitive world. *Valuing this diversity and enhancing mobility between areas of market and non-market activity is needed to counteract exclusion, poverty and persistent dependency.*

Changing life patterns

Men's and women's lifecycle patterns are changing. Diverse family types, new forms of employment and greater opportunities for lifelong learning result in increased heterogeneity – between individuals and across the lifecycle of any individual. Policies need to ensure that this diversity does not translate into poverty, persistent dependency or social exclusion and that individuals do not get permanently trapped in a situation appearing at a specific time in their lifecycle.

Policies have tended to focus on stimulating greater participation in employment. OECD Social Policy Ministers noted that "exclusion from the labour market brings with it not only financial costs but also the human costs of dependency, lowered self-confidence and reduced social interaction and activity" (*The Future of Social Protection*, 1988). Failure to acknowledge the value of non-market activities may have similarly negative effects on individual self-worth and social participation. People not currently in the labour force are rarely unproductive or "inactive" – their time is usually spent in useful and meaningful ways. Fostering participation in both employment and other socially valuable activities – such as voluntary and community work, family care, and civic and cultural activities – is fundamental to avoiding social exclusion and working towards an "active society".

Recognition of non-labour market activity

Domestic production and voluntary or community work is essential for keeping societies and their supporting economies functioning. Structural trends – such as state retrenchment in the provision of some health and welfare services, and the growing demand for services to the elderly – are increasing the pressure on that sector. At the same time, women's increasing labour market participation reduces the pool of people able to fulfil those functions.

The provision of an enlarged range and quality of services depends upon greater involvement in household production and community activities by a broader range of actors. Because family and community services have been mainly provided by women – especially home-based women – they have remained largely invisible and undervalued. This undervaluation, when coupled with the negative effects periods out of employment have on an individual's future labour market status, discourages greater involvement in the provision of these services. Without a significant revaluation of domestic and community activities, and improved mobility between non-labour market and labour market activities, participation in these tasks is unlikely to increase.

Unpaid activities such as childcare, services to the elderly, and managing community organisations, require significant skills, experience and responsibility – competences which are equally valuable in a labour market setting. The organisational and budgeting skills utilised by an individual setting up a community organisation are in no way inferior to those used by someone launching a similar project in a commercial context. Assessing the skills requirements of non-market activities, and the transferability of those skills, is instrumental in recognising and revaluing the social and economic utility of unpaid activities. It also promotes mobility between that sector and the labour market.

Improving the "conditions" under which unpaid domestic and community activities are carried out stimulates participation in those activities. This involves addressing needs in relation to leave, activity-related expenses, access to social protection and training. When paid workers become ill they are able to take leave, yet those engaged in informal sector activities – especially those involved in family care – have to struggle on. Individuals engaged in community work personally shoulder the activity-related costs – such as transport, and childcare expenses – yet the benefits of their efforts accrue to society as a whole. Social protection entitlements for individuals engaged in informal sector functions – discussed below – is another question requiring a policy response. Training would enhance the quality of services provided and, if it offers credentials, could transform informal sector experience into a recognised labour market asset.

Time-use surveys – being carried out in several OECD countries – are useful tools for assessing the nature, extent and economic contribution of non-market activities. The availability of this information can enhance economic and social planning. For example, it has revealed in one case that attempts to reduce government expenditure through withdrawal from the provision of some health and welfare services have resulted in cost shifts – from the public sector to households and the community – rather than cost savings.

Social protection and diversity

Diversity in life and employment patterns has not been matched by corresponding diversity in entitlements to social protection. Personal autonomy and choice depend on increased options to combine different forms of activity – such as combining parenting and community activities with some form of employment – and being able to change that combination at some later point. The risk of becoming trapped in a transitory life phase is especially real for women. Women have a higher chance of becoming dependent on social security or income derived from a male spouse, and are more at risk of falling into temporary or long-term poverty. The further feminisation of poverty is a looming threat.

Eliminating persistent dependency is a major challenge. Dependency traps are an unintended outcome of most social security systems. Policy responses to short-term situations can sometimes cause long-term problems. Transfer payments to lone parents is a typical example. High effective marginal tax rates applying to individuals moving off social security into employment can trap them into dependency, especially when they are only able to take on part-time work or when their expected wage levels are low. The costs associated with labour market re-entry, combined with a shortage of affordable childcare services, compel many lone parents – usually women – to remain on social security despite their employment readiness. It is important to recognise the costs of transition, by allowing individuals to move gradually from social security to employment. Assistance for work-related expenses (such as childcare, transport, and clothing needs) and other benefits (such as health care cover) would help to smooth that transition.

Poverty related to personal employment histories is a growing issue confronting OECD countries. The disadvantaged economic position of many older women signals a problem that may become more generalised. Private sector contributory superannuation schemes or insurance payments based on past earnings discriminate against those who have spent significant periods outside the labour market. Periods of non-market activity, in the case of women, are usually dictated by responsibilities for family care – including the care of children, grandchildren and elderly relatives – and are sometimes followed by early withdrawal from the labour market to coincide with a spouse's retirement. Time spent out of employment seriously limits women's ability to plan for income security in old age. When coupled with their relatively low lifetime earnings, this means that women's accumulated entitlements tend to be meagre. Older women are an increasingly vulnerable group, especially given the mounting pressure on state-funded old-age pensions.

More longitudinal research is required to assess the full economic effects of non-continuous employment histories. It should examine variables such as increased life expectancies, changing life and employment patterns, the age of entitlement for retirement pensions, and the extent to which those factors together affect the ratio of market to non-market activity across the lifecycle. This will indicate policy directions likely to lead to enhanced economic security for women.

There is clearly a need to introduce flexibility into social security schemes to match the diversity of personal situations. Schemes have to be redesigned to account for the whole range of employment situations, as well as diversity in family structures, and the needs of those performing socially necessary domestic and community functions. Preservation and portability of employment-related entitlements is important for ensuring long-term economic security over lifecyles that will increasingly include periods out of the paid workforce. Entitlements to social protection need to be established for those involved in informal sector activities, especially where contributory social insurance schemes are the primary means of income protection.

A social security system based on individual entitlements is likely to improve women's access to social protection. Joint-income testing – using the household as the unit of assessment – is based on the assumption that income is pooled and redistributed between family members. A woman finding herself out of work through unemployment or illness is likely to be refused a benefit on the basis of her partner's income – which she may or may not have access to. Joint-income testing also creates disincentives to women's labour market participation.

In most OECD countries the tax system is now based on the individual as the unit of assessment. Applying the same rule to social security enhances consistency and promotes the principles of personal autonomy and economic independence. It also helps to reject the notion that women's incomes are supplementary to and therefore dispensable portions of overall family income.

Co-ordination of social security regimes with social and labour market insertion programmes would promote mobility between market and non-market areas of activity. Social insertion programmes can assist the older and long-term unemployed to engage in activities that enhance their social participation. Participation in these programmes will be greater if the activities offered are meaningful and allow opportunities for skills enhancement. The revaluation of domestic and community activities is likely to enhance the status of social insertion programmes and to improve the take-up rate. The spin-off for society is the provision of socially necessary community services.

Directions for Action

Acknowledge the social and economic value of non-market forms of activity and the interdependence between market and non-market activities.

Develop mechanisms to assess the skills transferability and meet the training needs of individuals involved in non-market activities.

Address the long-term income and social protection requirements of individuals whose lifecycle includes periods of non-market activity.

Ensure that social security regimes and social and labour market insertion programmes increase the opportunities and incentives for both social and economic participation.

DECISION-MAKING: PARTICIPATION AND RESPONSIBILITY

Decision-making systems must be responsive to change. Increased participation by a variety of actors will enhance both the effectiveness and the democratic foundations of decision-making systems. *Empowering women to participate in collective decision-making is essential for effective structural adjustment. Monitoring forms an integral part of decision-making systems.*

A pluralistic decision-making system

Effective structural adjustment depends on decision-making systems that are responsive to structural change and the changing needs of the populations they serve. Active involvement by a multiplicity of actors will ensure that a broad range of needs and contingencies are accounted for. Participation by currently under-represented groups needs to be enhanced. This requires a decision-making process that is both transparent and accessible. Responsive decision-making systems will reinforce the effectiveness and coherence of decisions as well as their democratic foundations.

Women as decision-makers

Decisions that determine the shape of structural reform currently suffer from the lack of women's input. Those decisions are made in forums and groups that are predominantly masculine, and tend to reflect the values, perspectives and the life experiences of the people who make them. Improving women's participation in collective decision-making can make structural adjustment policies more responsive to women's needs and to the growing diversity in life and employment patterns. Creating an environment that encourages women to assume greater decision-making responsibilities depends on addressing the current structural barriers to involvement. That means developing positive action mechanisms to empower women and to improve their political efficacy as well as making the decision-making process more transparent and accessible.

The presence of women in the arenas of political and economic power is relatively recent. In a number of OECD countries, neither women's suffrage nor individual right to work was established until after World War Two. Women still lack the numbers to band together to influence decisions or to challenge the stronghold that men maintain over the bulk of "strategic" decision-making positions. Women in leadership positions often report feeling isolated by a lack of peer support and by having to operate according to rules of the game designed for and by men.

Specific measures are required to increase the numbers of female decision-makers, especially in representative decision-making bodies. These include programmes to encourage women to put themselves forward for positions, and setting up special structures to represent women's interests. Some political parties and unions have chosen quotas as one way of increasing women's participation. In a few OECD countries, legislation requires all public commissions and committees to include a given proportion of women – on the assumption that women are a distinctive group in society which requires specific representation. This has had positive effects on the relative priority attached to issues of concern to women in those countries.

Having a few women in positions of power does not necessarily mean that the multiplicity of women's views and life situations will be adequately represented. A general improvement in women's ability to articulate their needs and concerns into the decision-making process is also required. Women need a basic knowledge of how the system works and access to information about issues on the policy agenda. Establishing women in leadership positions, politicising issues of concern to women, and enabling women to have a say on the variety of agenda items, are all elements of a strategy to make decision-making systems more responsive.

Some aspects related to the functioning of the political decision-making process inhibit women's participation. Meetings held at times that are incompatible with family schedules, an absence of childcare facilities and services, rigid rules for making submissions and intimidating meetings procedures all tend to discourage women's political activity. New channels for enabling women to have input into the decision-making process are required. Community consultations, and seeking advice from the organisations and groups that women belong to – rather than limiting consultation to groups that are already vocal and articulate (such as business or men's community groups or clubs) – can help to solicit women's views. Appointing one or two women to a committee and expecting them to speak for all women is not enough. Building up networks is also necessary. This calls for a broadened definition of "social partners" that includes a wider range of representative organisations.

Women's influence in both the public and private spheres where economic decisions are made also remains rather limited. Women are now relatively numerous in middle management positions – as a result of their higher level of qualifications and their continuous labour force attachment. Despite this "feeder layer", they have not made significant inroads into the realms of top economic management. The notion of the "glass ceiling" suggests a lingering resistance to appointing women to high level posts. Specific tools, such as the compilation of "nomination lists", might serve to challenge this resistance.

An overall improvement in women's employment status will help to increase the pool of qualified women from which to select managers. Rigorous implementation of equal opportunities legislation and other positive action measures is essential for that purpose. Special training programmes for women returning to the workforce, campaigns to encourage women into non-traditional occupations, special schemes to assist women's career planning and quest for management positions, and the development of women's mentoring systems are all examples of positive action measures to improve women's access to decision-making roles. These specific measures will complement the more general strategies outlined in the previous section on occupational segregation.

Responsive decision-making and public policy

The appropriate balance between decentralised and centralised decision-making is a matter of active debate in the current context of structural change. The drive for flexibility and the desire to be responsive to a variety of needs increases the pressure for decentralised decision-making. Yet structural trends such as market globalisation and demographic ageing indicate a need to take into account the broader environment, which calls for a centralised focus.

These apparently contradictory pressures have implications for the functioning of decision-making systems. Maintaining national standards and ensuring that policy objectives are being met – such as achieving gender equity – is more difficult when decisions are decentralised. The role and methods of intervention by central government need to be redefined. Co-ordinating the different actors is a major challenge.

Coherent and consistent public policy also depends on effective co-ordination between policy-making bodies. The preceding sections have highlighted numerous instances where co-ordination between various government agencies is needed, to account for possible externalities and to achieve integrated and effective policy. For example: employment, social security, taxation and childcare policies all interact to influence the social and economic participation of lone parents. Responsive decision-making requires greater decompartmentalisation of policy.

Government agencies need to be responsive to their clients – female as well as male. The existence of specific women's ministries does not mean that other agencies should abdicate their responsibilities to address women's needs and concerns. Some OECD countries have taken this challenge on board, by implementing mechanisms that require government agencies to report publicly on the relevance of their policies and programmes for women, and to outline any specific women's initiatives. The purpose is to elevate women's concerns on the policy agenda.

Decision-making and the labour market

Redefining roles for the different levels of decision-making is particularly important in the context of the functioning of the labour market. Globalisation is driving rapid growth in the international labour market. Rules set at the national level for the national context, increasingly have to take the international environment into account. In parallel, there is a need for greater international involvement in rule-setting.

Regulation defined at the international level can only be very general. Legislation and collective bargaining will increasingly operate as complementary avenues for action at the national level. The relative role of each process in defining employment norms and working conditions depends very much upon the existing industrial relations system – the differences between OECD countries on that level are considerable. Despite these differences, there is a common need to strengthen women's participation in collective bargaining.

The process of structural reform has put considerable pressure on unions and employer organisations. Both devote increased attention to structural adjustment, especially in highlighting the need for training. Equal opportunities is also increasingly on their individual and joint agenda. However, like other institutions, neither employers organisations or unions have yet developed a comprehensive approach to incorporating equity and adjustment strategies into a coherent response to structural trends.

Increasing women's involvement in union and employer decision-making would help to develop an integrated approach to structural change. This is necessary to ensure that women's working conditions and positions are improved or at least maintained in the face of adjustment. Women's role in collective bargaining is currently limited by a range of factors. The dearth of women in senior management positions in enterprises means that they are also less likely to be represented in employer organisations. Women tend to be employed in areas dominated by small enterprises, where it is difficult to organise both employers and workers into the sort of negotiation models operating in other sectors. Women also increasingly work under atypical conditions of employment, most of which fall outside the collective bargaining process. As a result, women generally have lower rates of unionisation. Even where they are highly unionised – such as in the public sector or in countries where for institutional reasons the general level of unionisation is high – women are not well represented in decision-making positions.

Increased involvement by women in unions and employer organisations – particularly in decision-making positions – and the development of new innovative consultation and negotiating structures that include workers and employers currently under-represented in collective bargaining, would considerably reinforce the role of industrial relations in promoting adjustment based on better utilisation of human resources and responsiveness to workers' needs and aspirations. This would benefit all workers, regardless of gender.

Whichever way industrial democracy develops in future, there will be a role for central regulation in relation to setting minimum standards and conditions for a fair and just working environment – including rules against gender discrimination. Strict enforcement of these basic rules is required. Governments are currently re-evaluating a whole range of existing regulations – and the extent to which some need to be strengthened or removed. Whether the existing regulatory framework can accommodate adjustment or whether a totally new framework is indicated needs to be determined. The role of regulations in improving the situation of women needs to be addressed throughout.

Monitoring progress

The relative success of strategies introduced to enhance the responsiveness of the decision-making process needs to be assessed. Setting goals and timetables is essential for achieving cumulative results, and also offers a sound basis for monitoring progress. Effective monitoring presupposes the development of comprehensive data and information on women's employment status, as well as indicators of improvement or deterioration. This information is still lacking in many OECD countries; in some cases data are not even systematically disaggregated by gender.

Responsibility for monitoring and assessment needs to be defined. Many OECD countries already have machinery of government that could assume this function. Women's ministries, equality councils and other similar organisations can collaborate with those responsible for the collection of national statistics to develop equity indicators. It is crucial that statistics on women are part of mainstream data collection and are given full visibility.

Directions for Action

Implement positive action measures to improve women's direct representation in economic, social and political decision-making forums.

Promote effective and accessible channels for women to articulate their needs and concerns into the decision-making process.

Improve the coherence and consistency of policy as it impacts on women, in particular through effective co-ordination of the actors.

Set goals and timetables for achieving women's full participation in the process of structural change.

Monitor structural reform and develop appropriate statistics and indicators to assess the position of women.

ENHANCING INTERNATIONAL CO-OPERATION

Globalisation and increased interaction between national labour markets call for cross-country monitoring and greater international co-operation.

Globalisation brings increased interaction and interdependence between national economies. A new international division of labour is being driven by the global restructuring of production. This affects migration flows and the conditions of competition and employment on national labour markets. The need for international co-operation and a co-ordinated approach to structural reform is reinforced under these circumstances. This

43

report has stressed that structural reform needs to address the economic and social status of women. International organisations provide an ideal forum for inter-country comparisons of structural adjustment, and for fostering dialogue on approaches to integrating gender equity issues into the international policy-making process.

The OECD has an existing mandate to conduct multilateral surveillance of structural reform. The monitoring process – including gathering and disseminating information and conducting regular country reviews – should apply to the performance of Member countries in meeting equality objectives in the context of structural reform. Including gender equity within the agenda of structural adjustment requires that those issues also penetrate the work of the various OECD committees dealing with this matter. New models of interaction – bringing together groups and issues that have hitherto been separated institutionally – would facilitate cross-fertilisation of ideas and approaches to structural change. This is consistent with efforts to develop an integrated and coherent approach to policy both within the Organisation and in national capitals.

There is a definite role for international organisations to foster dialogue on integrating gender equality issues into the international policy-making process. Additional "rules of the game" specifically related to women and structural adjustment have to be defined at the international level. Attempts to orient structural change, along the lines indicated in this report, at the national level will not produce full results if international flows – trade and labour mobility – continue to be based on the acceptance of female workers as cheap labour. Enhanced international co-operation is needed to promote the economic status of women at the international level.

Directions for Action

OECD to include the status of women in the context of cross-country comparisons and surveillance of structural reform.

OECD to foster dialogue on approaches to integrating gender equality issues into the international policy-making process.

Part Two

WOMEN AND EMPLOYMENT RESTRUCTURING

Report by the Secretariat

Chapter 1

OVERVIEW

During the last decade major forces have reshaped the economic and social environment of the OECD countries, both nationally and internationally. Trade expansion and fiercer international competition, the spread of new technologies, more flexible regulation in a number of sectors and industries, the redefinition of the role of government, and demographic trends have all had an impact.

Employment patterns and the functioning of labour markets had to adjust to the combined effect of these factors. A new division of labour was established among countries and, in given countries, among population groups. New forms of employment and work organisation were introduced in response to the adjustment strategies pursued by the various actors. The extent and nature of the changes have put even the industrial relations system under strain.

The employment of women was affected as well. For a proper understanding of the changes in their employment situation over these ten years it is necessary to have this context in mind. This opening chapter outlines the main changes that occurred in the OECD countries over the 1980s with respect to employment, particularly those that had a significant impact on the employment of women. The following chapters will deal in greater detail with specific factors that have brought about changes: the greater participation of women in the labour market, part-time employment, and recruitment policies in the service and public sectors. The policy implications of the observed changes will be assessed in the last chapter, special attention being paid to equal opportunity measures.

Towards a service sector economy and an increasingly female labour force

The dynamics of growth in service sector employment

In the OECD area as a whole, the share of the service sector in total employment continued to grow in the 1980s. While net job losses occurred in agriculture, the level of employment in industry, which had deteriorated in the early 1980s, picked up towards the end of the decade but, save in a few countries, still remained lower in 1989 than ten years before. The service sector was in fact the only one where employment grew steadily over the whole period and in all the countries.

As in the past, the expansion of the service sector favoured the employment of women. In several countries, four out of five women in employment are in the service sector and elsewhere the trend is in that direction. Overall, women increased their share of employment: today they account for over 40 per cent of total employment in the majority of OECD countries.

In the future, female employment will increasingly depend on the situation of the service sector. Although the divide between service and industrial activities is becoming blurred owing to similar developments in production and marketing conditions, the service sector still retains some distinctive characteristics that have come to apply to the employment of women: working conditions and work organisation, abilities and skills, but also vulnerability to cyclical downturns and wage-setting processes (see Chapter 4).

Two trends emerging in the 1980s deserve closer attention as they indicate a change in the nature and quality of jobs. The first is the slowdown in public sector growth and the privatisation of certain services previously supplied by government (see Chapter 5). The second is the ''contracting-out'' of services previously provided within firms and government for their own consumption. As a result, female employment tends to rise faster in small private service firms. These firms are vulnerable to cyclical downturns and competition pressures and their small size does not allow for full implementation of specific policies.

Women and structural unemployment

In the OECD area as a whole the female labour force grew on average at an annual rate of 2 per cent over the 1980s. This resulted as much from an increase in the working-age population as from an increase in participation rates (see Chapter 2). Over the same period, total employment rose by only just over 1 per cent a year. Even though women benefited more than proportionately from the growth in employment, there was still a major job gap relative to the pool of available female labour. In several countries the gap persisted and even widened, generating large-scale unemployment for new job-seekers, mainly young girls leaving school and women returning to the labour market after having devoted several years to raising their children.

At the same time, many women lost their jobs because of structural adjustments in agriculture and industry. In agriculture job losses were appreciable in many countries. The labour-intensive industries – often highly feminised – were obliged to modernise rapidly or to relocate abroad to cope with international competition and adjust to new demands. In vulnerable sectors, women are as much at risk as men. They were particularly hard hit by wholesale labour shedding in some industries – textiles in particular. Those who lost their jobs in agriculture and industry were generally older and unskilled and retraining was difficult in their case. Moreover, the new jobs are seldom located in the rural areas or regions most adversely affected by economic change. When women lose their jobs, their only alternative to long-term unemployment is all too often permanent withdrawal from the labour market. In some countries, one-half to three-quarters of female unemployment is long-term and this underestimates the size of the problem.

Underemployment and underutilisation of available human resources are today a feature of most OECD economies. The growth of service sector employment was thus not sufficient to absorb the workers shed by other sectors in addition to first-job-seekers. This situation perpetuates the problems of access to employment for many women, even if other groups are equally affected. However, the emphasis usually given to ''access'' should not conceal the fact that jobs are not all of equal ''status'' and that the very nature of employment is changing very radically.

Enterprises' adjustment strategies and changes in employment practices

The pervasiveness of new technologies, broader and keener competition in all sectors, and greater versatility of demand have obliged firms to display greater flexibility in their production and functioning.

The linkage that is forged between the production factors, capital and labour, is one of the key aspects of the flexibility strategy adopted by the enterprise. Two very different strategies with a specific impact on labour utilisation are to be found today. The first is based on lowering production costs as much as possible, the other on quality and innovation. Firms seek above all, in the first case, to enhance their external numerical flexibility, and in the second, to improve their internal functional flexibility. Employment models are radically changing under the impact of these two strategies, and this cannot but have implications for women's employment.

External numerical flexibility

Numerical flexibility enables the volume of labour to be closely adjusted to fluctuations in demand. It is often accompanied by efforts to keep costs down, particularly labour costs; labour is here considered as a cheap factor of production expandable according to demand. Moreover, it enables the firm to have access to special skills without having to bear the cost of training or retraining workers, which would only be warranted if there were a permanent need for those special skills.

This type of flexibility has spawned a variety of atypical forms of employment: part-time, temporary or casual, fixed-term, self-employment (which is often closely tied to a firm under subcontracting arrangements). Because of this, secure, full-time, dependent employment is no longer the norm. On present trends, the so-called norm could well apply only to a minority of jobs in the years to come.

In several countries, the growth in atypical forms of employment is the result of derestriction of the regulations applying in this area. Many labour market policies have also contributed to the development of atypical forms of employment. Labour market regulations and social security systems, on the other hand, continue by and large to be based on the notion of secure, full-time, dependent employment.

Somewhat paradoxically, while firms claim to be pursuing flexibility primarily for reasons of international competitiveness, it is in fact service sector firms, including the less vulnerable public sector, that are the keenest proponents of flexibility. Women are thus very seriously affected since the vast majority of them are employed in the service sector and, in some countries, in the public sector.

While women are concerned by all forms of atypical employment, there is one form of flexibility that is considered to be a particularly "female", namely part-time employment (see Chapter 3). In the 1980s the number of full-time jobs filled by women fell in several OECD countries whereas the number of part-time jobs rose in all of them. The question is then whether the trend might not be towards the replacement of full-time jobs by part-time jobs, with a redistribution of employment over a greater number of women.

Part-time work has the undeniable advantages of creating new employment opportunities for many women and making it easier to combine work and family life. But it has also several drawbacks because of the way it has expanded. Part-time jobs tend to be "inferior" on a whole range of criteria. Moreover, to the extent that there is substitution and as full-time jobs become relatively scarce, part-time employment is imposed on women for lack of alternative choice. Finally, part-time employment, in that it is largely confined to women, compounds job segregation according to gender which goes against the objectives of equal opportunity policies.

On balance, all forms of atypical employment offer fewer safeguards than "normal" employment in some very important respects: job and income security, social protection and enterprise training. The proliferation of different forms of employment within a given enterprise, which means more individualised labour relations, reduces the influence that collective bargaining can have on the terms and conditions of atypical forms of employment.

Internal functional flexibility

A widely-held view is that in the long term, the best strategy for firms in OECD countries is one based that on product quality and reliability, and customer service that can be achieved because of technological progress and the highly skilled labour force in these countries. Human capital is central to this strategy. The productivity gains that new technologies could bring will be achieved only if firms have a skilled and highly adaptable workforce.

In the process of rationalisation and modernisation, firms must redefine job content and work organisation. They must also bring in new skills, the development of which requires a genuine human resource management policy in conjunction with a major initial and further training effort. A revision of traditional job classifications and appraisal methods is part and parcel of the modernisation process. The new classifications must serve as a device for career management and occupational mobility, for upskilling and for developing new work organisation methods.

At the end of the process, new mobility patterns within the enterprise will have emerged. Opportunities for women to progress inside enterprises seem considerably better in this new context where both horizontal and vertical mobility will be facilitated. Women tend on the whole to have some of the new skills that modern firms need. As these skills are now recognised, a positive impact on women's earnings will follow. Moreover as firms increase their training efforts, women should be able to acquire the skills needed in their own enterprise.

There remains, however, a major question regarding how women may be affected by this strategy based on functional flexibility: what will occur to women employed in the lowest jobs that will eventually disappear?

A twofold polarisation

In the real world, the two strategies coexist, sometimes even within the same firm. An employer's decisions are dictated by the human resources available both within the firm and on the external labour market. Moreover, prospective planning of jobs and occupations is still in its infancy as a management tool.

Today, a twofold polarisation of jobs is occurring: a new distinction has been superimposed on the traditional skill-based one that is geared to how labour is used. Workers' position is thus defined first according to whether they occupy a skilled or unskilled job and, second, according to whether or not they form part of the firm's stable core.

The distribution of women across these different forms of employment means that the diversity of individual employment situations and problems is growing. This diversity raises the question of what policies are the most effective for improving the employment situation of women.

The need for adjusting policies

The 1980s were thus a period of great upheaval in the world of work. The evolution of women's employment is marked by contrasting developments. The considerable rise in women's employment undoubtedly reflects the greater role they are playing in the economy. But alongside the growth in women's employment, there was increasing inequality in working conditions. Nowadays, jobs do not always bring the same security and income to their holders as in the past. And while today women are to be found in every occupation, they are over-represented in less secure and part-time jobs. The diversification of forms of employment, may well open up more job opportunities, but it does not necessarily imply freedom of choice: self-employment is often simply a means of avoiding unemployment, and part-time employment appears as a last resort solution when a full-time occupation would have been preferred.

Women's employment today depends on a whole series of interesting factors, among which trends in demand, technological innovation, production processes and work organisation. Policies must take due account of the impact these factors may have on the utilisation of labour, particularly female labour. The risk, otherwise, is that of leaving the door wide open to new forms of inequality and discrimination that would simply replace or compound long-standing problems.

Policies likely to promote the employment of women include among others equal opportunity policies directly targeted on women. Significant results can also be achieved by ensuring that women derive all possible benefits from general measures in other policy areas.

Responding to the new employment situation

While the restructuring of employment throughout the 1980s was characterised by an increasing feminisation of the labour force and of employment, by the tertiarisation of the economy and by diversified forms of employment, economic, social and labour market policies and the institutional structures continued to be modelled along the standards of the past: the man as sole breadwinner, the large industrial firm, secure full-time employment. Women would derive much more benefit from policies if these were redesigned to reflect the real world.

The increasing labour force participation of women, particularly married women, invalidates the model of "the man as the sole breadwinner". It challenges the traditional organisation of work and raises the problem of how to reconcile work and family life. So far, this problem has nearly always been considered as concerning only women, as if their new economic role could not affect their traditional role. The way part-time work has developed as a form of flexibility for women illustrates this quite well. Other solutions are needed today, that would not only allow to combine paid work with family life, but also enable women to have a full career. This implies a fairer sharing of family responsibilities between men and women. These solutions must be part of a broader debate on flexible working time arrangements and employment in general. Structural adjustment policies should also focus much more directly on household production given its complementary and interdependence with the other sectors, enterprises and government. The current difficulties in resolving the problem of ageing populations are highlighting the limitations of an approach that does not take into account the domestic and informal production sector.

Because of the growing importance of the service sector, analysis and policies based exclusively on the industrial sector are becoming less and less representative and relevant. There are in fact great and many differences across the two sectors: in the degree of exposure to international competition, in company size and structure, in the qualifications and skills of the workforce, in wages and other working conditions, in the number of casual and part-time workers, and in the degree of unionisation and bargaining power. Current institutional structures, such as collective bargaining, have been designed for the large industrial firm but they are not necessarily effective in a quite different context. Adjustment strategies in the service sector – where most women are employed – need to be based more on new ways to achieve efficiency and equity, and on small businesses.

Although secure, full-time, dependent employment is accounting for an ever smaller share of total employment, it is still the norm on which employment conditions – wage rates in particular – and most social protection measures are based. In some cases, the norm needs to be changed while in others, systematic reference to employment should be eliminated. This would help to do away with some of the discriminations affecting many workers today. It could also promote the principle of employment flexibility as a factor in structural adjustment.

If policies are to be brought in line with the real situation, there needs to be an information system that will make it possible to monitor developments more closely and to detect changes as soon as they occur. In particular there is a need for innovation in the fields of research, statistics and indicators. The policy debate could then take place on firmer and broader foundations.

Equal opportunity policies and trends in employment

In the early 1980s, equal opportunity policies were essentially aimed at opening up the primary labour market to a greater number of women. These policies may need to be redefined to take into account the development of new employment practices spreading as a result of *de facto* deregulation (see Chapter 6).

The growing diversity of women's individual employment situations points also to the need for policies to identify special target groups. Older women workers are likely to be particularly vulnerable in the years to come given the nature of current structural changes. As employment restructuring is largely based on retraining workers, the older ones run a great risk of being excluded from the labour market. Early withdrawal from the labour market, or any lengthy period of work in atypical jobs, would seriously affect older and unskilled women's pension income at a time when population ageing is putting a high pressure on the public purse.

Chapter 2

PATTERNS OF LABOUR MARKET PARTICIPATION

The rapid feminisation of both the active population and overall employment is perhaps one of the major structural changes to have occurred on OECD labour markets in the past decades. The evolution observed since the early 1960s continued everywhere during the 1980s under the combined effect of the supply of and demand for women workers.

This chapter sets out the principal labour market indicators, highlighting the present share of women in the active population, in employment and in unemployment throughout the OECD area. The same indicators also serve to identify more qualitative differences in the situation of men and women on the labour market: the age profiles of labour force participation, the share of part-time work and the causes of unemployment. The immediate objective is not to explain the developments observed but to set up useful markers for the following chapters. Thus, even if global indicators do not have a great analytical bearing, they draw our attention to changes as they occur and also the sometimes quite remarkable differences between countries.

In order to identify the structural changes that affected the situation of women during the 1980s, this study will compare the years 1979 and 1989 which correspond to the peaks of the last two economic cycles in most OECD countries. Examining the differences between the situation of men and women in each country appears more significant than directly comparing the situation of women from country to country. In fact, the level of each indicator (activity rate, unemployment rate) reflects structural characteristics specific to each country.[1]

The first section of this chapter focuses on the development of labour force participation rates in OECD countries during the 1980s; it shows that the rapid rise in female participation rates observed throughout the 1960s and 1970s continued thereafter. The second section attempts to provide a dynamic interpretation of participation rates and to throw some light on the continuity of women's presence on the labour market over their lifecycles. The last section examines to what extent observed trends of participation rates (supply) are matched by similar trends in employment rates (demand). It will be shown, in particular, how the unemployment and part-time employment situation of women varies from country to country.[2]

TRENDS IN FEMALE PARTICIPATION RATES DURING THE 1980s

The participation rate is the indicator used to measure the mobilisation of human resources on a national labour market. It indicates the ratio of the economically active population to the population of working age, the economically active population being made up of all those present at a given moment on the labour market, *i.e.* the employed as well as those in search of a job. The participation rate is the most appropriate indicator of labour force supply.

Overall participation rates

The mobilisation of the female population on the labour market – as measured by female participation rates – has increased considerably in all OECD countries over the last decades (OECD, 1988). Nevertheless, if this has been a general tendency, it has taken place at a very different pace in different countries: in some, the female participation rates are rapidly converging towards male rates, while in others there is still a considerable gap. On the other hand, the fluctuation of women's economic activity according to the economic cycle is now rarely observable and women's labour market participation has become a more structural factor (see Statistical Annex, Table A).

The increase in female participation rates was particularly marked in the Netherlands (16 points, or 50 per cent, in 10 years) and New Zealand (15 points); it was also steep (more than 1 point a year on average) in Australia, Canada, Greece, Norway and the United States. In some countries (France, Ireland, Portugal), on the other hand, it increased by only a few points.[3]

While female participation rates are on the rise everywhere, male participation rates are on the decline in many countries. Gender differentials are therefore diminishing overall while remaining very pronounced in certain places. In 1989, the gap between male and female rates had been reduced to 5 points in Sweden, while in Ireland it was still 45 points.

Age-related participation rates

It is difficult to interpret developments and variations in participation rates without recourse to a breakdown by age group. Whether or not one is present on the labour market depends not only on gender but also on age. Thus, the labour market behaviour of the youngest age group (16-24) and of the oldest (55-64) is much influenced by such external factors as education and health or by educational and retirement policies. Such policies vary a great deal from country to country as does the size of a particular age group relatively to the overall working-age population.

For a variety of reasons, age is an important factor when comparing the situation of men and women. Participation rates vary according to age, but differently between the sexes. It is obviously very important to isolate the age group corresponding to the years during which families are raised; as in both extreme age groups, the participation rates of women in this central age group are affected by external factors including cultural traditions and equal opportunity policies which vary greatly from country to country. Furthermore, there is still today a generation effect in the case of women which causes considerable differences in labour market behaviour between successive cohorts. Finally, in certain countries, there is a difference of several years in the age at which women and men can claim their retirement pensions. This in turn can cause a difference in the activity rates of men and women within the oldest age group.

In most OECD countries the curve of female participation rates according to age showed a similar shift over the 1980s: an upward movement of the curve and a flattening out of any depression for the 25-35 age group (Graph 2.1). In several countries, however (France, Ireland, Portugal and Spain, in particular), the curve was higher only in the middle group since the participation rates for the youngest and oldest groups were lower in 1989 than they had been in 1979.[4]

Table 2.1 illustrates how the gap between male and female participation rates has varied for each age group. No substantial difference was found in the participation rates of young men and women aged 15 to 24. While the rates for young men were generally higher than those for young women (except in Japan), the gap was usually under 10 points. This gap narrowed in most countries during the 1980s and, judging by the rate at which it is moving, it might, in some cases, very well disappear altogether in a few years' time.[5]

The situation of the oldest age group – 55 to 64 – varies a good deal from country to country. Most often, the gender differential is the widest for this group, which may be due to a generation effect (still observable for women) or to the fact that women can claim their retirement earlier than men. Where the gap in the participation rates of men and women in this age group diminished during the 1980s, it was also due to declining male rates.

Apart from a few countries such as Finland and Sweden, the disparities between the participation rates of men and women in the 25 to 54 age group are still very significant. In 1989, the gap still ranged from 20 to 30 points in most countries, and was much wider in Ireland, Italy and Spain. But it dwindled considerably – by 10 and sometimes even 15 points – during the 1980s. If this trend continues, the participation rates of men and women in the 25 to 54 age group could well be at the same level in some countries by the year 2000.

THE CONTINUING PRESENCE OF WOMEN ON THE LABOUR MARKET

The intensity of participation in economic activity is measured by two factors: the number of those taking part and the length of their participation. Knowing that there is an increasing number of women on the labour market at a given moment is not enough. We must also determine whether women's professional paths have become more continuous.

There have been, up to now, considerable differences in the labour market behaviour of women and men. Men usually remained on the labour market from the time they entered working life until their retirement. Women, on the other hand, were much more likely to interrupt their working lives, possibly returning to the labour market later. This process could be repeated several times and reflected the fact that priority was being given to family responsibilities.

Graph 2.1a. Labour force participation rates by age and sex

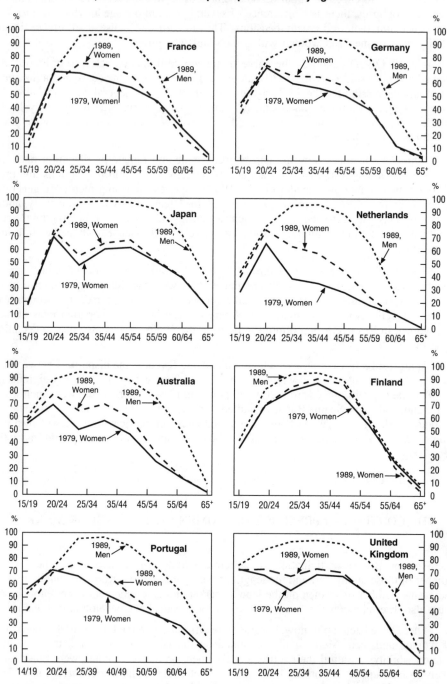

Source: OECD, *Labour Force Statistics*.

Graph 2.1b. Labour force participation rates by age and sex

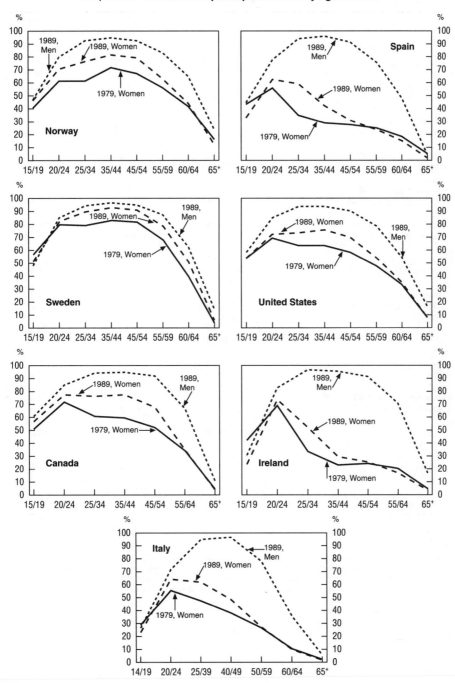

Source: OECD, *Labour Force Statistics.*

57

Table 2.1. **The participation gap,**[a] **by age**

	15-24	25-54	55-64
Australia			
Remaining gap in 1989	6.9	27.4	39.7
Decrease in gap 1979-89	(6.4)	(15.7)	(9.5)
Canada			
Remaining gap in 1989	5.6	19.3	31.7
Decrease in gap 1979-89	(4.7)	(17.9)	(10.8)
Finland			
Remaining gap in 1989	9.0	6.2	4.4
Decrease in gap 1979-89	(2.1)	(4.9)	(10.6)
France			
Remaining gap in 1989	7.1	23.6	15.6
Decrease in gap 1979-89	(1.3)	(9.7)	(15.9)
Germany			
Remaining gap in 1989	4.9	29.5	32.4
Decrease in gap 1979-89	(0.6)	(10.0)	(6.1)
Ireland			
Remaining gap in 1989	7.8	57.5	54.1
Decrease in gap 1979-89	(6.9)	(9.9)	(3.7)
Italy[b]			
Remaining gap in 1989	5.1	42.3	25.4
Decrease in gap 1979-89	(3.7)	(12.1)	(1.6)
Japan			
Remaining gap in 1989	−1.7	33.7	36.3
Decrease in gap 1979-89	(1.3)	(7.3)	(3.5)
Netherlands			
Remaining gap in 1989	3.3	37.1	29.5
Decrease in gap 1979-89	(−0.4)	(22.0)	(21.4)
Norway			
Remaining gap in 1989	5.9	14.4	20.7
Decrease in gap 1979-89	(−4.0)	(12.4)	(12.1)
Portugal			
Remaining gap in 1989	8.4	27.8	33.6
Decrease in gap 1979-89	(6.2)	(12.5)	(9.6)
Spain			
Remaining gap in 1989	13.8	49.0	43.0
Decrease in gap 1979-89	(7.6)	(16.3)	(12.8)
Sweden			
Remaining gap in 1989	0.4	4.1	10.5
Decrease in gap 1979-89	(1.7)	(10.2)	(14.3)
United Kingdom			
Remaining gap in 1989	7.3	21.2	28.4
Decrease in gap 1979-89	(3.2)	(11.1)	(15.4)
United States			
Remaining gap in 1989	8.8	19.4	21.9
Decrease in gap 1979-89	(4.1)	(12.2)	(8.6)

a) The gap is defined as the difference between the labour force participation rates of men and women in the same age group. A negative sign for the gap in 1989 indicates that the labour force participation rate of women is higher than that of men; a negative sign for the trend over the period 1979-89 indicates an increase in the gap.

b) Age groups 25-49 and 50-64.

Source: OECD, *Labour Force Statistics.*

The participation rate analysed in the preceding section is a static indicator which gives no hint as to whether the situation measured is provisional or permanent.[6] However, the rise in female activity rates usually reflects a longer and a more continuous presence of women on the labour market.

This is shown by working life expectancy, which is a composite indicator based on participation rates according to age at a given time. In 1977, the US Bureau of Labor Statistics estimated women's working life expectancy at 71 per cent of men's. At the age of 25, a woman could be expected to work for a further 23 years and a man for 33; comparing the situation with that in 1970, women had gained four years and men had lost one (Smith, 1982). In 1986, similar Australian calculations established working life expectancy for women at 26 years (Young, 1990).

Other types of data provide detailed information on work experience and work interruptions over a given period. These data are derived from longitudinal or retrospective studies and are available only for a few countries and generally for a single year or for a somewhat remote period. They hence cannot be used to determine trends over the 1980s. Neither are they homogeneous from one country to another, making direct comparisons problematic. Nevertheless, they contain a store of information and provide useful benchmarks. They are used here to highlight the principal characteristics of women's career paths in some OECD countries.

Work interruptions

The results of retrospective surveys[7] show that the trend seen throughout this century towards an increase in the participation of women in the labour market has been accompanied by a progressive change in their working life patterns. In the past, women would go to work only after their last child was considered old enough; later on, they worked up to the birth of their first child, at which point they interrupted their work until the youngest child was old enough to go to school; today most women remain active over the whole working-life cycle, with shorter or longer interruptions at the birth of each child.

A first observation is that almost all women today work at some point in their lives. In Canada, in 1984, the lowest proportion of women having worked (81.6 per cent) was found among women between the ages of 50 and 64. In the United Kingdom in 1980, only 4 per cent of the female population had never worked. In France, the corresponding rate in 1982 was 4.5 per cent; the proportion of women never having worked reached its lowest rate around the age of 30; one woman out of six aged 50-54 and above had never worked.

But this is not to say that women's professional paths are necessarily continuous. In fact, continuous paths characterise only a minority; most women's working life has interruptions whose length and frequency depend on a number of factors.[8] In Canada, in 1984, among those 30 years and older, two women out of five had never experienced a break of more than a year; three out of five had experienced at least one such break, and one out of five had had at least two. In 1982, half of the women in France between the ages of 35 and 39 had experienced a continuous professional path (meaning in this case with no break exceeding two years).

These data confirm that women's paths are more discontinuous than men's, and they also provide an explanation. Family reasons appear predominant, especially at certain ages, but they are in no way the only cause. Thus, whereas half of women's breaks in France at the end of the 1970s were due to family reasons (45 per cent of the first interruptions taking place at a birth or in order to raise a child), at the beginning of the 1980s breaks were increasingly caused by economic factors such as unemployment. A similar situation was observed in Spain[9] and the United Kingdom.

Interruptions tend to be longest when they occur for family reasons, even though the duration of these is decreasing. They are also shorter and less frequent among women of a higher educational level. In the United States, in 1984, breaks over six months represented overall 14.7 per cent of the potential working time in the case of women (1.6 per cent in the case of men). Educational level introduced a considerable differential: in the 30 to 44 age group, the amount of time lost represented 16 per cent in the case of women who had not completed secondary education, and only 9 per cent in the case of those who had attended university.

Withdrawal from the labour market at childbirth

The birth of a child is one of the main reasons why women withdraw – at least temporarily – from economic activity. The considerable development of maternity, parental and other types of family leave in OECD countries in the 1980s is worth mentioning here (see Chapter 6). Women's behaviour is very much affected by these measures.

An American study shows how the patterns of women's withdrawal from the labour market on the birth of their first child have changed over the past 20 years (O'Connell, 1990).[10] The study compares the periods 1961-65 and 1981-85. After a 20-year lapse, more women were found to have worked by the time of their first pregnancy, in addition to which they stayed at work longer during pregnancy and returned to work sooner after confinement. On average for 1981-85, 75 per cent of all women had at least six months work experience at the time of the birth; 65 per cent had worked during their pregnancy, and among these, half had worked to within a month or less of confinement (the corresponding figures for 1961-65 were 60 per cent and 44 per cent). Over the same period, 28 per cent of women who had worked during their pregnancy voluntarily gave up their jobs after giving birth, half were granted leave which guaranteed their return to the job, and one out of five had taken leave with no guarantee of re-employment. The decrease in "voluntary" resignations in favour of leave with a guarantee also became more pronounced during these five years.

Among the women who were entitled to leave with a job guarantee, the proportion receiving at least partial financial compensation also increased (four out of five in 1981-85). But the most remarkable change is the increasingly early return to work after confinement. In 1981-85, 44 per cent of all women were back at work six months after the birth of their first child; the percentage was still higher (71 per cent) in the case of women entitled to leave with a job guarantee. In 1961-65, only 14 per cent had gone back to work within six months of the birth of their first child. Thus, in most cases, it appears that withdrawal for the birth of a first child does not constitute a real break as much as a temporary interruption. In the United States, today a quarter of the female population interrupt their working life for three months or less at the birth of their first child and only a third for more than a year.

Sweden provides another interesting example because it is the country in which measures concerning parental leave are the most developed. E.M. Bernhardt analysed the results of the 1981 fertility survey. She notes that it is becoming increasingly rare for a woman to be still "at home" a year after the birth of her first child and that the extension of parental leave – which is a year long and sometimes more – means that this phenomenon can no longer be regarded as a "withdrawal" from working life (Bernhardt, 1987). Most of the women who went back to work less than a year after confinement went back to part-time work, while 70 to 75 per cent were working full-time prior to birth. The continuity of Swedish women's working lives is increasingly associated with shorter working hours. This can be considered as a "combination" strategy, i.e. combining career and family life, halfway between the "housewife" strategy (on the decline)[11] and the "career woman" strategy (restricted to a minority of highly qualified women).[12]

In all countries for which data are available it can be observed that leave entitlement at the time of birth and in the subsequent period has positive effects on the continuity of women's working lives because it prevents definitive and premature withdrawals from the labour market. The duration of these breaks is increasingly linked to the length of the leave entitlement itself. However, women do not always take full advantage of the leave they are entitled to. This is true of both the least and the most qualified women, but for different reasons. In the first case, the reasons are purely economic and result from the fact that income replacement is either not guaranteed or insufficient. In the second case, the reasons are professional, since any prolonged absence from the workplace risks jeopardising normal career progression. Finally, flexibility in working time at the end of leave is certainly conducive to a more prompt return to the labour market.

Today, women are returning to the labour market after the birth of a child more frequently and more rapidly than they were in the past. As a result, they also return to work more frequently in between births. Thus, in Sweden before 1968 (according to the survey mentioned previously), half of the women who had not returned to work a year after their first birth started a second pregnancy without having returned to the labour market; after 1975, this was only true of 15 per cent. In the future, it is likely that the problem of the integration or reintegration of women who have spent many years away from the labour market raising their children will become less acute (this is a particularly thorny problem in certain countries today as will be seen in the section below on unemployment). On the other hand, the problem of aged parents is increasingly critical and is likely to cause many women on the labour market to withdraw not towards the beginning but at the end of their career path.

The problem of elderly dependants

In OECD countries today, an increasing number of elderly people are becoming dependent on the help and care provided either by members of their families or by public or private services. Within families, women have traditionally had the responsibility for looking after the elderly. Since age-related dependence begins mainly after the age of 75 – according to an American survey, nearly one out of every five persons of this age group has to be assisted in order to perform certain acts of daily life – it is usually at the onset of their 50s that women have to take on this new burden.

The constraints that this burden represents and the impact on women's employment may be considerably aggravated in the future. An increasing proportion of adults will have very elderly parents due to longer life expectancy.[13] The new cohorts reaching the age where they have to take care of their parents usually belong to relatively small families which means that the burden of elderly dependants cannot be shared by several siblings.

Furthermore, since a great majority of women today are employed, very few are likely to take care of elderly dependants who are not members of their family on a voluntary basis. If services for the elderly are not implemented rapidly and on a large scale – which is unlikely – the responsibility for taking care of the elderly will rest mainly with the family. This can create a very heavy additional burden for working women. And since parents are having their children later on in life, the need to look after elderly dependants will be present from 40 onwards, a crucial period in terms of career.

Surveys on this matter are still few in number, but the scant information available confirms that the need to look after elderly parents can have a profound impact on women's employment. In Japan, the task of looking after the elderly invariably falls on the female population. In 40 per cent of cases, working women who had to take main responsibility for an older member of the family – a parent or other person – had to give up or change their job (Japanese Ministry of Labour, 1989). In the United States, a 1982 survey came to similar conclusions on a possible conflict between employment and the need to look after aged relatives. According to this survey, 31 per cent of people responsible for older members of their families with functional disabilities had a job and another 10 per cent had had to give up work. Of those who carried on working, 29 per cent had to rearrange their working hours, 21 per cent were obliged to reduce them and 19 per cent had to take unpaid leave.[14] In the United Kingdom, as elsewhere, women are the main providers of care for dependants. Some of these women claimed they had to adopt "compromise" strategies in order to keep their jobs (Finch and Mason, 1990).

EMPLOYMENT, UNEMPLOYMENT AND INACTIVITY

Conventional labour market analysis identifies three activity states: employment, unemployment and non-participation. The criteria developed for the statistical observation of the labour market establish well defined boundaries between each of these states. In reality, each one of these terms applies to a large range of situations: employment may be stable or insecure, full-time or part-time. In the same way, unemployment situations vary according to their duration. Additionally, the boundaries between each of these states can better be described as large and not very clearly defined zones in which states may overlap. During the 1980s, employment, unemployment and non-participation became still more diverse, and the distinctions between each state became more blurred. These factors are of a particular importance in comparing the situation of women and men.

This chapter provides a general picture of the distribution of the working-age population of OECD countries according to activity status: employment, unemployment, and non-participation. As mentioned previously, it is always useful to distinguish between age groups when analysing labour force participation. When dealing with gender comparisons the central age group (from 25 to 54) is the most interesting and it will be the focus of most of our observations.

Employment rates

Because participation rates include workers in search of employment as well as employed workers, they provide a clearer indication of the mobilisation than the utilisation of human resources in the economic sphere. In order to apprehend the actual utilisation of these resources it is necessary to use employment indicators reflecting the matching of supply with demand on the labour market. Part-time employment introduces a most fundamental distinction in the concept of employment and it is essential to identify it. Graph 2.2 shows the distribution of women aged 25 to 54 in 20 OECD countries, according to activity status in 1989. The graph distinguishes between full-time and part-time employment. To describe this distribution the concept of employment rate is used; it indicates, for a given population, the proportion of all those employed.

If we first consider full-time employment only, Finland seems to have an exceptionally high rate: in fact eight women out of ten in between the ages of 25 and 54 are employed full-time. North American countries and Portugal also have relatively high full-time employment rates (nearly six women out of ten), whereas Spain and Ireland have relatively low levels (fewer than three women out of ten). Australia, Germany and the United Kingdom differ very little from this last group with only slightly higher rates. The Netherlands, on the other hand, is on the opposite end of the scale from Finland, with fewer than one in five women in full-time employment. In all other countries, about half the women in this age group work full-time. Full-time employment seems to be the norm for men in the same age group (80 to 90 per cent). Thus, in 1989, the situation of women was markedly different from that of men with respect to full-time employment, with the exception of Finland.

The picture concerning part-time employment is quite different.[15] The highest part-time employment rate for women in the central age group is found in Sweden: four women out of ten work part-time. In Norway, the Netherlands and the United Kingdom, more than three women out of ten are in this situation, and just under this in Australia and Denmark. In Mediterranean countries, on the other hand, only one woman out of 20 is employed part-time.

The share of part-time employment in total employment for women in the central age group varies considerably from country to country. Here again, the Netherlands stands out with practically two part-time jobs for every full-time job. In Sweden and the United Kingdom there are nearly as many female part-timers as there are full-timers. Everywhere else full-time employment is predominant, although part-time employment remains significant (around one-third) in Australia, Denmark, Germany, Japan, and New Zealand and, in smaller measure, in Belgium, France and North America. Part-time employment is marginal in the Mediterranean countries, Ireland, Luxembourg, and, of course, Finland (owing, in this last case, to the very high level of full-time employment).

If one now considers total employment of women in the age group 25 to 54 (part-time together with full-time) the classification of countries initially established on the basis of full-time work only is significantly changed. Australia, the Netherlands, the United Kingdom and Sweden considerably improve their ranking while Greece, Italy and Portugal fall behind. But the leaders are still Denmark, Finland, Norway and North America whereas Ireland and Spain once more bring up the rear. Since part-time employment for men in the central age group is everywhere marginal (in general less than 2 to 3 per cent of the male population), the gender gap in employment rates is considerably reduced due to the part-time employment of women.

Graph 2.2. **Activity status of women aged 25-54, 1989**

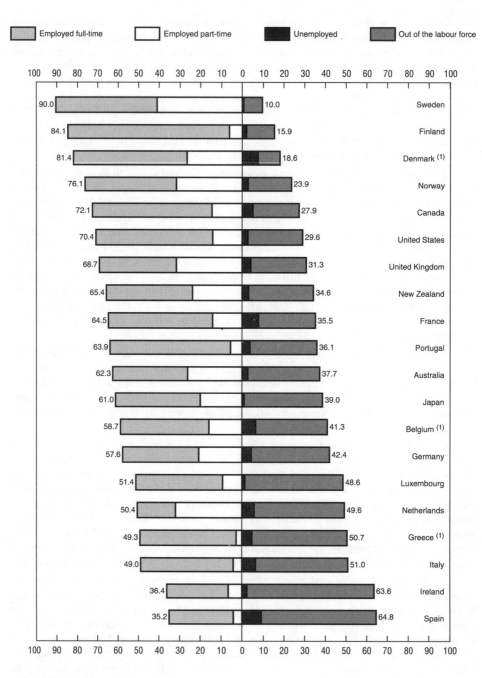

1. Data refer to age group 25-49 and year 1990.
Source: National Labour Force Surveys.

The trends in the employment rates of women in the age group of 25 to 54 from 1979 to 1989 show a great deal of diversity from country to country. For example, in Australia both full-time and part-time employment rates increased; in the United States, the full-time employment rate showed a marked rise while the part-time employment rate stayed the same; in France, on the contrary, the full-time employment rate stayed the same while part-time employment increased significantly.

The employment rates of women in OECD countries show that while it is possible to imagine a situation in which full-time employment would constitute the norm for women as well as for men (such as in Finland), most countries have chosen a different path with a mix of full-time and part-time employment in the case of women.

Female unemployment

According to the conventional definition, unemployment is a measure of the human resources which, although actively offered on the labour market and immediately available, are not used at a given moment. The interpretation of unemployment can be fairly ambiguous. Unemployment may first be regarded as the most directly accessible labour reserve which allows for labour market dynamics. On the other hand, a high unemployment rate for a particular population group is a sign of that group's specific difficulties in integrating into the labour market. A situation of high unemployment can cause discouragement and lead some unemployed workers to discontinue their job search activity, which is interpreted as a withdrawal from the labour market. This introduces a certain amount of uncertainty in the distinction between employed and non-active workers.

Unemployment rates according to gender and age

The gap between the unemployment rates of women and men is one of the most commonly used indicators of gender inequality on the labour market. A simple comparison of the overall unemployment rates of men and women gives no idea of the full disparity in unemployment according to gender, whether in quantity or kind. For this, it is also necessary to examine the structure of unemployment according to its duration, its origin and the age of unemployed workers.

Male and female unemployment levels were higher in 1989 than in 1979 in nearly every OECD country, in absolute as well as relative terms[16] (see Statistical Annex, Table B). The structural and permanent nature of the unemployment problem became increasingly marked over this period. In some countries, this situation affected men more than women, serving to reduce the gender gap in unemployment rates though these were at higher levels for both men and women. However, the gap widened in Europe with the exception of the Nordic countries, where unemployment increased considerably.

There is a great deal of variation in the gender gap throughout the OECD area, irrespective of what age group is considered (Graph 2.3). This variation is particularly strong among the adult population. Thus, in 1989, unemployment rates for the central age group were twice as high for women as for men in the Mediterranean countries. In France, Germany, the Netherlands and Japan the female rates were some 50 per cent higher than the male rates. In the United States and in the Nordic countries the rates were much the same for both men and women. In Ireland and the United Kingdom, on the other hand, female unemployment rates were lower than male rates by half.

Graph 2.3. **Unemployment rates 1989**

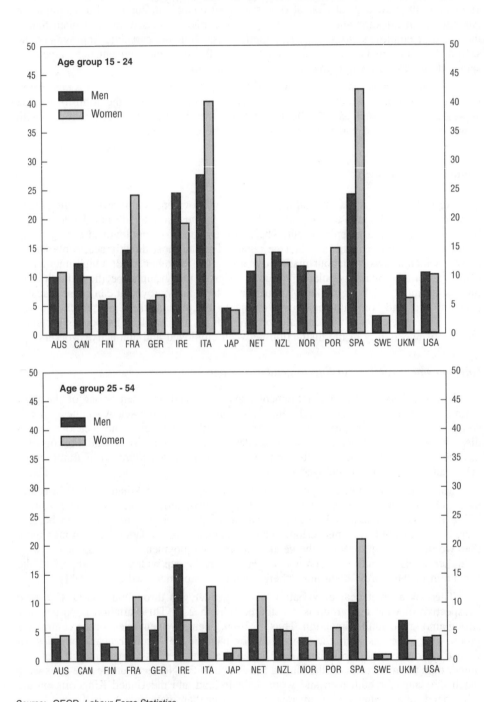

Source: OECD, *Labour Force Statistics.*

In almost all countries, the unemployment rates among both men and women are higher for young people than for the adult population. Germany is an exception with the unemployment rate of the youngest women slightly under that of middle-aged women. However, the differences between the unemployment rate of young people and that of adults vary from one country to another. The gender gap in unemployment rates generally follows the same pattern for both age groups, although it is relatively smaller for young people. In Canada and Japan, however, the gap is reversed: there is less unemployment among young women than among young men. In Finland, on the contrary, adult women seem to enjoy a slight advantage over men which younger women do not. In countries where both gender and age introduce a gap in unemployment rates, young women suffer a double disadvantage. In Spain and Italy, the unemployment rate of young women between the ages of 15 and 24 is over 40 per cent, a clear sign that integration into the labour market is particularly difficult for this group.

The structure of unemployment according to origin

Unemployment is as a rule a transition phase either between non-participation and employment (and vice versa), or between two jobs. Unemployment rates might be expected to be higher in the case of women since the frequency of their entry or re-entry on the labour market is also higher. The fact that integration into the labour force is increasingly through casual or insecure jobs, *i.e.* those leading sooner or later to unemployment, further reinforces this trend towards higher rates.

Table 2.2 shows the distribution of the unemployed population in the 25 to 54 age group according to both gender and the origin of unemployment.[17] The data are from the European labour force survey and are therefore not available for all OECD countries. The survey distinguishes between three categories: the unemployed in search of their first job, the unemployed in search of a job after a period of non-participation and the unemployed in search of a job after losing one. This last category covers both redundancies and the termination of casual or fixed-term employment.

The results are quite revealing. Apart from in Belgium and Denmark, there are appreciable differences in the structure of unemployment according to origin for each gender. The search for a first job is generally marginal for the unemployed of either gender in this central age group; this is not however the case in Greece and Italy, both of which have a high proportion of unemployed looking for a first job, even among men; this is also true, though to a lesser extent, in Spain and Luxembourg, but only as far as women are concerned. However, the gender-related difference lies mainly in the distribution of the unemployed between the ''job search after non-participation'' and ''job search after loss of employment'' categories. The first of these categories is much more frequently at the origin of unemployment for women than for men, while for the second, the opposite holds true. In Greece, Ireland, Italy, Luxembourg, the Netherlands, Portugal and the United Kingdom women's unemployment is caused by redundancy in fewer than one out of three cases. On the contrary, two-thirds to four-fifths of men's unemployment is caused by redundancy in all the countries surveyed with the exception of Italy and Portugal. The imbalance between the relative size of each category in the case of women and men varies considerably according to the country.

As Table 2.2 shows, a return to the labour market after a period of non-participation is particularly characteristic of women and is a non-negligible cause of their unemployment. It accounts for more than two-thirds of the unemployment of this category in

67

Table 2.2. **Distribution of the unemployed in the age group 25-54 by reason for seeking employment, 1989**

Percentage of total unemployment

	Men			Women		
	First job	After inactivity	After loss	First job	After inactivity	After loss
Belgium	7.7	13.8	78.4	4.3	20.2	75.5
Denmark	0.1	15.0	84.9	0.0	14.7	85.0
France	1.7	21.1	75.1	6.7	33.9	57.7
Germany	3.3	19.4	76.7	3.8	39.8	56.2
Greece	22.4	8.7	68.9	40.4	30.2	29.4
Ireland	1.7	9.8	88.3	3.9	66.4	29.7
Italy	39.5	35.7	24.0	48.5	42.2	8.9
Luxembourg	0.0	0.0	100.0	28.6	57.1	14.3
Netherlands	7.2	23.1	69.3	6.4	69.7	23.7
Portugal	3.1	46.9	50.0	16.3	52.9	30.4
Spain	10.1	4.7	85.2	25.8	15.1	59.1
United Kingdom	1.6	23.3	74.7	2.3	64.8	32.9

Note: Totals do not always add to 100 per cent due to a number of "reasons not stated".
Source: Eurostat, *Labour Force Survey, 1989.*

Ireland, the Netherlands, and the United Kingdom and from a third to more than half of the unemployment of this same category in other countries. Since working life expectancy after an interruption for family reasons is estimated at approximately 20 years for the present generation, it is not surprising that some governments are looking at this category of unemployed with particular concern[18] (see Chapter 6).

Long-term unemployment and discouraged workers

In 1989, the proportion of long-term unemployed workers – *i.e.* those continuously unemployed for more than a year – had increased everywhere in relation to 1979 (see Statistical Annex, Table B) although the exact proportion varies from country to country. It is particularly high in the countries of western and southern Europe where, in 1989, more than one in two of those unemployed were long-term unemployed (the corresponding figure for Belgium was more than three out of four). Although, in general, the share of long-term unemployment in overall unemployment does not vary much according to gender, it was found to be much higher for women in Spain, Greece and Portugal. On the contrary, it was much higher for men in Australia, Ireland, Japan, the Netherlands and particularly in the United Kingdom.

Long-term unemployment can lead to withdrawal from the labour market as a result of discouragement. Women form the majority – the large majority in Australia, Japan and Norway – of discouraged workers, and it is therefore important to take this factor into account when dealing with female unemployment (OECD, 1987).

68

CONCLUSIONS

Towards the end of the 1980s, the question of an increase in women's participation played an important role in discussions on the labour market in several OECD countries. This was closely linked to a perceived risk of a labour force shortage, especially of qualified labour which was seen in these countries as a major threat to stable and sustainable economic expansion. Under these circumstances, an increase in women's labour market participation appeared to be an ideal solution to labour force shortages, in both quantitative and qualitative terms.

While there is still a considerable difference in the participation rates of women and men in most countries, these differences are the strongest for the central and oldest age groups. If women are not present on the labour market, it should be remembered that this may be due to specific obstacles, such as the lack of qualifications among older women, or the incompatibility of working life and family life in other cases.

The example of countries in which women's activity rates are very high for all age groups (Finland, for example) suggests that these obstacles are not necessarily insurmountable. In fact, in OECD countries, fewer and fewer women remain completely outside the labour market and if, for many, working life remains interspersed with interruptions and re-entries, withdrawals from the labour market are more often temporary and increasingly short. Introducing parental leave has done much to prevent these interruptions from having a disproportionate impact on women's working lives and careers. The need to take care of elderly parents will undoubtedly create an additional source of pressure in the future but at a more advanced stage of their professional career.

In some countries, during the 1980s, the only increase in women's employment was through part-time work. There is no doubt that part-time work has the advantage that women who are committed to other priority or constraining activities still have access to employment. Nevertheless, in order to accurately understand the significance of part-time work for women, it is important to know whether it has been "freely" chosen. Whenever this is not the case, part-time employment may, in fact, be a reflection of hidden unemployment.

Family responsibilities remain an obstacle to women's full participation in economic activity; however, this is not the only factor: economic structures and the workings of the labour market play just as important a role. There has been a tendency in the past to place the emphasis on supply factors, especially as concerns the situation of women on the labour market. Economic developments, gender segregation, the increase in different forms of employment flexibility, as well as other institutional labour market characteristics all, however, play a major part in determining the level of employment and unemployment among women.

Structural factors explain, in particular, why, in some countries, women's unemployment is much higher than men's despite women's higher educational levels. Some of women's specific attitudes towards the labour market, such as not registering for unemployment or withdrawal, may be more easily explained by institutional factors rather than cultural factors, such as the way women perceive their role in society.

As female participation rates increase and converge towards those of men, the question of mobilisation of female resources is becoming less important and more attention needs to be paid to the utilisation of these resources, both from the point of view of quantity and quality. This requires information much more detailed than that given in traditional labour market statistics.

Notes

1. Thus, there are some significant differences in male participation rates from one country to another (for example, there is a difference of almost 20 points between Belgian and Swiss rates); comparing female participation rates without taking this structural factor into account could lead to faulty interpretations.

2. This chapter relies on and updates the information provided in *Employment Outlook, 1988,* Chapter 5.

3. The rise in participation rates must of course be understood in terms of their absolute level. The situation in Sweden, where the female participation rate rose by 9 points from a very high level, is thus particularly remarkable.

4. It should be noted that these are all countries where activity rates did not increase much and unemployment remained high even during the 1980s upturn.

5. A rise in the participation rates of this age group should not be too hastily interpreted as a sign of progress, since this might be due to a premature interruption of their studies.

6. This is true of other labour market indicators such as the unemployment rate. For instance, a female participation rate of 60 per cent only reveals that, at the time of the statistical survey, 60 women out of 100 aged 15-64 were present on the labour market. The same proportion might be obtained by the next survey (a month or a year later), but there will be nothing to show whether it is still the same 60 women who are on the labour market and the same 40 who are not, or whether there has been a change of status in either direction for a number of women.

7. Reference is made here to the following surveys: Australia, *Survey of Families,* 1982; Canada, *Survey of Families,* 1984; United States, *Survey of Income Program Participation,* 1984; France, *Enquête sur les familles,* 1982; United Kingdom, *Women and Employment Survey,* 1980.

8. In the retrospective surveys, only interruptions above a given duration are recorded. As this duration varies considerably from survey to survey, their results are not directly comparable.

9. Findings of a 1987 survey of a sample of workers aged 18 to 64 living in the major cities. Interruptions applied to periods over six months. Whatever the age and reason, a higher proportion of men than women (three out of ten as against one out of four) withdrew from the labour market at least once for more than six months. Among women in the 18-30 age group, two-thirds of the interruptions were due to employment difficulties and only one out of ten to family reasons (less frequently mentioned than resuming education). Family reasons were responsible for a break in slightly under four cases out of ten for women aged 31-40 and in more than three cases out of four for women over 40.

10. Maternity leave entitlement was only introduced at federal level in the United States in 1993; previously, this entitlement existed only if it was provided for at state level or in collective bargaining agreements.

11. Indeed, the "permanent housewife" has become rare in Sweden: of the women who had their first child at the beginning of the 1960s, only 7 per cent had never had a job during the next 16 years.

12. Strategy choice is greatly influenced by tax and other policies.

13. By way of example, a 1984 survey in the canton of Geneva revealed that the parents of half of the 51-55 age group were still alive.

14. *1982 National Long-Term Care Survey,* US Department of Health and Human Services.

15. Part-time employment is of great importance for the analysis of women's employment and is the subject of Chapter 3. Problems relating to the definition and interpretation of part-time employment will be raised in that chapter.

16. It should be remembered that these two years were each at the peak of the economic cycle.

17. It is not very meaningful to compare the structures of unemployment by cause for all unemployed workers (from 15 to 64) because the importance of young unemployed in overall unemployment is not the same from country to country (this, by implication, is also true of "unemployed workers looking for their first job"). Thus those seeking their first job represent fewer than 10 per cent of all unemployed in Denmark and Germany, but more than half of the unemployed workers in Greece and Italy.

18. A survey concerning women "re-entering" the labour market was carried out in Belgium in 1990 (Ministry of Labour, 1990). It was estimated that out of ten housewives, between one and three would like to have a job, which represents 55 000 to 165 000 women between the ages of 25 and 50. This survey shows that these women form a heterogeneous group. In comparison with working women, women re-entering the labour market are older (a third of them are under 35, half of them between 35 and 45 and 15 per cent over 45) and less qualified (more than half of them did not go beyond a lower secondary school diploma). On the other hand, women re-entering the labour market are slightly younger and certainly more qualified than other housewives. Only 5 per cent of them do not have dependent children; 3 per cent still have a child under the age of six. In four cases out of five, women re-entering the labour market have a professional history, which is true of only half of other housewives. However, they have not worked for an average of ten years (much longer than even they had originally expected). The work interruption is not always voluntary: in a third of the cases it is the result of redundancy or the termination of a contract. This is still more often the case of younger women. Eighty per cent of women re-entering would have preferred an alternative to a complete withdrawal from the labour market. A recent German survey also studied the situation of women going back to work after an interruption (Engelbrech, 1987). On average, from 1980 to 1985, they were 320 000 per year.

Bibliography

BERNHARDT E.M. (1987), *Labour Force Participation and Childbearing: The Impact of the First Child on the Economic Activity of Swedish Women,* University of Stockholm, Stockholm Research Reports in Demography, No. 41, September.

DESPLANQUES G., RATON I. and THAVE S. (1991), *L'activité féminine,* INSEE Résultats, No. 118, Paris: INSEE.

DEX S. (1984), *Women's Work Histories: An Analysis of the Women and Employment Survey,* Research Paper No. 46, Department of Employment, London.

ENGELBRECH G. (1987), "Erwerbsverhalten und Berufsverlauf von Frauen: Ergebnisse neurer Untersuchungen im Überblick", *MittAB,* 2/87.

FINCH J. and MASON J. (1990), "Gender, Employment and Responsibilities to Kin", *Work, Employment and Society,* Vol. 4, No. 3, September.

GLEZER H. (1988), *Maternity Leave in Australia: Employee and Employer Experiences,* Monograph No. 7, Australian Institute of Family Studies.

INSTITUTO DE LA MUJER, Ministerio de Asuntos Sociales (1989), *Encuesta sobre discriminacion salarial,* Madrid.

JAPAN MINISTRY OF LABOUR (1989), *The Labour Conditions of Women,* Tokyo.

MARTIN J. and ROBERTS C. (1984), *Women and Employment: A Lifetime Perspective,* Department of Employment, London: HMSO.

MINISTÈRE DE L'EMPLOI ET DU TRAVAIL (1990), *Femmes au foyer à la recherche d'un emploi,* Brussels.

O'CONNELL M. (1990), "Maternity Leave Arrangements: 1961-85", in *Work and Family Patterns of American Women, Current Population Reports,* Special Studies Series P-23, No. 165.

OECD (1987), *Employment Outlook,* Paris: OECD, Chapter 6.

OECD (1988), *Employment Outlook,* Paris: OECD, Chapter 5.

ROBINSON P. (1987), *Women's Work Interruptions: Results from the Family History Survey,* Ottawa: Minister of Supply and Services.

SERVICE DE L'ÉMANCIPATION SOCIALE, ministère de l'Emploi et du Travail (1992), *Les femmes dans la population active, l'emploi et le chômage,* Brussels.

SMITH S. (1982), "New Worklife Estimates Reflect Changing Profile of Labor Force", *Monthly Labor Review,* Vol. 105, No. 3.

US BUREAU OF THE CENSUS (1987), *Male-Female Differences in Work Experience, Occupation and Earnings: 1984, Current Population Reports,* Series P-70, No. 10, Washington D.C.: US Government Printing Office.

US DEPARTMENT OF HEALTH AND HUMAN SERVICES, *1982 National Long-Term Care Survey/Survey of Caregivers,* Washington D.C.

YOUNG C. (1990), *Balancing Families and Work,* Canberra: Australian Government Publishing Services.

Chapter 3

PART-TIME EMPLOYMENT*

One of the most dramatic changes in the structure of labour markets in industrialised Western countries has been the increase in forms of employment that differ from permanent full-time work. Part-time employment is one form of this "atypical" work and one which mainly affects women.

Part-time employment is not a new phenomenon. However, growth in its variety and extent and the fact that certain economic sectors are now largely organised on a part-time basis, is a relatively new development.

Part-time employment ranges from "short" part-time employment – with very few hours of work a week or month – to employment where working hours are similar to full-time employment. Labour regulations concerning part-time work vary between countries. While some efforts have been made to upgrade it and to integrate it into equal pay, dismissal and other regulations, as a form of non-standard employment part-time employment often falls outside the realms of protective labour regulations.

The implications of part-time employment for women appear rather ambiguous. On the positive side, part-time work creates employment opportunities for women and enhances their attachment to the labour force. On the negative side, it usually means lower income and less choice in terms of sectors and occupations, and fewer chances for career progression.

This chapter examines the development of part-time employment in OECD countries over the last decade. Comparisons over time and between countries are difficult to make, because of the definition and measurement problems outlined below. Data presented in the chapter – which reflect mainly regular part-time working – include a variety of definitions and are therefore only roughly comparable. Broad-based conclusions, however, can still be drawn.

The following discussion describes the characteristics of part-time employment and highlights new divisions between different groups of part-time workers. The factors influencing the growth of part-time work are also analysed, including the gender division of labour, employer and union approaches to part-time work, and the impacts of government economic, social and labour market policies. Some conclusions are drawn on the future development of part-time employment.

---

* This chapter is an abridged version of *Women and Employment Restructuring: Part-time Employment,* edited by Friederike Maier [OECD/GD(91)211].

The term "part-time" applies to employment which involves fewer than the normal weekly or monthly hours of work. It covers a range of arrangements, to include:

- regular part-time employment involving a set of hours specified for a week or a month;
- irregular part-time employment where the number of hours per week is unspecified and may fluctuate from one week to another;
- temporary part-time employment which recurs on a seasonal basis (and may involve re-employment of the same person each year);
- "on-call" part-time employment, where the workers are hired on an occasional basis, as the need arises.

When part-time employment is defined as any amount shorter than legally or collectively regulated full-time working hours, then the definition of part-time employment in terms of hours worked will need to change in accordance with modifications to full-time or "standard" employment. What then constitutes "typical" employment in OECD countries today in terms of working time?

Full-time employment is in most cases regulated and defined by fixed weekly, monthly or – more recently – annual number of hours. In OECD countries the legally fixed working week varies between 38 and 48 hours, while in collective agreements it varies between 33 and 48 hours. Nowhere is there a uniform standard working week across all industries or occupations. In addition, the general decline in working time, combined with flexibility patterns in daily, weekly or monthly working time, creates major definitional variations across countries. A 33-hour working week is regarded in the Netherlands as normal full-time employment for workers in the metal industry on rotating shifts, whereas in Portugal, shiftwork is on the basis of 44 hours per week (Bosch, 1989).

National definitions of part-time work and comparability problems

Different definitions of part-time work are used for various purposes. Statutory definitions are designed for administrative purposes, while statistical definitions are intended to divide the employed population into two groups, full-time and part-time.

There is no uniform statutory definition in the OECD countries. Reviewing the definitions used in 16 OECD countries in Europe, the *European Industrial Relations Review* noted that: "There is no statutory definition whatsoever in 11 of the countries. Of the five where such a definition exists, there is a wide variation; in the cases of West Germany and Italy, less than normal/standard hours; ...in France less than 80 per cent of normal hours; in Spain lower than two-thirds of standard hours" (IRS, 1990).

National statistical definitions are also problematic. The two basic methods for defining part-time work are self-assessment and the application of cut-offs to usual hours of work. In practice countries may adopt a more complex definition partly to exclude anomalous cases; for example self-assessed part-time workers who report more than a certain number of hours of work, either on an actual or usual basis. The treatment of people with two part-time jobs is also not uniform. Under self-assessment, respondents generally refer to their main job, while in some countries, an hours cut-off is applied to total usual hours in all jobs. In addition, household-based surveys, conducted in a specific reference week, may produce misleading results if there are inconsistencies between the number of hours usually worked and those worked during the reference week.

Definitions of part-time workers in labour force surveys (1991)

Australia	Persons who usually work less than 35 hours a week and did so during the survey week.
Austria	Persons who usually work less than 35 hours a week. Persons working less than 13 hours a week are not considered employed.
Belgium	Persons who declare themselves to be on part-time work.
Canada	Persons who usually work less than 30 hours a week for all jobs.
Denmark	Persons who declare themselves to be on part-time work at their main job.
Finland	Persons who usually work less than 30 hours a week. Unpaid family workers who worked less than one-third of normal working time are not considered employed.
France	Persons who declare themselves to be on part-time work.
Germany	Persons who declare themselves to be on part-time work.
Greece	Persons who usually work fewer hours than those provided for in collective agreements for this type of job.
Ireland	Persons who declare themselves to be on part-time work.
Italy	Persons who usually work fewer hours than those normally worked in this type of job.
Japan	Persons who were at work and worked less than 35 hours during the reference week.
Luxembourg	Persons who declare themselves to be on part-time work.
Netherlands	Persons who usually work less than 35 hours a week at their main job.
New Zealand	Persons who usually work less than 30 hours a week.
Norway	Persons who usually work less then 37 hours a week, except for those usually working 30 to 36 hours who state that their work is full-time.
Portugal	Persons who declare themselves to be on part-time work.
Spain	Persons who declare themselves to be on part-time work.
Sweden	Persons who usually work less than 35 hours a week.
United Kingdom	Persons who declare themselves to be on part-time work.
United States	Persons who usually work a total of less than 35 hours a week for all jobs. Unpaid family workers working less than 15 hours a week are not considered employed.

Within countries there are also discrepancies between different statistical sources and between statutory and statistical definitions. The United Kingdom provides a useful example: most official sources – such as Department of Employment's Historical Series on Employment – define part-time work as regular employment with no more than 30 hours a week. Data from the Women and Employment Survey 1980 revealed that roughly 1.5 million women officially counted as "non-working" did casual and occasional part-time paid work. On average, these jobs involved only five hours' work a week with earnings below the thresholds of National Insurance or income tax. In the Family Expenditure Survey, this kind of employment is not considered to be a "job". The New Earnings Survey excludes all employees earning less than the thresholds of National Insurance (Hakim, 1989).

International definitions

Comparable statistics must be based on common definitions. Since 1963, when the first major international study on part-time work was conducted by the ILO, little progress has been made in developing international definitions. The definition proposed by the ILO: "part-time employment is regular, voluntary employment carried out during working hours distinctly shorter than normal" raises two problems:

i) The word "regular" excludes all casual and temporary workers.

ii) The word "voluntary" raises the issue of whether workers choose to work part-time or are "involuntary" part-time workers because full-time positions are not available, or because they have been put on reduced schedules by employers responding to poor business conditions (OECD, 1990*a*).

The European Community Commission (ECC) defines part-time work as a "relationship involving shorter working hours than statutory, collectively agreed or usual working hours". However, it does not specify the degree to which hours of part-time work must be shorter than those of full-time work and it excludes workers whose average weekly working time is less than eight hours. This definition is designed to reflect the ECC's broader approach to "atypical" work, and the related concern that the absence of uniform definitions inhibits the development of policies to improve the status of and protection extended to those in non-standard employment:

"'Atypical' forms of work ... constitute an important component in the organisation of the labour market. For example, part-time working in all its forms, casual work and fixed term working have grown considerably in recent years, often in a quite anarchical manner. Unless safeguards are introduced, there is danger of seeing the developments of terms of employment such as to cause problems of social dumping or even distortion of competition, at community level." (EIRR, 1990).

The lack of uniform definitions of part-time work within countries and between countries raises several problems. It restricts both the ability to detect changes in the level and extent of part-time work over time and prevents making valid comparisons across countries. It also interferes with the development of policies related to this category of workers.

DEVELOPMENT AND CHARACTERISTICS OF PART-TIME EMPLOYMENT

The growth of part-time employment

Table C in the Statistical Annex indicates a variety of developments in the size and composition of part-time employment in OECD countries since the late 1970s:

- Denmark, Norway and Sweden had a high proportion of part-time employment both at the end of the 1970s and in the mid-1980s. Since then the proportion decreased, although more than 23 per cent of the employed still work on a part-time basis.
- Australia, the Netherlands, New Zealand and the United Kingdom had major increases in part-time employment, from a medium to a high level between 1979 and 1990. The proportion of part-time employees in these countries now matches or even exceeds those in the Nordic countries above. In Belgium and France the increase was also high, albeit starting from a low level at the end of the 1970s.
- Canada, Germany, Japan and the United States had a medium level of part-time employment at the end of the 1970s and moderate increase during the 1980s (in the United States, however, the proportion decreased during the late 1980s).
- Austria, Finland, Greece, Ireland, Italy, Luxembourg and Portugal began the period with a low level of part-time employment and experienced little or no increase during the 1980s.

The proportion of part-time workers in total employment increased virtually everywhere over the 1980s though to a greatly varying degree. In the Nordic countries and in the United States a peak was reached at the end of the 1980s and the proportion is now decreasing. The differences between OECD countries as they enter the 1990s are high: in Southern Europe – Greece, Italy, Portugal, Spain – and in Austria, Finland, Ireland and Luxembourg the proportion of part-time employment is below 9 per cent, while the Netherlands have more than 33 per cent. These wide variations imply similar variations in the relevance of part-time employment for national economies.

Over the 1980s female employment grew faster than men's employment in all OECD countries. In some, the growth in female employment was due solely to the growth in part-time employment (Table 3.1). This trend is most pronounced in Belgium, France, Germany, the Netherlands, the United Kingdom, where the number of women employed full-time actually fell, and particularly so in the two last countries. In these countries, even if more women were employed in the late than in the early 1980s, the average number of hours worked per female employee may have decreased. The opposite situation occurred in Canada, Denmark, Finland, Ireland, Italy, Luxembourg, Norway, Sweden and the United States, where the growth of full-time work contributed more than part-time employment to overall growth in female employment.

These divergent trends point to the fact that part-time work does not play the same role in women's employment in each country. While in all OECD countries women make up the vast majority of part-timers (between 64 and 90 per cent), the proportion of women working part-time varies considerably from country to country. As many as 40 to 60 per cent of all employed women work part-time in Australia, Denmark, the Netherlands, Norway, Sweden, and in the the United Kingdom. In contrast, in Austria, Finland, Greece, Ireland, Italy and Portugal only a minority (less than 20 per cent) work part-time, and more than 80 per cent of employed women have full-time jobs.

Table 3.1. Contribution of part-time
to cumulative growth of female employment, 1979 to 1986

	Percentage growth of total female employment	of which:	
		Due to part-time	Due to full-time
Australia	28.8	16.0	12.8
Belgium	6.4	7.5	−1.1
Canada	28.0	9.1	18.9
Denmark	13.6	1.3	12.3
Finland	10.4	2.1	8.3
France	4.6	7.3	−2.7
Germany	2.3	2.9	−0.6
Greece	24.3	..	..
Ireland	5.6	1.9	3.7
Italy	9.8	−0.2	10.0
Japan	11.5	6.2	5.3
Luxembourg	15.7	0.7	15.0
Netherlands	24.6	37.1	−12.5
Norway	19.9	8.1	11.8
Sweden	11.6	4.3	7.3
United Kingdom	2.9	7.3	−4.4
United States	22.2	5.2	17.0

Source: OECD Employment Outlook, 1988, Table 5.5.

The proportion of men working part-time is still uniformly low, varying between 15.8 per cent of all male employed persons in the Netherlands and 1.6 per cent in Austria. However, male part-time work has increased in nearly all countries and is relatively high in Australia, Canada, Denmark, Japan, the Netherlands, New Zealand, Norway, Sweden, the United Kingdom and the United States, all countries with a similarly high rate of female part-time employment.

Increased polarisation of part-time work

Recent trends show the development of different forms of part-time work as well as emerging differences between various groups of part-time workers.

Long versus short part-time work

"Short" – less than 10 or 15 hours a week – and "long" part-time work are two very distinct forms of part-time employment. In many cases social security regulations set thresholds for eligibility that exclude "short" part-timers. Protective labour regulations – such as protection against dismissal, the right to a written contract or the right to equal pay – are also often based on a given number of hours worked weekly or monthly on a regular basis.

"Short" part-time work is not always included in employment statistics. However, where data exist they indicate that it is increasing rapidly in some countries. Graph 3.1 shows the distribution of male and female part-time workers in six EC countries by usual weekly hours. There are high proportions of both male and female "short" part-timers in the Netherlands and the United Kingdom, but smaller proportions in Belgium, France and Germany. In Denmark "short" part-time is especially high among men working part-time and is lower among women. Table 3.2 shows a rapid increase in male "short" part-time in all six countries. For women the developments are less uniform. Thus, whereas in France the increase is not so pronounced and in Germany there is even a decline, "short" part-time increased disproportionately in the remaining four countries.

Men working part-time, especially on "short" hours, are typically students in Denmark, the Netherlands and the United Kingdom. In 1988, 48.7 per cent of the men in "short" part-time work (and 25.9 per cent of all male part-timers) in the Netherlands were undertaking education and training. The equivalent percentages were 64.4 per cent (and 34.7 per cent) in the United Kingdom and 80.5 per cent (and 67.2 per cent) in Denmark. With the exception of Belgium (where a majority of men working short part-time declare that they could not find a full-time job) the majority of men working "short" part-time are single and under 24 years old. In Denmark, the Netherlands, and the United Kingdom, between 48 per cent and 65 per cent live as a "dependent child" with their family.

In contrast, the vast majority of women in "short" part-time jobs are married – between 75.6 per cent in France and 83.7 per cent in Germany. The remarkable exception is Denmark where only 29.4 per cent of female "short" part-timers are married, a large majority (73.2 per cent) working "short" part-time because of educational commitments.

Voluntary and involuntary part-time

A growing number of families depend on the part-time income of women for their subsistence. There are increasing numbers of sole parents, mainly women, in this situation (OECD, 1990b). In all countries an increasing proportion of female part-timers say

Table 3.2. **Development of part-time employment by groups of hours and by sex, 1983 to 1988**

1983 = 100

	Belgium		Denmark		France		Germany		Netherlands		United Kingdom	
	M	W	M	W	M	W	M	W	M	W	M	W
"Short" part-time												
1-15 hours/w	168	148	200	139	143	104	161[a]	95[a]	423	157	186	124
16-19 hours/w	60	152	224	82	165	114	80[a]	30[a]	326	203	187	132
"Long" part-time												
20 hours and more	105	137	98	102	152	153	141	214	159	136	165	116
Total part-time	105	141	155	106	151	134	137	109	237	149	176	120

M: men   W: women.
a) Data for Germany are for the following groups of hours: 1-10 hours and 11-19 hours. Therefore they are not comparable with other countries.
Source: Maier (1991c), Table 10.

79

Graph 3.1a. Distribution of part-time employment by hours worked
Employees - 1988

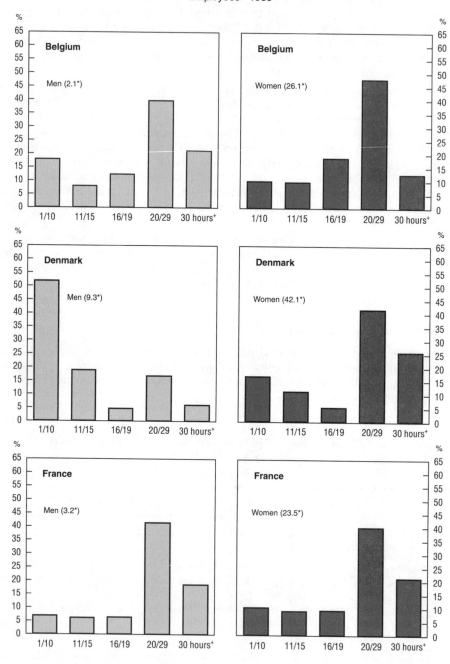

* Share of part-time employment in total employment.
Source: Maier, 1991c, Table 9.

Graph 3.1b. Distribution of part-time employment by hours worked
Employees - 1988

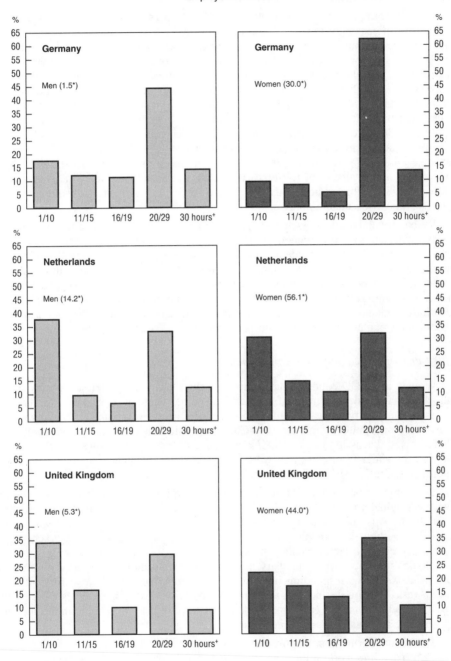

* Share of part-time employment in total employment.
Source: Maier, 1991c, Table 9.

they are the main earners in the family. Even among those on "short" part-time, between 10 and 15 per cent consider themselves to be main earners.

Income from part-time work rarely covers fully a person's living support. Part-time workers are increasingly having to combine several sources of income, often through more than one part-time job. That leads to two apparently contradictory developments: in most countries a growing number of women want to work part-time (and are unemployed because there is a shortage of jobs of that kind) and at the same time another growing number report that they want or need to work more hours or even full-time. In Germany and the United Kingdom, while a high proportion of women working "short" part-time declare that they do not want to work full-time (71.3 per cent in the former Federal Republic of Germany and 60 per cent in the United Kingdom), this does not exclude the possibility that they may wish to increase their hours of work. There are studies reporting that some groups of part-time employees, especially those on "short" part-time, wish to work longer hours, albeit not full-time (Bielenski and Strümpel, 1988; Statistiska Centralbyran, 1988). This indicates that some part-time employment is involuntary and represents disguised underemployment.

Research conducted in Quebec suggests "a growing polarisation of part-time work closely associated to two particular groups of workers with diverging characteristics and preferences. The first one is made up of youths, women with no more dependent children and old people; this group also counts a certain number of women with young children who see this type of employment as a way to reconcile working life with other activities. The second group is quite different, part-time work appears here as a constraint, a kind of precarious work not wanted as such. Most often, these people are looking for full-time jobs but must content themselves with part-time work." (Langlois, 1990).

Skilled and unskilled part-time employment

Women in OECD countries have improved their access to higher status jobs, especially through the development of the service sector. These jobs, however, are rarely available on a part-time basis. Skilled opportunities are mainly found in banking/insurance/finance and public administration. Chapter 5 will deal with public administration. The following discussion of the banking/insurance/finance sector shows that even when there is a potential to offer skilled work on a less than full-time basis, part-time work opportunities are largely confined to unskilled jobs.

The demand for extra staff to cope with peak workloads and longer opening hours gave the original impetus to the development of part-time work opportunities in this sector. In the Australian banking sector, for example, part-time employment was introduced during the 1960s in response to labour shortages, and part-time workers were originally used in a supplementary capacity. More recently, the introduction of new technologies into the banking industry has led to rationalisation and a reorganisation of work tasks with a corresponding increase in the number of jobs suitable for part-time work. "Tasks that are distinct and separate from other work lend themselves more easily to part-time employment... Part-time workers are employed to do specific duties and are kept separate from the normal career structure..." (Lewis, 1990).

Studies on German banking/insurance companies reveal a similar trend. The introduction of part-time work in the 1960s was aimed at "non-working" women as supplementary workers, but the recent process of restructuring and reorganisation of work tasks has resulted in even qualified women doing routine work. Therefore, although the banking sector offers women access to more qualified clerical work, part-time work opportunities have been largely confined to routine jobs which are only loosely connected to internal training and job advancement paths (Figge and Quack, 1990).

The way part-time employment has been introduced – even into areas with the potential to offer skilled work on a less than full-time basis – has contributed to the development of a mismatch of skills, jobs available and working-time conditions. This situation prevails in most OECD countries, although there is evidence that change may be occurring, albeit slowly. Employers facing severe recruitment problems, for example in specialised clerical work or in the nursing occupation, are starting to offer their skilled female employees part-time employment – usually for a transitional period – to ensure the retention of skilled staff. Given demographic trends which signal future labour shortages, this new trend is likely to continue.

Economic implications of part-time work

Part-time employment and earnings

The gender-based wage gap – due to the fact that highly feminised industries and occupations typically pay workers a less-than-average hourly wage – is exacerbated by the fact that part-time jobs pay even less per hour than their full-time equivalents.

There are pay differentials between women working full-time and part-time. A Canadian Committee of Inquiry into part-time work reported that, in 1981, women employed part-time received only 90 per cent of the hourly earnings of women employed full-time (Commission of Inquiry, 1983). This gap seems higher in Great Britain; in 1989 female part-timers earned only 75 per cent of full-time employed women, and the gap had widened since 1980 (Rubery, 1991).

These pay differentials appear even greater when compared to male earnings. The aforementioned Canadian Inquiry revealed that women working full-time received 78 per cent, and those working part-time only 71 per cent of the average male full-time wage. Similar results appear in Germany. Amongst semi-skilled and unskilled manual workers, women employed full-time received 78 per cent, regular part-timers 76 per cent and marginal part-timers only 74 per cent of male full-time wages (Büchteman and Quack, 1989).

The earnings gap between men and women, and between full-time and part-time employees, is common to most OECD countries. The differentials between female part- and full-timers can be explained in part as the result of direct wage discrimination against part-timers. Some countries have minor differentials – like Australia or Germany. In other countries the differentials are very pronounced. This is also the result of the institutional framework of wage-setting and wage regulations. Only in some countries do the wage-setting regulations cover all economic sectors (like in Germany or the Scandinavian countries). In Canada, Great Britain and the United States, the level of unionisation appears as another relevant variable. Canadian data show that wage differentials between women working full-time and those working part-time disappear in unionised jobs, although the general male/female earnings gap remains.

Part-time work and career

While most women claim their choice to work part-time is a voluntary one, they often ignore the long-term implications of that decision. Such a choice may well turn out to be an irreversible one and have negative impacts on future career progression. Because men and women follow different part-time employment patterns, the same scenario does not usually apply to men (Graph 3.2).

For men, part-time work is generally concentrated among very young and older men. It therefore coincides with the beginning or the end of their working lives, and rarely involves career interruption. Rather, part-time work operates in that case as a transition into or out of the workforce. Some employers use part-time work as a recruitment tool – as a means of "checking out" potential employees. It then acts as a probation period which offers young men a step into employment and a chance to obtain work skills. For older men, part-time work opens up a smooth transition to retirement.

Female part-time work, on the other hand, typically coincides with the family-intensive phase and often involves career interruption, although this varies between countries. While a great number of German women in the age group 25-34 leave the labour market altogether and re-enter on a part-time basis at a later date, French women have a constant high participation rate with minor increases in part-time employment. In Denmark, female participation rates increase with age (and are very similar to male participation rates) with a decrease in full-time employment among women over 25. The British pattern is similar to Germany's showing a decrease in participation rates in the 25-34 age group, followed by an increase in both part-time and full-time work among women over 35.

German data indicate a greater tendency to move from full-time into part-time work and from "non-working" into a part-time job than from part-time to full-time work or from "non-working" into full-time. Eighty per cent of female part-timers had worked full-time in previous years, whereas only 10 per cent of women working full-time had worked part-time during their previous working life. Only a minority of marginal part-time workers made the transition to regular part-time work (33 per cent) or to full-time work (10 per cent); the majority stayed in a marginal job or moved out of work (Büchtemann and Quack, 1989).

The switch from full-time to part-time employment and vice versa is regarded as normal practice in Sweden, although this generally only applies to women with full-time or stable employment contracts. In addition, the development of part-time work in Sweden – partly a result of the right of full-time employees to switch to part-time, and partly a product of public policies to create part-time employment – seems to have limited the number of full-time jobs available for unemployed women or women with part-time contracts seeking full-time work.

Since women are now having fewer children, career interruptions or periods of part-time work for family purposes will be increasingly short. Yet, many women still find it difficult to make the transition back into full-time work. Because part-time work has a negative impact on future employment prospects, it currently represents in most cases a significant work "trap" for women.

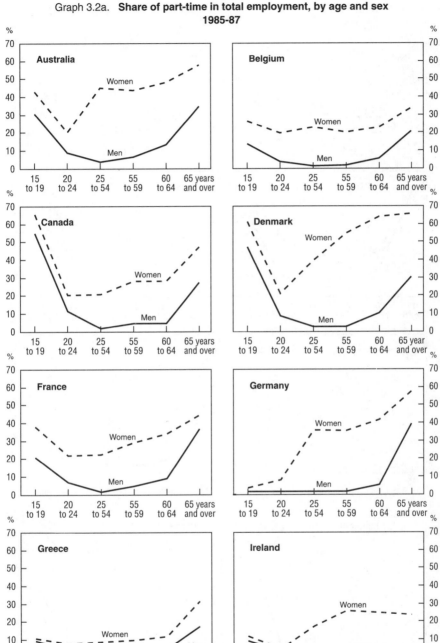

Graph 3.2a. **Share of part-time in total employment, by age and sex**
1985-87

Source: OECD, *Employment Outlook 1988,* Table 1.4.

Graph 3.2b. Share of part-time in total employment, by age and sex
1985-87

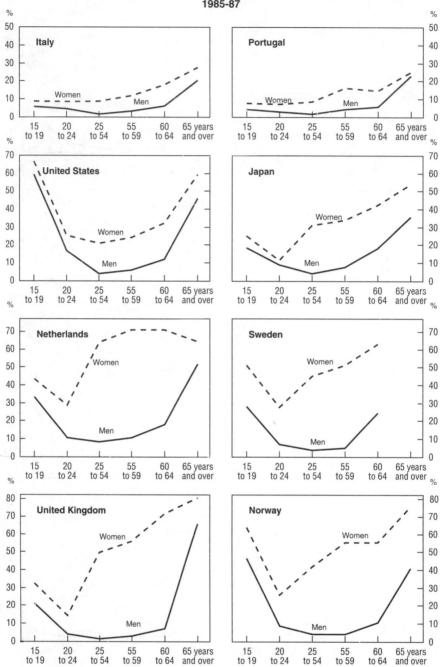

Source: OECD, *Employment Outlook 1988,* Table 1.4.

FACTORS INFLUENCING THE DEVELOPMENT OF PART-TIME WORK

The development of part-time work must be seen in the context of women's overall level of labour market participation, changing industrial and occupational structures and the wider socio-economic framework that shapes labour market supply and demand, including the gender division of labour, employer and union approaches to part-time work and the institutional framework of economic, social and labour market policies.

Increasing female labour force participation

All industrialised countries have experienced growing female labour force participation rates over the last 20 years (see Chapter 2). The general assumption that higher female participation goes in parallel with an increase in part-time work – the availability of part-time jobs attracting into the labour market married women who otherwise would not have worked – is true for only some countries. Countries with relatively high participation rates (like Finland and France) have a low proportion of part-time employment, while others with nearly the same participation rates have high part-time shares. In some countries female participation rose without any increase in part-time employment. Female labour force participation rates cannot therefore fully explain the level of part-time employment in the OECD countries (Drew, 1990) [Graph 3.3].

Graph 3.3. **Trends in female participation rates and in the share of part-time in total female employment, 1979 to 1990**

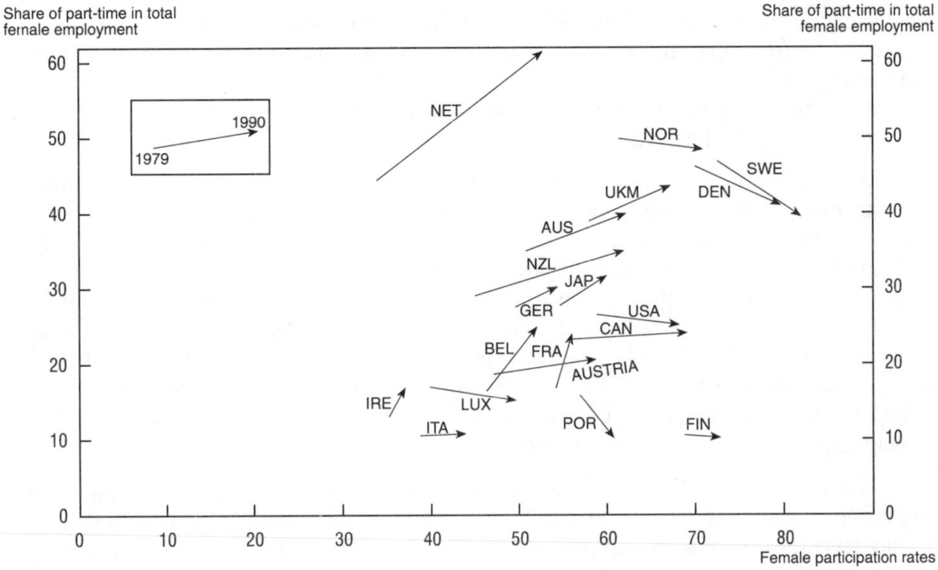

Share of part-time in total female employment

Share of part-time in total female employment

Female participation rates

Source : Statistical Annex, Tables A and C.

87

Changing economic and occupational structures

Economic developments, especially the changing occupational and sectoral structures of national economies, might partly explain increases in the level of part-time employment, and its variations between countries. Part-time work is an intrinsic element of the gender-segregated labour market structures. As a rule, men and women are unequally distributed among occupations and economic sectors – women being more likely to be employed in the service sector and in service-related occupations – and female part-time employment is even more concentrated in certain industries and occupations than full-time employment.

Service sector employment contributes heavily to the level of part-time employment. Most female part-timers in OECD countries work in "other services" or "distributive trades, hotels and catering". Variations in the size of the service sector, however, does not fully account for variations in the amount of part-time work as the extent to which the service sector utilises female part-time workers varies considerably across countries.

A study of six EC countries – Belgium, Denmark, France, Germany, the Netherlands and the United Kingdom – shows both similarities and differences in the occupational and sectoral distribution of part-time work (Maier, 1991*b*; and Table 3.3). Within industries, using the NACE classification (*Nomenclature des activités économiques dans les Communautés européennes*), group 60 (distributive trades, hotels, catering) and group 90 (other services, excluding public administration) employ the highest proportion of women, both full-time and part-time. However, the ratio of full-time to part-time women workers in these two sectors differs from country to country. In Denmark, the Netherlands and the United Kingdom, over half of all female employees in "other services" are part-time workers, whereas in Belgium, France and Germany the proportion is around a third.

A similar sectoral distribution of part-time employment occurs in other OECD countries. In Australia, almost half of the part-time workforce is employed in only two industries: retail trade and community services (mainly nurses and teachers). In the United States, the increase in part-time work is concentrated in the retail and personal services, while part-time work is declining in other sectors.

In terms of occupational structures, service-related employment is also significant for part-time work. In Australia part-time employees are concentrated in three major occupational categories – clerks, salespersons and personal service workers – which accounted for nearly 75 per cent of all part-time workers in 1991. Data on occupational structures collected by the Statistical Office of the European Community show the expected concentration of female part-time workers in the "clerical and related" occupations, "service workers" and "sales workers", but also an unexpectedly high proportion in "professional and technical related jobs". The latter group covers teachers, scientists and doctors where female employment is more likely to be on a part-time basis than in managerial or administrative occupations (Maier, 1991*b*).

There are country-specific differences in the extent to which certain occupations are organised as part-time jobs. Sales work in Germany is more likely to be part-time than in France, where service workers are more likely to be employed as part-time workers than in Denmark. A comparison between employment structures in Japan and the United States shows that in the latter country female part-timers are more likely to be employed

Table 3.3. Female part-time employment by economic sector, 1987

NACE group	Belgium (1)	Belgium (2)	Belgium (3)	Denmark (1)	Denmark (2)	Denmark (3)	France (1)	France (2)	France (3)	Germany (1)	Germany (2)	Germany (3)	Netherlands (1)	Netherlands (2)	Netherlands (3)	United Kingdom (1)	United Kingdom (2)	United Kingdom (3)
0 Agriculture	..	..	..	0.9	0.9	41.0	0.8	1.0	28.5	0.9	0.8	22.7	1.2	1.1	50.5	0.8	1.0	53.3
1 Energy and water	0.4	0.3	19.7	0.7	0.2	20.5	0.7	0.4	14.8	0.7	0.5	19.1	0.5	0.2	26.1	0.8	0.3	18.8
2 Minerals, chemicals	2.0	1.2	15.1	3.6	1.0	31.3	2.0	0.6	6.8	3.6	2.5	18.9	1.4	0.9	33.0	1.8	0.8	20.3
3 Metal	4.9	2.9	16.1	10.3	2.0	25.6	5.5	1.7	7.1	10.3	6.1	17.9	2.4	..	..	5.3	2.5	21.2
4 Other manufacturing	11.6	4.4	10.0	10.8	6.6	30.2	9.5	4.5	10.7	10.8	9.1	27.6	5.8	2.2	21.2	8.7	4.9	25.0
5 Building, engineering	0.6	0.8	36.3	1.7	1.2	39.2	1.2	1.4	24.7	1.7	2.2	41.5	1.3	1.3	56.7	1.6	1.6	45.1
6 Trade, hotels	15.8	24.0	40.5	21.8	16.9	51.9	16.1	19.0	26.5	21.8	25.3	35.6	21.9	21.5	55.5	25.0	34.0	60.6
7 Transports, communicat.	2.7	1.8	17.7	3.6	1.3	26.9	4.3	4.3	22.6	3.6	4.5	36.0	3.4	2.7	44.8	3.2	1.7	24.1
8 Banking, insurance	8.5	7.3	23.0	9.4	7.0	30.8	10.5	8.0	17.2	9.4	8.5	27.2	9.6	6.9	40.8	11.2	6.7	26.7
91 Public administration	11.2	10.5	24.9	8.9	7.6	38.4	11.9	13.6	25.8	8.9	8.8	28.6	4.9	3.7	42.1	6.8	4.2	27.6
90 Other services	42.2	46.4	29.3	28.2	55.7	50.2	37.4	45.0	27.1	28.2	31.7	32.6	47.6	54.5	64.6	34.8	42.0	53.7
Total	100	100	26.6	100	100	42.8	100	100	22.5	100	100	29.0	100	100	56.0	100	100	44.5

(1) Distribution of total female employees (full-time and part-time) by economic activity (NACE groups).
(2) Distribution of female part-time employees by economic activity (NACE groups).
(3) Female part-time employees as a percentage of all female employees in the NACE group.
.. Not available.
Source: European Labour Force Survey, 1987.

as professionals, clerical and service workers whereas in the former part-time work among women is concentrated in production-related and sales jobs.

The gender division of labour

Some sociologists have analysed the increase in part-time work in terms of a shift in preferences towards more leisure time and a change in attitudes towards working time in general. Fixed hours seem less acceptable as individuals attempt to exert greater control over the hours they work. Researchers also discovered a desire for more flexibility in working time over the lifecycle, and for a smooth transition into and out of the workforce (Weiermair, 1988).

If attitudes towards working time have changed, this is not reflected in actual time allocations, especially among male workers. While female labour market participation has changed towards an increase in part-time and "on-call" or occasional work, the male part of the labour force is – despite overall reductions in "standard" working time – working longer hours. Even in countries where men have the right to reduce their working time for the purpose of childcare, as in Sweden, they do not generally claim for this right.

In all industrialised countries, women still assume primary responsibility for child and other dependant care, as well as the bulk of household duties. Even in countries with high female labour force participation, there has been no substantial change in the gender division of domestic labour. Time-budget studies show that women living in households with more than one person spend twice or three times more time on "reproductive work" than their male counterparts, whether children are present or not.

This division of labour shapes the integration of women into the paid economy. Typical male paid work patterns – full-time continuous employment across the life-cycle – impose an external constraint on families' time-budgets; women provide the flexibility. Although most women define their decision to work part-time as "voluntary", the decision is based on the household division of labour.

Gender-based labour market segmentation – reflected in women's lower incomes, lower access to qualified and better paid jobs and to career advancement – entrenches the domestic division of labour. If a woman's potential income is lower than her partner's, it seems logical that she should assume primary responsibility for the provision of unpaid family services, and where necessary combine those responsibilities with part-time work. The typically low income earned by part-time workers subsequently hinders any reversal of the original decision to divide family and employment roles.

On the supply side of the labour market, part-time employment can be characterised as a coping strategy between paid work and family responsibilities. There is now a larger pool of women who – due to domestic constraints, economic necessity and personal aspirations – offer themselves as part-time workers. On the surface it appears that the growth in part-time work is a result of well-matched labour market supply and demand. As a Japanese government report remarked: "Employers pointed out that demand for part-time workers has increased because they are sufficiently qualified for the type of work needed and because they provide cost advantages over full-time employees. From the supply side perspective, the number of housewives desiring part-time employment has grown because this form of employment provides better opportunities for them to work, while fulfilling household responsibilities such as childcare" (Prime Minister's Office, 1990).

Part-time work and childcare provision

How women combine family care and paid work depends heavily on childcare provisions. The birth of a child is likely to be connected with withdrawal from the labour market in Germany and the Netherlands; with part-time work in Sweden and the United Kingdom; and with full-time work in Denmark, France and Finland (OECD, 1988, 1990a). In general a high number of women working part-time can be related to limited childcare provisions. This seems to be the case especially in the United Kingdom, somewhat less in the United States. On the contrary, the high proportion of women working full-time in France seems to be the result of the extensive public childcare and school systems (Dex and Walters, 1989; Gregory, 1987).

Where childcare services are expensive or inaccessible, the "choice" of employment for workers with limited disposable income is limited to work undertaken at times when others can look after the children without financial compensation. Women with children typically seek jobs that can be carried out in the mornings (especially in Germany, where the school day ends at lunch-time), in the late evenings (when other family members can look after the children) or on weekends. Childcare provision and school systems influence the extent to which women have to work with "unusual" time schedules.

Women with children and limited access to childcare facilities are forced to work part-time, or to withdraw from the labour market altogether, which, it is generally recognised, creates high barriers to labour market re-entry: not using professional skills devaluates those skills, while the skills gained in childcare or other family work are rarely perceived as labour market assets. There is less awareness that switching to part-time, especially part-time work that is available at unusual times, has similarly negative effects on career progression. Because jobs with this characteristic are heavily concentrated in low-paid traditional female occupations, women seeking employment with hours that fit in with family care schedules often end up – despite their professional skills – in unskilled or semi-skilled low-paid work.

In countries where childcare facilities are publicly provided – such as France or the Scandinavian countries – the responsibility for family care does not necessarily mean a withdrawal from the labour market or working unusual hours. Danish, Finnish, French and Norwegian data show that women with young children are more likely to work full-time than women in other countries, and that part-time work is characterised as a temporary or transitional situation within a professional career. The latter is especially true in Sweden. However, in general, even women working part-time during a transitional period are often disadvantaged in terms of career progression compared with equally educated men with equal length of employment.

In the future, ageing populations and, in some countries, State withdrawal from the provision of some health and welfare services will mean that the lack of access to services to care for the elderly and ill will increasingly impact on women's ability to take on paid employment (in the same way that the lack of access to childcare services already does).

Employer strategies

Employers increasingly use part-time workers as an element of a flexibility strategy. Employers hire part-time employees as a way of responding to changing market conditions by adding and subtracting from the peripheral part-time workforce as needed while maintaining a high commitment to a core of full-time employees. Relative to other forms of labour adjustments – such as taking on additional permanent staff or requiring existing staff to work overtime – the use of part-time workers has a number of cost and productivity advantages:

- part-time workers display higher levels of work intensity and lower levels of absenteeism, which raises labour productivity;
- part-time employment allows adjustment to fluctuating work loads and related staffing requirements, thus facilitating a closer match of hours worked and hours paid;
- part-time employees have lower costs of hiring, screening and induction compared to full-time workers;
- workers seeking part-time work often have more skills than are required for the job;
- wages paid to part-timers are generally lower than those paid to full-time employees in comparable occupations, jobs and industries, and there is often no obligation to contribute social security schemes;
- to the extent that the employment of part-time workers can reduce overtime and allow a better match between hours worked and hours paid, it can also contribute to a better allocation and utilisation of capital investment in equipment, thereby further raising productivity.

On the other hand, the use of part-time workers often involves higher administrative costs, since administrative overheads (notably payroll and supervision) have to be written off against fewer hours of work. Where additional equipment is required because of the greater number of employees, part-time employment may lead to higher capital costs (Lewis, 1990; Weiermair, 1988). Employers will only increase the proportion of part-time employees if the additional costs involved do not exceed the cost savings. Employers recognise that the advantages exceed the disadvantages in most cases. However, the net impact of part-time profitability will vary from industry to industry and from country to country.

Part-time work as a flexibility mechanism is highly concentrated in female occupations and industries. Male-dominated occupations or industries – and even male workers in female-dominated sectors – are subject to other forms of labour flexibility. For example, the rise in demand instability in the manufacturing and construction sectors in the 1970s and 1980s did not result in corresponding increases in part-time employment. Instead, other flexibility mechanisms were utilised – such as short-time, overtime and temporary contacts – which were regulated by collective agreements or labour law and often extended wage compensation to the employees affected.

The majority of part-time work remains organised in low-paid and low-skilled sections of service industries. Most women working part-time are therefore relegated to peripheral sections of the labour market which employers draw from as the need arises. This scenario is seen in the United States, where part-time work is an element of employer strategies to achieve external flexibility (Levitan and Conway, 1988). In this case, part-time work is associated with precarious employment and limited access to internal labour markets.

Recent changes in work organisation in response to technological developments bear implications on the utilisation of part-time workers. In the past it has proved profitable to separate certain tasks and organise them on a low-skilled/low-paid part-time basis. In most countries the trend is now towards more integrated forms of work. Part-time employment of the traditional kind does not appear suitable for jobs involving high levels of co-ordination, group problem-solving, or process-based production. Part-time employment is increasingly being offered as a means to retain trained skilled female workers in their jobs, especially by employers facing severe recruitment problems. In this case it is more likely to be integrated in the firm's internal labour market and to be covered by legal and collective rights.

The overall integration of female part-time work into internal labour markets is most advanced in the Scandinavian countries which show another scenario for the future of part-time work. The necessity to gain flexibility and profitability by using low-paid and low-skilled part-time labour has not disappeared in these countries, but it is now concentrated in a different fragment of the labour force; the flexible workforce is no longer just women, but increasingly young people, including young men.

Unions' attitudes

In most industrialised countries trade unions have strongly opposed the introduction of part-time work, fearing that it would be used as a means to undermine conditions of "standard" employment and worker solidarity. This was especially the case in the early 1980s, when unions were campaigning for an overall reduction in full-time hours of work.

Unions accepted the introduction of part-time work only to the extent that it did not affect the status and conditions of core workers. Negative trade union attitudes towards part-time employment resulted in its exclusion from collectively bargained rights, thereby influencing the development of a peripheral and unprotected workforce which, in return, saw no advantages in joining a union (Weiermair, 1988; Drew, 1990; Nassauer, 1989).

In the service and trade sectors, where unions are typically weak, increases in part-time work have created large segments of low-skilled and low-wage jobs. There is increasing union recognition that part-time work is no longer confined to a small proportion of married women, and that it is not a temporary phenomenon. Unions have thus been faced with the challenge of integrating part-time work into the collective bargaining process.

Trade unions' strategies in industries where employers have systematically substituted cheaper part-time labour for full-time employees now include efforts to improve the status, wages, employment rights and working conditions of part-time employees. However, in only a few countries – mainly the Nordic countries – have those strategies resulted in an equalisation of wages and fringe benefits between full- and part-time employees. In most other countries, part-time work is still not covered to the same extent by collectively bargained rights as full-time employment.

Union action to improve the working conditions of part-timers is more likely if a large proportion of the actual or potential union membership consists of women. However, recent studies found that female jobs, especially part-time jobs, are located in less unionised sectors which impacts on the lower women's unionisation level. Evidence suggests that this may be changing with women now forming the majority of the membership of some unions, especially in the service sector (OECD, 1991).

Impact of policies

Each country's policy framework – in particular labour and social security regulations, labour market measures and tax policies – creates incentives and disincentives which influence the growth of part-time employment and its structure.

Statutory social security schemes

Only limited protection is sometimes afforded to part-time workers in social security schemes. Where rigid thresholds apply, they tend to exclude certain groups of part-time workers from the schemes. In a number of countries unemployment and pension benefits, and to a lesser extent maternity or sickness payments, only apply to those who work a specified number of hours per week or earn a minimum income. Social security schemes often treat marginal part-timers as "non-working" persons. Access tends to be greater for those working more than 20 hours a week than for those working "short", casual, or irregular part-time. Exclusions may be broad as in Austria, Germany, the Netherlands and the United Kingdom (Table 3.4).

Exclusion from social security schemes acts as an incentive for employers to offer and for employees to accept work that falls outside the social security system. Employers save costs if they are not obliged to contribute to social insurance, while employees have a higher net income if social insurance payments are not deducted from their earnings. However, when these employees have to stop working – because of unemployment, maternity or illness – they do not receive any compensation for loss of income. In this case, they usually become dependent on public welfare schemes or the family. The treatment of marginal part-time work in social security schemes means that while employers save costs, those costs are often borne by the Welfare State and individuals in private households at some later date.

Protection for part-timers is severely limited under unemployment insurance schemes, due to exclusionary thresholds and the fact that benefits are calculated on previous earnings. Protection is slightly better under pension schemes. Some countries – such as Austria, Belgium or Germany – link retirement pensions to years of affiliation and contributions paid. This means that a full retirement pension is only paid to those who have worked full-time for their entire working life (30 to 40 years). Periods of part-time work reduce the pension entitlements over-proportionally, while some marginal part-timers are totally excluded. Other countries – such as France, the Netherlands, Norway and Sweden – base pension schemes on length of residence. Part-time workers are then treated on the same basis as all citizens. These countries also have an additional pension scheme which grants extra payments in proportion to total contributions paid. The threshold for this additional pension scheme is a weekly working time of at least 15 to 30 hours, which discriminates against "short part-time" workers. However, in France, Norway and Sweden pensions are calculated on the basis of the years where the highest income was earned. This means that if a person has worked full-time for a number of years, periods of part-time work do not reduce their retirement pension (Hohenberger et al., 1989; Maier, 1991a, b).

Table 3.4. **Minimum thresholds for social security coverage (1991)**

	Minimum thresholds		Unemployment	Exemption from employers' contributions
	Health, maternity	Pensions		
Austria		8 hrs/week and min. earnings	8 hrs/week and min. earnings	yes
Belgium	400 hrs over 6 months	4 hrs/day	8 hrs/week	no
Denmark	40 hrs over 4 weeks	10 hrs/week[a]	15 hrs/week	no
Canada			15 hrs/week and minimum earnings	yes
Finland			18 hrs/week	no
France	200 hrs over 3 months			no
Germany	15 hrs/week and minimum earnings	15 hrs/week and min. earnings	18 hrs/week	yes
Ireland	minimum earnings		min. earnings	yes
Italy	24 hrs/week[b]			no
Japan			22 hrs/week	no
Luxembourg			20 hrs/week	no
Netherlands		10-16 hrs/wk[a]	8 hrs/week	no
Norway			min. earnings over 3 years	no
Sweden			17 hrs/week	no
Switzerland		min. earnings	min. earnings	no
United Kingdom	min. earnings		min. earnings	yes
United States			min. hours[c]	no

a) For supplementary pensions.
b) For maternity benefits.
c) Depending upon state legislation.
Source: Information supplied by national authorities.

Employment protection

If little progress has been made in integrating part-time employment into social security schemes, in most countries the integration of part-time work into labour law and collective agreements has improved over the last decade (Blanpain and Köhler, 1988; ILO, 1989). All part-time workers are included in general labour regulations in Belgium, France, Germany, Portugal, the Scandinavian countries and Spain. Those regulations may relate to equal pay for work of equal value, working hours, protection from dismissals, and entitlements to paid holidays. In some cases it is stated explicitly that the employer is obliged to treat part-time in the same way as full-time workers. However, for rights that exceed the legally guaranteed minimum – like additional wages and bonuses, additional paid holidays, company schemes offering additional pensions, special premiums (over-time rates, wage premiums for work at "unusual" hours, or night work) – part-time workers in general or those who work less than 50 per cent of the full-time hours are often excluded. This has a substantial effect on the level of their earned income relatively to full-time workers.

In countries where no general labour legislation applies, the rights of part-timers are often very poor. For example, in the United Kingdom only part-timers working more than 16 hours a week, who have been with the firm for more than two years (or more than 8 hours if they have been with the firm for at least five years) are protected against unfair dismissal. In the Netherlands an employee must work more than 14 hours a week to earn the right to a guaranteed minimum wage, to be protected against unfair dismissal or to vote for the workers' representatives (ILO, 1989; Maier, 1991b).

The national institutional framework influences not only the number of part-time jobs offered but also the occupational distribution and the volume of hours worked. In the United Kingdom, where the wage threshold for employers' contributions to social security schemes is one of the highest, the share of marginal part-time work in total employment is one of the largest. In the Netherlands, where part-time workers with less than 14 hours are not covered by legal protection, a dramatic increase in this type of part-time work has occurred.

Workers who change from full-time to part-time work can in most countries be severely penalised in terms of pensions, unemployment benefits and other benefits. Only a few countries have regulations giving priority for full-time jobs to workers who wish to change from part-time to full-time. Sweden has the strongest regulations allowing transition from full-time to part-time work and back again (Hohenberger et al., 1989). In fact, Swedish researchers have shown that the increase in full-time employment and the decrease in part-time work among Swedish women in the mid-1980s were mainly due to women who were formally employed part-time increasing their hours to full-time employment (Sundström, 1991).

Labour market measures

In the early to mid-1980s, many countries adopted measures to encourage employers to expand part-time work opportunities through financial incentives – such as wage subsidies granted for a specific period of time – or by removing cost-related legal barriers, e.g. disincentives with regard to social security costs. However, in most countries the main emphasis has been on phased retirement and part-time job creation programmes for unemployed young workers.

Subsidies to firms promoting part-time work are in most cases now being phased out. The results of these programmes were often very disappointing. Where the subsidies were bound to certain conditions (regular contracts, hours or income above the threshold, part-time in sectors where it is uncommon, part-time for male workers or in highly paid occupations), the take-up rate was quite low. Where the standards set by the programme were low, the results showed that most of the subsidies went to firms which would have increased their part-time workforce anyway.

Public programmes were therefore reoriented towards offering financial incentives to workers. Almost all phased retirement schemes offer some financial support to encourage workers to accept part-time work. In some countries this arrangement does not decrease future pension entitlements. More countries are offering support to full-time employed persons who want to work part-time for family reasons or to undertake further training. Paid or unpaid parental leave, which can be combined with part-time work and the right to return to full-time employment, is a statutory right in Belgium, France, Germany and the Scandinavian countries. Large firms are starting to offer similar arrangements to ensure staff retention. Financial compensation varies considerably, from high benefit in Sweden (nearly 90 per cent of lost income) to no payment at all in schemes offered by some private firms.

To encourage the unemployed who were formally full-time workers to accept part-time work, some countries – such as Belgium, France and Sweden – pay partial unemployment benefits. In France, for example, a scheme was introduced to give part-time workers the right to receive benefits up to the level of their previous unemployment benefit, if the wage of the part-time job is lower than that previous benefit.

Employment creation programmes – especially those designed to give young people work experience – are more and more often based on part-time employment (for example in France, Italy, Spain and the United Kingdom), and usually include a training component. The public sector is also offering more part-time positions. The Belgian government, for example, hires new recruits only on a part-time basis; after a certain probationary period they are entitled to shift to full-time employment. The Dutch government has in the past offered part-time jobs in its public service; it now offers special subsidies to employers hiring young people on a part-time basis.

CONCLUSIONS

Part-time employment has become a growing and permanent segment of the labour markets and employment structures of industrialised countries, although there are marked differences across countries. It creates employment opportunities for those who wish or have to remain involved in another sector of activity, such as childcare and housework, education and training. On the other hand, part-time employment imposes a "restricted choice" on workers. Part-time jobs are in most countries largely confined to certain industries and occupations, they are typically low-skilled and low-paid and offer little access to training, benefits, or occupational mobility. As part-time employment is mainly women's work, many women are confronted with those limited job possibilities.

Current institutional arrangements have acted as an incentive for the substitution of full-time workers with cheaper and unprotected marginal part-timers. Part-time work, especially on short hours, often falls outside the framework of legally guaranteed social security and labour law regulations. The upgrading of part-time work requires the equalisation of wages and working conditions between full-time and part-time workers in equivalent jobs.

Access to training activities and career progression remain closely connected to full-time employment. Complementary mechanisms are required to allow workers to make the transition from full-time to part-time employment and back again, and to open up access to training and career advancement to all workers. Only with these changes in policies and practices could employees be considered to work part-time on a "voluntary" basis.

Strategies to upgrade part-time work will likely broaden the range of jobs that can be performed on a less than full-time basis and allow for a better balance between part-time and other forms of flexibility. There is a need to develop working-time and employment flexibility in general, through a greater variety of flexibility forms applicable to both men and women workers.

Bibliography

BIELENSKI, H. and STRÜMPEL, B. (1988), *Eingeschränkte Erwerbsarbeit bei Frauen und Männern,* Edition Sigma, Berlin.

BLANPAIN, R. and KÖHLER, E., eds (1988), *Legal and Contractual Limitations to Working Time in the European Community Member States,* Office for Official Publications of the European Communities, Luxembourg.

BOSCH, G. (1989), *Wettlauf rund um die Uhr? Betriebs- und Arbeitszeiten in Europa,* Dietz-Verlag, Bonn, p. 69.

BÜCHTEMANN, C. and QUACK, S. (1989), "Bridges or Traps? Non-standard Employment in Germany", in G. and J. Rodgers (eds.), *Precarious Jobs in Labour Market Regulation,* International Institute for Labour Studies, Geneva, pp. 109-148.

COMMISSION OF INQUIRY INTO PART-TIME WORK (1983), *Part-time Work in Canada,* Report of the Commission of Inquiry into Part-time Work, Minister of Supply and Services, Ottawa.

DALE, A. and GLOVER, J. (1990), *An Analysis of Women's Employment Patterns in the United Kingdom, France and the United States,* Employment Department, Research Paper No. 35, London.

DEX, S. and WALTERS, P. (1989), "Women's Occupational Status in Britain, France and United States: Explaining the Difference", in *Industrial Relations Journal,* Vol. 20, No. 3, Autumn 1989, pp. 203-212.

DREW, E. (1990), "Part-Time Working in Ireland", in *Equal Opportunities International,* Vol. 9, Nos. 3, 4, 5.

EIRR (1990), "EEC: Draft of a Typical Work Directives", in *European Industrial Relations Review,* No. 200, September 1990, pp. 12-16.

EISENSTEIN, Z. (1979), "Capitalist Patriarchy and the Case for Socialist Feminism", *Monthly Review Press,* New York/London.

EUZEBY, A. (1988), "Social Security and Part-time Employment", in *International Labour Review,* Vol. 127, No. 5, pp. 545-556.

FIGGE, K. and QUACK, S. (1990), *Die Auswirkungen des europäischen Binnenmarktes auf die Beschäftigung von Frauen im Kreditgewerbe der BRD,* Wissenschaftszentrum Berlin, discussion paper FS I 90-15.

GREGORY, A. (1987), "Le travail à temps partiel en France et en Grande-Bretagne", in *Revue Française des Affaires Sociales,* No. 3, July/September, pp. 53-60.

GONÄS, L. (1989), En *Fråga om kön, Kvinnor och män om strukturomvandlingens spar* (A Question of Sex – Men and Women in Patterns of Structural Change), Arbetslivscentrum, Stockholm.

HAKIM, C. (1989), "Workforce Restructuring, Social Insurance Coverage and the Black Economy", in *Journal of Social Policy,* Vol. 18, Part 4, October, pp. 471-503.

HOHENBERGER, L., MAIER, F. and SCHLEGELMILCH, C. (1989), *Regelungen und Förder-programme zur Teilzeitarbeit in Schweden, Norwegen, Grossbritannien, Frankreich, Niederlande, Belgien und Österreich,* Dokumentation des Bundesministers für Jugend, Familie, Frauen und Gesundheit, Materialien zur Frauenpolitik 3/1989, Bonn.

HORRELL, S., RUBERY, J. and BURCHELL, B. (1989), "Unequal Jobs or Unequal Pay", in *Industrial Relations Journal,* Vol. 20, No. 3, pp. 176-191.

ILO (1988), *Working-Time Issues in Industrialised Countries,* Tripartite Symposium on Working Time Issues in Industrialised Countries, International Labour Office, Geneva.

ILO (1989), International Labour Office, "Part-time Work," *Conditions of Work Digest,* Vol. 8, 1/1989, Geneva.

InforMISEP 28 (1989), "Part-time Work", in *InforMISEP,* No. 28, Winter.

IRS (Industrial Relations Services) (1990), "Non-Standard Forms of Employment in Europe", *European Industrial Relations Review,* Report Number Three, London.

LANGLOIS, S. (1990), "Le travail à temps partiel – vers une polarisation de plus en plus nette", *Relations Industrielles,* Vol. 45, No. 3, pp. 548-564.

LEVITAN, S. and CONWAY, E. (1988), "Part-Timers: Living on Half Rations", in *Challenge,* May/June, pp. 9-16.

LEWIS, H. (1990), *Part-Time Work: Trends and Issues,* Department of Employment, Education and Training, Women's Research and Employment Initiatives Programme, Australian Government Publishing Service, Canberra.

MAIER, F. (1991a), "Part-Time Work, Social Security Protection and Labour Law: an International Comparison", in *Policy and Politics,* Vol. 19. No. 1.

MAIER, F. (1991b), *The Regulation of Part-Time Work: A Comparative Study of EC Countries,* Wissenschaftszentrum Berlin, discussion paper FSI91-9.

MAIER, F. (1991c), *Women and Employment Restructuring: Part-time Employment,* OECD/GD(91)211, Paris.

NASSAUER, M. (1989), "Gewerkschaftliche Tarifpolitik zu Teilzeitarbeit. Skizze der Geschichte eines 'verqueren' Regelungsbereichs", in Müller, U. and Schmidt-Waldherr, H. (Hrsg.), *Frauensozialkunde,* AJZ-Verlag, Bielefeld, pp. 58-73.

NATIONAL INSTITUTE OF EMPLOYMENT AND VOCATIONAL RESEARCH (1988), *Women Workers in Japan,* NIEVR Report No. 4, Tokyo.

NOU (Norges Offentlige Utredninger) (1987), *Arbeidstidsreformer* (Working Time Reforms), NOU 1987: 9A, Oslo, Bergen, Stavanger, Tromsö.

OECD (1988), *Employment Outlook,* Paris, September.

OECD (1990a), *Employment Outlook,* Paris, July.

OECD (1990b), *Lone Parent Families: The Economic Challenge,* Paris.

OECD (1991), *Employment Outlook,* Paris, July.

PRIME MINISTER'S OFFICE (1990), *Japanese Women Today,* Report of the Headquarters for the Planning and Promotion of Policies Relating to Women, Japan.

RUBERY, J. (1991), "Pay, Gender and European Harmonisation: Some 'Societal Effects' in the Determination of the Gender Pay Differential", manuscript, Manchester School of Management (UMIST).

STATISTISKA CENTRALBYRAN (1988), "Deltidsarbete – Omfattning och orsaker" (Part-time Work – Scope and Reasons), *Information om arbetsmarknaden* No. 2, Stockholm.

SUGENO, K. (1990), "Flexibility in Working Time in Japan", in *Japan Labor Bulletin,* June (Part 1, pp. 5-8) and July (Part 2, pp. 5-8).

SUNDSTRÖM, M. (1991), *The Growth of Full-Time Work Among Swedish Women in the 1980s,* Working Paper, Stockholm, Arbetslivscentrum.

TAKANASHI, A. (1989), ''A Challenge to Economic Progress: Changing Aspirations and Labour Market Problems'', paper for the OECD Conference on Japanese Employment in the Context of a Changing Economy and Society, Paris.

THURMANN, J. and TRAH, G. (1990), ''Part-Time Work in International Perspective'', in *International Labour Review,* Vol. 129, No. 1, pp. 23-40.

WEIERMAIR, K. (1988), ''Part-Time Labor: Causes and Consequences for Managerial Discretion'', in Dlugos, G., Dorow, W. and Weiermair, K. (eds.), *Management under Differing Labour Market and Employment Systems,* Berlin/New York, pp. 335-349.

Chapter 4

THE SERVICE SECTOR: A LABOUR MARKET FOR WOMEN*

Service employment has been the major contributor to employment growth in OECD countries over the past 25 years. If the developments which have occurred in this sector have had a bearing on employment overall, women have been disproportionately affected because they are overwhelmingly concentrated in service sector occupations and industries.

Analyses of service sector employment are hindered by difficulties associated with classification. Two problems arise: how to group together production activities which are similar enough to form a coherent subset (such as producer or administrative support services), and how to specify the boundary between service and non-service activities.

The most common method of classifying services as economic activities is by industrial sector[1] but analysing them by occupation is more problematic. In a manufacturing industry, for example, there are clear distinctions between white-collar and blue-collar occupations in terms of skills and functions. In many service industries, however, occupational distinctions must be made among a predominantly white-collar workforce. Since these intra-industry distinctions are relatively new and since many service occupations have also been profoundly affected by the introduction of micro-electronic technologies, international comparisons by occupational category are often more difficult.

This chapter analyses significant changes occurring in the service sector and their impact on women.[2] It illustrates differences and similarities in the production of service outputs in national contexts, and describes shifts in the share of female employment within service industries. It also assesses the effects of increased internationalisation of services; changes in the skill level of service jobs; the development of internal labour markets; and the implications of changes in service sector employment for equality policies. Due to the lack of comparative data at an international level, this discussion will rely mainly on illustrative examples. Finally, as Chapter 5 deals with women's employment in the public sector, thus public services, this chapter will focus mainly on marketable services.

---

* This chapter is an abridged and edited version of *Women and Employment Restructuring: The Service Sector,* by Susan Christopherson [OECD/GD(91)212].

Trends in overall employment

Women's increasing employment in services and the dominance of service employment overall must be seen in the context of changes in the structure of OECD economies. As was the case in the United States and Canada during the early part of this century, a significant share of the recent proportional growth in service employment in European countries can be attributed to a decline in primary sector employment in absolute terms (see Statistical Annex, Table D). In many industrialised countries with relatively low levels of female labour force participation – such as Ireland, Italy and even Japan – women are still employed as non-salaried family workers in the primary sector. Decreases in agricultural employment in these countries will likely contribute to proportional growth in service employment in the future. In addition, OECD countries such as France, Germany,[3] Italy and the United Kingdom were affected by serious downturns in manufacturing employment in the 1980s, which also contributed to a proportionally higher representation of service employment.

Service activities are at present the fastest growing area of employment in most OECD countries, accounting for over half of all employment. Growth in financial and business services, as well as in community services and wholesale trade, has been a common feature of OECD economies over the past decades. Another common feature is

Graph 4.1. **Growth in service sector employment and in female participation rates, 1980 to 1990**

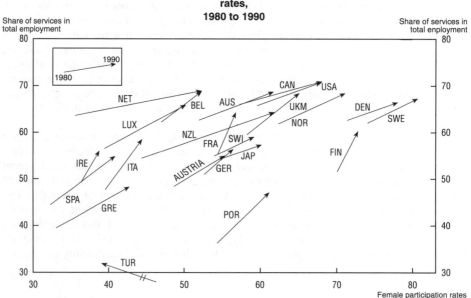

Source: Statistical Annex, Tables A and D.

Graph 4.2a. **Female employment in service activities, 1989**

Wholesale and retail trade, restaurants and hotels
Financing, insurance, real estate and business services

Transport, storage and communication
Community, social and personal services

Distribution of female employment by sector

Feminisation rates

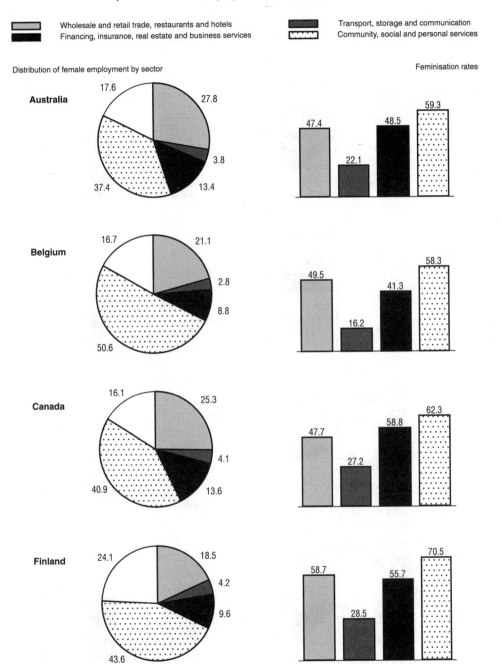

Source: OECD, *Labour Force Statistics.*

Graph 4.2b. Female employment in service activities, 1989

▨ Wholesale and retail trade, restaurants and hotels	■ Transport, storage and communication
■ Financing, insurance, real estate and business services	⬚ Community, social and personal services

Distribution of female employment by sector

Feminisation rates

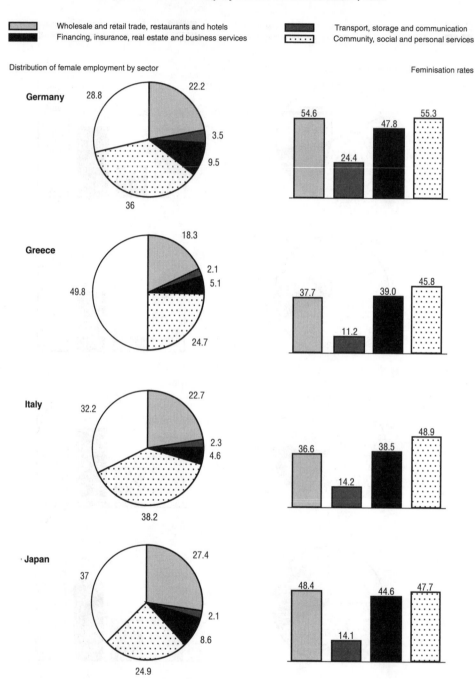

Germany

Pie: 22.2, 3.5, 9.5, 36, 28.8

Bars: 54.6, 24.4, 47.8, 55.3

Greece

Pie: 18.3, 2.1, 5.1, 24.7, 49.8

Bars: 37.7, 11.2, 39.0, 45.8

Italy

Pie: 22.7, 2.3, 4.6, 38.2, 32.2

Bars: 36.6, 14.2, 38.5, 48.9

Japan

Pie: 27.4, 2.1, 8.6, 24.9, 37

Bars: 48.4, 14.1, 44.6, 47.7

Source : OECD, *Labour Force Statistics.*

Graph 4.2c. **Female employment in service activities, 1989**

Wholesale and retail trade, restaurants and hotels
Financing, insurance, real estate and business services

Transport, storage and communication
Community, social and personal services

Distribution of female employment by sector

Feminisation rates

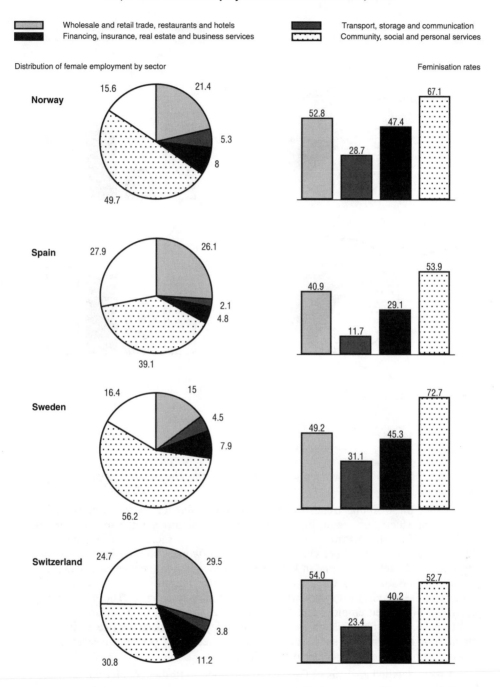

Source : OECD, *Labour Force Statistics.*

Graph 4.2d. **Female employment in service activities, 1989**

Wholesale and retail trade, restaurants and hotels

Financing, insurance, real estate and business services

Transport, storage and communication

Community, social and personal services

Distribution of female employment by sector

Feminisation rates

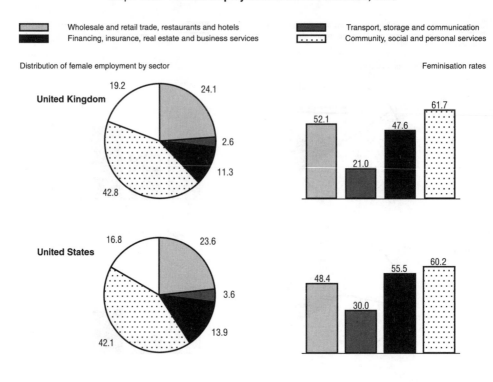

Source : OECD, *Labour Force Statistics.*

the high concentration of women's employment in the community services and public sector activities.

Despite these similar trends there are striking differences between national female employment patterns by sector. First of all, there are variations in the structure of female employment (*i.e.* the distribution of women in different sectors): for example, in the United States in 1989, 56 per cent of all employed women worked in community and financial service activities while in Japan the corresponding figure was only 33.5 per cent. Second, feminisation rates for a specific activity (*i.e.* the proportion of women among workers in the activity) also vary widely from country to country. Those with a higher proportion of women employed in the agricultural, industrial or manufacturing sectors tend to have lower feminisation rates in community or financial service activities. The feminisation rate in public, social and personal services is 72 per cent in Sweden, 55 per cent in Germany and only 47 per cent in Japan.

A more detailed analysis of the data would point to further country variations in the distribution of female employment among occupations. While occupational data by sector are not available at an international level, distribution by occupation in the whole economy can give an indication of the representation of women in "service" jobs. These data show that employment in the "service occupations" tended to decline across OECD countries from 1980 to 1989 as a percentage of total female employment. For instance, although in many countries there were increases in the absolute number of women employed in clerical occupations, the proportion of women in those occupations remained stable or declined slightly, relative to other occupational categories, particularly professional, technical or managerial occupations (Table 4.1). Some of the relative decline of women's employment in "service occupations" may in some cases be attributed to rationalisation of public sector activities which historically have employed a large number of women in this category (see Chapter 5).

Observed differences in female service employment across countries can be attributed to several factors:

i) The means by which personal or consumer services are provided: in countries such as Germany, Italy and Japan services such as food preparation, laundry services and childcare are still primarily provided by women in the home. In other countries – such as Sweden and Norway – some of these services, particularly childcare and care of the elderly, have been redefined as collective responsibilities and are carried out by women employed in the public sector. In still another set of cases – most notably the United States and to a lesser extent the United Kingdom – these services are privatised and are provided by women who are self-employed or employed by private firms.

ii) The degree to which service activities are subcontracted: when services previously integrated within a large manufacturing firm are sub-contracted, employment in the service sector increases at the expense of employment in the manufacturing sector. This apparent increase is simply a statistical artefact.

iii) The size of firms carrying out service sector activities: where service provision in activities such as tourism or health care is carried out in small firms, employment in those sectors will tend to be more labour-intensive than in cases where services are provided through large firms, or, in the case of the public sector, large organisations.

iv) Changing consumption patterns related to women's labour market participation and urbanisation: where an increasing portion of the female workforce works full-time, there has been a secondary spurt of growth in the consumer service sector, particularly in restaurants and prepared food. In addition, higher rates of urbanisation contribute to increased purchases of services.

v) The way in which regulation constricts or expands employment opportunities for women: regulation which severely limits shop opening hours both constrains the number of part-time jobs available and creates difficulties in provisioning for people with full-time jobs. In some countries, health and safety regulations eliminate women as competitors for certain jobs or confine them to unrecorded work for family firms. On the other hand, social regulation mandating maternity and other benefits, such as "personal days", has made the task of combining childcare and wage work easier. All of these regulatory practices affect female labour supply and impact on women's ability to enter and remain in the workforce.

In addition, in societies that maintain traditional structures, female employment (and unemployment) is undercounted because it is disguised within family firms. Thus in

Table 4.1. **Distribution of female employment by occupation**[a] **1980 and 1989**

Percentages

Country [b, c]	Professional, technical and related	Administrative and managerial	Clerical and related	Sales workers	Service workers	Agriculture and related	Production and related
Belgium							
1983	25.9	1.4	24.4	13.7	18.6	2.8	13.2
1988	28.2	1.4	27.3	14.6	14.4	2.1	11.6
Index (1983 = 100)	118	113	122	116	84	86	95
Canada							
1980	19.1	5.4	34.5	10.0	18.3	2.8	9.9
1989	20.9	10.7	30.5	9.9	17.0	2.2	8.9
Index (1980 = 100)	143	185	114	123	122	98	113
Finland							
1980	19.8	1.4	21.8	8.6	22.3	10.5	15.5
1989	31.2	1.9	22.7	11.5	16.2	6.5	10.0
Index (1980 = 100)	172	147	113	145	79	66	70
Germany							
1980	14.1	1.3	30.7	12.9	16.3	6.9	15.9
1986	16.2	1.5	29.8	12.8	16.1	5.5	13.3
Index (1980 = 100)	118	115	99	102	102	83	86
Greece							
1981	10.7	0.7	12.9	9.0	9.7	41.6	15.5
1989	14.4	0.8	14.6	10.8	11.5	34.0	13.9
Index (1981 = 100)	156	130	131	138	137	95	104
Japan							
1980	9.6	0.5	23.1	14.3	12.7	13.1	26.5
1989	11.4	0.8	26.4	14.4	11.4	8.8	26.5
Index (1980 = 100)	173	132	116	104	77	116	250
Norway							
1980	23.6	2.2	19.2	12.8	24.9	5.9	11.2
1989	28.3	3.5	19.8	12.4	22.3	3.9	9.4
Index (1980 = 100)	141	188	121	114	106	78	99
Spain							
1980	8.7	0.2	13.2	15.4	25.6	18.2	18.7
1989	15.2	0.4	18.2	15.4	25.2	11.1	14.4
Index (1980 = 100)	202	280	160	116	114	70	89
Sweden							
1980	30.6	0.8	21.6	8.7	22.8	3.0	12.4
1989	42.0	n.a.	21.9	9.3	13.2	1.8	11.7
Index (1980 = 100)	154	n.a.	114	120	65	66	106
United States							
1980	16.8	6.9	35.1	6.8	19.5	1.2	13.8
1989	18.1	11.1	27.8	13.1	17.7	1.1	11.1
Index (1980 = 100)	136	202	99	243	115	115	101

a) Major groups of the International Standard Classification of Occupations (ISCO).
b) Not all countries publish data according to ISCO. Countries in which occupational classification systems have changed during the relevant period are omitted.
c) The index indicates the growth in total numbers employed in the occupation over the decade.
Source: ILO, *Yearbook of Labour Statistics.*

Germany, Ireland, Italy, Japan, Portugal and Spain, a large percentage of women workers are involved not only in agriculture, but also in trade, hotel and catering activities, all of which are highly dominated by family firms.

Developments in service industries in the 1980s and their implications for women's employment

Employment prospects in specific sectors

While employment in the service sector has increased overall, this growth has not occurred evenly across service sector activities. Two sectors have played a particularly significant role in the past decades: the public sector and business and financial services. Those countries with the fastest growth in women's employment have combined both large national and municipal public sector activities with growth in business and financial services.

Women's employment in the future – in terms of both the quantity of jobs available and the quality of these jobs – will depend on the set of complex trends occurring within these service industries which employ increasingly large numbers of women. The crucial question is whether these trends will result in more, and more skilled, jobs for women. Since the public sector is analysed in Chapter 5, the following provides examples mainly from the business and financial services.

The expansion in financial and business service activity initially stimulated strong employment growth in clerical work. In Japan, where business and financial service growth has been dramatic, clerical employment expanded from 17.5 per cent of all non-farm employment to 26.6 per cent between 1960 and 1980. But recent technological advances, particularly the computerisation of much office work and the reorganisation of clerical positions, have significantly slowed the growth in clerical employment in all countries which experienced expansion in the 1960s and 1970s (Eichenwald, 1991).

In the 1980s the deregulation of financial markets and increased capital mobility stimulated extensive growth in financial service activities, creating new financial products and leading to a demand for highly-skilled service workers. Although this workforce was predominantly male, women with advanced degrees in business and management also benefited. More recently, however, because there has been less volatility in financial markets, there has also been less employment growth in these fields, a trend that can be expected to continue.

In general, business and financial services – as well as retail trade – have been strongly affected by trends towards computerisation, self service and rationalisation. These trends, albeit uneven, are observed across OECD countries. They suggest a general slowdown in employment growth in these types of services in the 1990s. However, in countries with a concentration of specialised financial and business services, there will be positions for women with the requisite skills, especially in the highly-skilled professional service sector (advertising, law, accounting, marketing, etc.).

With respect to public sector activities, similar trends are apparent. In health services, for example, a rationalisation process is occurring in many OECD countries, together with increased privatisation of public sector services. Health care has always been highly feminised, largely because of its proportion of nurses. In the 1980s, however, other segments of the health care sector began to be characterised by increases in the proportion of women employed. The proportion of female physicians, for example, has increased in the majority of OECD countries. Thus, as in financial services, low-skilled jobs may be rationalised and reduced in number while demand will grow in a smaller number of more highly-skilled positions.

Although some areas of service provision – particularly those amenable to computerised rationalisation – may not generate as much employment in the 1990s, other areas of service provision show good growth potential. There are strong indications that there will be a small but significant increase in demand for labour in services related to manufacturing, especially of high-technology products, including customisation services, design services, and maintenance services. The dramatic changes which have been occurring in the computer industry are a good illustration of this trend. These changes are the consequence of:

  i) standardized industry-wide systems;
  ii) decreasing profits from capital equipment; and
  iii) increasing demand for integrated information technology, based on a combination of hardware, software and communications equipment.

Profit margins in the computer hardware industry declined from 9.2 per cent in 1984 to 3.6 per cent in 1989. On the other hand, software and services have increased their share of the market from 19 to 25 per cent and have maintained both higher growth and higher profits than hardware industries.

Technological innovation has played a major role in altering labour demand in the service sector. In health care services for example, technological innovations are used as a source of product differentiation. A firm may provide highly-specialised diagnostic services that are not available in routine care centres. Technological innovations may also be used to reduce costs through methods such as aiding the closer scheduling of personnel according to demand for their services. The choice of technology-based strategies directly affects labour demand but also makes it difficult to draw conclusions about demand across firms within the same industry. In the future, employment prospects and opportunities will be as affected by the firm in which one is employed as by the sector.

There is clearly a trend across OECD countries towards higher levels of skill and a concomitant demand for more qualified, highly trained workers. This is a result of the rationalisation of lower-level white-collar jobs – particularly clerical jobs – and the use of fewer workers to do more demanding jobs. It also reflects the reorganisation of some activities, such as banking, away from the provision of routine services and towards more specialised services and sales. Although some service sector activities still employ large numbers of low-skilled workers (catering, hotel, some health care activities, etc.), the combined effects of automation in routine work, more self-service, and advances in firm management methods, add up to increasing complexity in service jobs and increasing demand for skilled workers.

The higher qualifications required for some financial and business service jobs and the elimination of routine clerical work are changing the gender composition of specific service activities in some countries. In Germany, the feminisation rate in finance and insurance rose from 44.3 per cent in 1970 to 50.2 per cent in 1975 and then declined to 48.3 per cent in 1986 despite growth in the relative share of employment in these activities in the overall economy. In the same country as well as in Japan, the number of female workers in banking started to decline in the 1980s, decreasing overall female representation in the sector and possibly contributing to slow increases in female labour force participation rates (OECD/CERI, 1989). In the United States, the greater access of qualified women to more skilled positions in the financial and business services means that this reversal has not been as extensive.

Variability in working hours and contracts

The expansion of service employment has been paralleled by an increase in the variability of employment contracts across OECD countries[4] (Tables 4.2 and 4.3). This is particularly pronounced in countries where service employment dominates. Women constitute the majority of workers on non-standard contracts, particularly in part-time jobs but also in temporary work on fixed-term contracts, and in seasonal work. However, as stressed in Chapter 3, it is difficult to make absolute statements about non-standard working hours because what is "standard", "typical", or "normal" differs considerably across countries and, within countries, across industries.

There are also important differences among countries in the way in which women working on non-standard contracts are integrated into the workforce. Workers on non-standard contracts in the Scandinavian countries seem to be more fully integrated into the economy than elsewhere. Relative to other economies, reduced work schedules are not as associated with erosion of skills or reduced opportunities for career mobility. This may be related to the higher percentage of men who also work on reduced work schedules, particularly in the public sector (see Chapters 3 and 5).

Labour law is perhaps the key factor differentiating economies with large numbers of workers on non-standard contracts from those with fewer such workers (Standing, 1989). But there has been expansion in the relatively less regulated service sectors even in countries where labour legislation and collective bargaining agreements regulate the extent of part-time employment (Bertrand and Noyelle, 1990).

A central debate related to non-standard employment contracts questions whether this form of labour demand is primarily cost-driven or is a response to employer demands for more flexibility in allocating work hours. Evidence from the British retail and hotel industries indicates that in large service firms with multiple establishments, local managers are allocated fixed budgets for labour and therefore utilise employees on a range of flexible employment contracts in order to contain costs. According to this study, employers justified paying lower wages to women on part-time and temporary contracts on the following grounds: *i)* a lower level of "commitment" to the organisation despite evidence of the long-term stability of many of these workers; and *ii)* the perceived relative income needs of the worker. In no case were lower wages justified by lower productivity (Walsh, 1990). This contrasts with recent research in the United States which shows that employers use non-standard contracts to adapt to short-term changes in labour demand and for purposes not directly related to labour cost. For example, internal temporary pools are being used by firms as employment screening devices (Christopherson *et al.,* 1990).

The increased tradeability of services

The concept of "tradeability" in services, while complicated, is increasingly important for understanding how the service sector as a labour market for women will change in the years to come. There is a conventional distinction between services provided on the market (tradeable) and those provided through the public sector (and non-tradeable). The concept of tradeability, however, may also be used to distinguish between local, regional,

Table 4.2. **Part-time employment**[a] **as a percentage of total employment in service sector activities, 1985/86**

	Wholesale and retail trade, restaurants and hotels (ISIC 6)	Transport, storage and communications (ISIC 7)	Financing, insurance, real estate and business services (ISIC 8)	Other services (ISIC 9)	Public administration (ISIC 91)
Australia	25.4	9.5	18.1	—— 24.2 ——	
Belgium	11.2	2.8	10.0	17.4	7.4
Canada	23.5	6.1	11.6	24.4	7.0
France	12.1	6.7	10.8	19.4	13.4
Ireland	9.7	4.3	4.7	12.5	2.5
Italy	5.1	1.6	3.3	7.7	1.7
Japan	16.2	7.5	10.7	14.3	7.1
Luxembourg	8.6	4.3	5.7	12.5	7.0
Netherlands	24.9	12.1	19.8	45.5	33.7
Norway	29.7	15.3	17.3	—— 32.4 ——	
Sweden	28.9	14.9	21.2	—— 36.5 ——	
United Kingdom	35.5	6.5	15.3	38.8	10.3
United States	29.7	7.6	10.7	22.4	6.2

a) See Chapter 3 for definitions of part-time employment.
Source: OCDE, *Employment Outlook 1987*, Tables 1.4 and 1.5.

Table 4.3. **Temporary jobs**[a] **as a proportion of total wage and salary employment in service sector activities, 1989**

European Community countries

	Wholesale and retail trade, restaurants and hotels (ISIC 6)	Transport, storage and communications (ISIC 7)	Financing, insurance, real estate and business services (ISIC 8)	Other services (ISIC 9)	Public administration (ISIC 91)
Belgium	4.9	2.3	3.8	8.5	8.6
Denmark	13.1	5.1	6.2	11.7	11.9
France	10.9	3.9	7.5	9.5	5.9
Germany	13.6	6.4	10.1	15.4	15.9
Greece	19.3	12.6	9.9	12.3	3.0
Ireland	10.3	3.5	6.0	14.7	1.9
Italy	8.1	1.4	4.3	7.0	2.3
Luxembourg	5.2	1.8	2.2	5.4	2.7
Netherlands	9.6	5.9	7.8	10.9	7.4
Portugal	23.3	8.9	11.2	17.3	9.8
Spain	31.7	15.9	19.3	22.8	10.3
United Kingdom	7.6	2.7	4.1	8.8	3.2

a) Figures should be interpreted with caution as questions asked in surveys differ significantly across countries. Temporary work comprises many sub-categories, including fixed-term contracts, employment with temporary agencies, seasonal employment, casual employment and certain types of government schemes.
Source: OECD, *Employment Outlook 1991*, Table 2.11.

or national markets. This reflects the influence of spatial scale in the concept of tradeability. Services provided exclusively in a local market are not tradeable because they provide no positive exchange value to the local economy. However, services may also be defined as non-tradeable if they have only a national domestic market and are not traded internationally. Moreover, tradeable and non-tradeable service functions may coexist within a given industry. In banking, for example, consumer deposit service functions are not tradeable, yet the sale of specialised financial products may be. Significant problems arise when attempts are made to disentangle the external trade aspects of international financial transactions, making it difficult to interpret trade statistics.[5]

Taking into account these conceptual difficulties, it appears that more services are becoming tradeable as a consequence of the deregulation of financial services in some countries (notably the United Kingdom and the United States) and the privatisation of public services across the range of OECD countries. Increased tradeability is occurring within national economies as local service firms develop national markets (Beyers, 1990). Services such as nursing care, formerly provided in the home or in the public sector, are now increasingly provided by profit-making firms. As these services are privatised they have also become more concentrated in higher order urban centres.

Although non-tradeable services account for the greatest portion of female employment, there is evidence, at least in France, Canada, the United Kingdom and the United States, of a gradual shift in female employment from non-tradeable to tradeable services. The increased tradeability and commodification of services has at least two implications for women's employment. First, there will be increased productivity pressure on privatised, tradeable services, possibly promoting the redefinition of the service product itself or encouraging the application of technology to reduce labour costs. The second consequence may be a delocalisation of service provision and the restructuring of labour markets to use a more highly skilled workforce and more capital-intensive work organisation. Both of these developments will change the content of many service jobs as well as their working conditions. As discussed below, pressure to increase the tradeability of services will presumably build up as markets become more internationalised.

Firm competitive strategies

Changes in national regulatory structures in some countries in the 1980s – aimed at making national firms more competitive internationally or in response to the emergence of regional markets such as the European Community – have encouraged mergers, acquisitions and strategic alliances among firms.

As large firms have emerged as dominant players in a more international economy, several trends have developed. First, there is an increasing demand for highly-qualified workers in the international commercial sector (Commission of the European Communities, 1990). Second, the relationships between large distributor firms and their suppliers are now more oligopsonistic than in the late 1970s and early 1980s. Closer and more controlled – or "streamlined" – relations with suppliers are driven by the desire for greater control over the cost and quality of output. A possible by-product may be the elimination of some small firms. Given that many women have been employed in the small firm sector because of its greater employment access and flexibility, this "streamlining" process may have adverse consequences for women workers – especially those employed by subcontractors providing routine inputs, such as building maintenance and catering. However, even for specialised services – in areas such as graphic design, law, media, and accounting where highly-qualified women have made professional inroads – a greater degree of industrial concentration may limit employment opportunities.[6]

The ways in which individual firms compete in service sector industries translate into quite different tendencies in terms of labour deployment. One strategy is to compete in terms of cost: providing services at low cost by employing a low-cost, less-skilled labour force, typically on fixed-term work contracts. A second strategy is to compete on the basis of product differentiation, specialisation, or value-added services. This kind of competitive strategy requires a quite different labour force, one which is skilled and highly productive. In this case, labour cost is less significant than the skills and productivity of the workforce. Firms may utilise either of these two strategies depending on both the nature of competition in the service activity and the characteristics of labour supply. Both strategies may also occur within the same activity.

Although it is difficult to generalise, there appears to be a tendency to move away from competition on the basis of cost towards competition on the basis of worker productivity. This tendency is more pronounced in some service sector industries than in others, and in some countries more than others. For example, a large supply of female part-time workers at the local level in the United Kingdom encourages cost-competitive strategies in locally-provided services. In contrast, the relative decline in the portion of the female workforce willing to work part-time in the United States, along with the privatisation of public services, the spatial configuration of local labour markets, and the increased tradeability of services, has encouraged employers to pursue a productivity-driven strategy, employing a full-time, skilled workforce.

In Germany the trend towards service "intensification" has been exacerbated, at least in part, by the regulation of part-time work and of working hours in general. The lack of a cost-competitive alternative has forced firms to adopt managerial and technological innovations which increase labour productivity. They emphasize an internally-trained workforce as a means of decreasing staff turnover and reducing reliance on the external labour market. The productivity strategy has important implications for women workers; it creates a demand for skilled workers but also privileges those who work long hours and follow uninterrupted career paths.

Conclusion

There are indications that employment growth in the service sector will be slower in the 1990s than in the 1980s. Emerging growth activities are likely to be those which add value to manufactured goods or other services (such as commercial financial products), or those related to service enhancement or the international functions of some industries. It is also likely that there will be an increase in the demand for personal and social services as a result of women's increased labour market participation and the needs of the growing elderly population.

While there will be employment for women in some moderately-skilled positions, especially in customer services, clerical jobs are likely to be further rationalised and to decline relatively if not absolutely. Among the fewer newly-created jobs, more will require both technical skills and high levels of general qualification and will be associated with manufacturing. Some of these fields – drafting, design, computer programming, systems engineering – are relatively open to women. Special efforts will have to be made to encourage women to enter these occupations.

A set of new issues has emerged from the intensified internationalisation of the economy and the potential conflicts between a space of flows and a space of places. Possible outcomes of the internationalisation of services on the labour market will remain very much a matter of speculation until basic problems of definition and measurement are resolved. The labour market consequences cannot simply be derived from differences in regional or national wage rates, or social benefits, as is frequently assumed. Information technology and institutionally-created human capital undermine simple concepts of comparative advantage, and questions related to what types of economic activities will be located, and where, are quite complex. And as regulatory mechanisms to govern increasingly international processes are being developed by international bodies, *e.g.* the European Community, a systematic evaluation of how various changes in regulatory structures will affect women's roles in the economy seems also essential.

Internationalisation of services and international migration

The international migration of male unskilled workers is a relatively well-documented phenomenon. More recently there have been increases in the international migration of highly-skilled workers, in response to the opening of borders, internationalisation of business enterprises, and the development of international product markets. Both employers and job applicants are now looking beyond national labour markets. Since services are a major component of OECD economies and since women form a large portion of service workers, it is likely that emerging international migration streams will include a larger female component. Moreover, national regulatory systems which govern migration are responding to changes in labour demand and altering the composition of the migrant stream.[7]

The health professions provide an interesting case of international migration of skilled workers. Migration occurs mainly for economic reasons although there are some differences among types of skilled migrants. Physicians from less developed economies are frequently trained outside their own countries and have become accustomed to a level of diagnostic and treatment facilities which are unavailable in their country of origin. In addition, developing countries have an overwhelming need for general medical practitioners while the training in developed economies emphasizes specialisation. This means that fewer professional opportunities of the kind they have come to expect are available to these migrants in their home countries than in the country where they have studied. Migration is thus an avenue to professional development and recognition as well as higher levels of remuneration.

For nurses, the situation is quite different. Nurses are almost always trained in their home countries and acquire general rather than specialised skills. In several countries, most notably the Philippines, Korea and Pakistan, nursing graduates are trained for service in a world market rather than a national one. This is reflected in training texts and in symptoms of diseases studied (Ball, 1990).

While nursing migrants to the United States come primarily from Asia and also Ireland and Haiti, a new migration stream is developing from Eastern European countries into Western Europe, especially into Germany (*Social and Labour Bulletin*, 1989). Nurses typically emigrate for economic rather than professional reasons. Increased demand for this category of skilled female migrants in some economies, particularly in the United States but increasingly in Western European countries, is the result of a complex set of developments. As employment opportunities have opened for women in other occupations in these countries, nursing – with its extremely flat career hierarchy and generally low pay – has become less attractive. In addition, the restructuring of health services in some countries has further undermined working conditions for nurses, causing many of them to leave the profession (see below). These developments are affecting the supply of nurses across OECD countries. Given this shortage, there is considerable pressure to look to foreign sources to fill available positions.

Several factors indicate that, in the future, female migrant labour may become more important. First, as women in OECD countries become more qualified and specialised in particular occupations, they will be increasingly subject to occupational mobility requiring that they spend periods of time in another country. Second, as women in these economies assume more qualified positions, women immigrants may be used to fill the gap in routine service work. Female immigrant labour has already been used to meet the demand for personal services – such as domestic work and childcare previously provided in the home – stemming from women's increased labour market participation.[8] Finally, the hiring of immigrant women may be used as a strategy to reduce the cost of providing routine services.

Very few studies have focused on the implications of increased female labour migration in services which therefore remain rather unclear. There are both positive and negative aspects. On the one hand, migration provides a higher measure of economic independence for the migrant female worker and presumably more leverage with respect to critical life choices such as marriage. It may also allow those workers to acquire a higher level of skills. On the other hand, the use of low-paid, more vulnerable female labour may undermine a drive towards professionalisation of predominantly female occupations and the development of complex career ladders. Its effects will be felt more strongly among less skilled female workers. The use of an immigrant workforce to meet labour shortages may further exacerbate future shortages by discouraging native workers from entering the field. All of these trends lend support to the notion that a more bifurcated female labour market will emerge in the 1990s.

Internationalisation of services and international trade

How changes in trade regulations governing services will affect women's employment is very much a matter for speculation. While research so far has been minimal, there are hints of some significant consequences. For example, research conducted in Canada on the bilateral trade agreement between the United States and Canada raises several issues related to women's employment in the service sector (Cohen, 1987). First, there is a possibility that open borders and advances in telecommunications transmittal will encourage the movement of women's routine "back office" or data-entry jobs to low-wage areas outside the country where transactions originate. Second, the implicit assumption in trade agreements that all services are commodities and should be provided in the market may undermine state-supported functions in health and cultural activities. Because women, including professional women, are strongly represented in public sector activities, the reorientation of the economy and the privatisation stimulated by trade agreements may disproportionately affect them.[9] For instance, since public sector media services are historically more egalitarian in their hiring and promotion practices than private sector firms, the privatisation of these activities may reduce employment opportunities for women.

Other research on trade liberalisation has dealt with declining financial service boundaries in the European Community and their effects on German banks and on women's employment in banking (Figge and Quack, 1990). This study indicates that women, even highly-qualified, are relegated to employment in local credit institutions, in non-commercial activities and are overwhelmingly excluded from managerial jobs. As such, they would almost certainly not be in a position to receive the training necessary to work in the developing international commercial sector.

Some of these findings are generalisable: expansion into new geographic markets is of strategic importance for the future of most major firms. Given that the percentage of women in upper management positions is so low – about 4 per cent across OECD countries – it is not surprising that they are almost completely unrepresented in international business. Although these positions are small in number, they are critical because of their decision-making power, and women's lack of access to them constitutes an aspect of the "glass ceiling", creating a significant barrier to career development.

Internationalisation of services and local labour market impacts

There has been a reordering of regional labour markets in response to the global reorganisation of production, distribution and finance in OECD countries. Among these, one set of countries deserves special attention because they house emerging corporate command centres. In cities within these countries, functions related to corporate headquarters and accompanying business services have expanded dramatically. All cities with five or more of the top *Fortune* 500 companies are in the United States, the United Kingdom, France, Germany, Italy, Canada, Sweden and Japan. Business services have been a particularly important component of economic growth in these countries. This trend has had great consequences for female labour, concentrating the demand for professional services (and routine clerical work) in particular urban labour markets.

What is also notable about these local or regional labour markets is: *i)* a substantial expansion of demand in banking and insurance services that are predominantly female in employment and dominated by large firms; and *ii)* an expansion of demand for specialised services such as information services, research and advertising. In Japan, for example, employment in information services, research and advertising increased 134 per cent between 1975 and 1985 in comparison with a 36 per cent growth rate in services overall (OECD/CERI, 1989). In general, the expansion of corporate and business service activities has meant an increase in the use of external labour markets to provide specialised service inputs, and a parallel demand for professional and technical workers with specific skills. For these workers, status and mobility are less tied to seniority than to educational credentials and experience (track record). Workers in these activities generally possess skills that can be applied across industries (computer programming, graphic design), rather than firm- or even industry-specific skills.

Conclusion

Internationalisation is changing the way firms do business, including their production organisation and labour deployment patterns. New regulatory frameworks have been designed in response to internationalisation, yet little attention has been paid to how these changes will affect women or other workers. While this section has sketched some potential implications of change, further and more detailed analysis will be necessary before it is possible to make definitive statements about how women in various industries, occupations and national economies will be affected by the growing internationalisation in services.

SKILLS AND SERVICE OCCUPATIONS

The definition and redefinition of skills

Skills can be defined in terms of the amount of time it takes an average person to master the responsibilities of a particular job. This is a useful measure because training time determines the cost to managers of replacing an employee. The question of skill is relatively less problematic in manufacturing because of the clear relation of skill to technology and to the production of specific material products. Skills are more difficult to define in services because they relate to the manipulation of ideas, interaction with people, and presentation of self, as well as more traditionally defined technical abilities.[10]

The skills employers require from the service workforce include learning, communication, and problem-solving skills. Women are valuable members of the service workforce because they typically possess many of these, yet their skills are perceived differently because they are often acquired through socialisation and a general education rather than through formal training. Some skills, such as diplomacy, may be undervalued because they do not reflect formal training and because it is difficult to measure their attainment. Despite employers' testimony that such skills are at a premium, they still do not translate into higher wages unless they are combined with formal credentials. A positive step towards developing a more complex notion of skill would be to revalue skills learned on the job or in formal training against those acquired elsewhere.

The alteration of skill levels

Some labour market analysts have argued that changes in the organisation of work alter the skill levels of all workers in the same direction (Braverman, 1974). However, empirical work on changing occupations in a variety of industries suggests contradictory patterns, mainly as a consequence of different firm strategies. Firms adopt different practices with regard to training depending on the available labour supply and the competitive conditions within which they operate.

Two conclusions can be drawn from the available data: first of all, there is a tendency for jobs to become more highly skilled for the majority of workers and, second, automation is generally associated with a rising skill level. The Economic Council of Canada found that whereas in 1971, 21 per cent of Canadian workers held jobs requiring more than two years of training, in 1985 this figure rose to 25 per cent. Although women tend to be concentrated in jobs that require less formal training, gender differences in relation to required training did diminish between 1971 and 1986 (Economic Council of Canada, 1991). In general, prospects in the contemporary service sector labour market are more favourable for younger workers who are well qualified prior to entering the labour market and have multiple skills. Women with these characteristics have fared relatively better in service-based economies. The steady increase of highly-qualified women in professional positions in some countries, albeit small, is testimony to this trend. On the other hand, poorly-educated women and older women have been most disadvantaged by changes in the economy.

Table 4.4. **Distribution of employment according to occupational skill level by sector, Canada 1971, 1981 and 1986**

	High-skilled occupations[a]			Medium-skilled occupations[b]			Low-skilled occupations[c]		
	1971	1981	1986	1971	1981	1986	1971	1981	1986
Goods sector	7.7	11.5	13.1	90.6	87.1	85.6	1.7	1.5	1.4
Service sector	26.2	29.4	31.6	55.6	53.8	51.0	18.2	16.8	17.4
Dynamic services	16.3	22.6	25.5	79.4	73.7	70.5	4.3	3.7	4.0
Traditional services	4.5	6.7	7.5	64.0	61.6	59.1	31.4	31.6	33.4
Non-market services	53.4	57.0	60.1	27.0	26.0	23.8	19.7	17.0	16.0
Total	19.2	23.5	26.0	69.0	64.8	61.4	11.9	11.7	12.6

a) Managerial, administrative, professional and technical occupations.
b) Clerical, sales and "blue-collar" occupations (the latter include mining, fishing, farming, machining and construction).
c) Service occupations like food servers, guards, janitors, and clerks.
Source: Economic Council of Canada (1991), Table 6.3.

Upskilling and multiskilling and their effects on labour deployment

There are several major questions about how skills are changing in response to the growth of service jobs. The first of these is "how are changes in the organisation of service work, and especially the application of technological innovations such as computers, altering the skills required of service workers?". The simplification of one task may, among other things, allow the reorganisation of work to combine a set of simplified tasks into a new composite job. This has occurred in a number of office jobs (receptionist, switchboard operator) resulting in a more complex and demanding set of tasks for secretaries. For example, the suppression of tasks associated with filing and the subsequent replacement of the file clerk by computerised file systems (as in banking and insurance) resulted in the "folding-in" of filing tasks with other secretarial work.

The occupation of travel agent provides yet another example of this type of development. The computerisation of scheduling and ticketing information might have been expected to deskill the travel agent's job. In reality, this occupation has become more demanding because the volume of travel has increased along with the complexity of fare information. Skilled travel agents are much more than mere ticketing agents. They must remain up to date with rapidly changing travel information which could affect their clients. In addition, they must understand both the capabilities and the limitations of the computerised reservations and information system in order to provide the best fares and routes.

Many service jobs held by women are in industries undergoing intensive restructuring in response to new competitive conditions or, in the case of public sector employment, privatisation or rationalisation. These are frequently skilled jobs but which may involve routine as well as non-routine functions. These jobs have been significantly affected by changes in work organisation and the application of technological and managerial innovations to increase productivity.

The changing nature of nursing provides an illustrative example. Although this profession has specific historical characteristics, the changes affecting nursing replicate those in other traditional skilled female occupations. One clear trend across OECD countries is a small but perceptible decline in the proportion of women in these professions which may be attributed to:

> i) the entry of men, particularly in those situations where some aspects of the profession have become more technically-oriented or specialised; and
>
> ii) the opening up of other less gender-segmented professions for educated women.

In some cases, the movement of women away from traditional skilled occupations has contributed to labour shortages and has heightened pressure to make these professions more attractive to new entrants.

The nursing profession: a case study

To understand how the nursing profession is changing, it is necessary to examine how the functions of nursing have evolved relative to other health care occupations. Nursing involves different activities in different OECD countries and it is difficult to disaggregate effects. However, a review of available literature reveals surprising similarities in the processes affecting the nursing profession across OECD countries.

First, nursing has become more technically oriented. Nurses are required to be computer literate as well as able to understand and operate complex diagnostic and treatment equipment. Contemporary nursing requires administrative as well as technical and caring skills, although these may not be required from the same individual at the same time or at the same level of competence. There is therefore increasing differentiation among nursing jobs with some requiring a much greater degree of training and experience than others.

Nurses face increasingly intensive and difficult patient care as health systems in OECD countries are reorganised to provide more out-patient treatment and fewer and briefer hospital stays, except for the seriously ill. Work intensification is also exacerbated by nursing shortages. In Germany, for example, it is estimated that nurses as a group work approximately 50 million hours of overtime every year.

The skills hierarchy is also changing. Nursing at the highest level of skill – bedside nursing in intensive care wards – requires more training, experience and professional responsibility than all but a few administrative posts, but the existing nursing occupational hierarchy only allows nurses to advance in status and salary by going into management roles. Nevertheless, there are hints that some recognition is being given to the more complex skills required of nurses and to the internal differentiation of this occupation.

This has advanced most rapidly in countries with national health care services where it is possible to implement nation-wide changes in the organisation of the profession. In France, for example, negotiations between unions and hospital administrators through a government agency has resulted in an agreement both to revise pay levels in accordance with newly recognised levels of qualification and to develop new lines of career development for different types of health care professionals.

Germany is illustrative of how qualification systems can inhibit occupational mobility. Nursing training in Germany is specific to the profession. It is not associated with other forms of advanced education such as a university degree as in some other countries. This training system produces a highly-skilled cadre of trained nurses whose qualification certifies them for only one occupation and who cannot advance without obtaining further credentials. The lack of a mobility path is a partial explanation for the shortage of nurses in Germany.

Salary scales in nursing have traditionally reflected a rather homogeneous occupation based on caring skills and a limited range of technical skills. The assumption is that these skills are acquired in nursing school and then applied with little alteration throughout the nurse's working life. In the United States, nurses' salary progression – which measures the difference between an occupation's average starting salary and average maximum salary – is only 69 per cent. In contrast, accountants can expect a salary progression of 209 per cent and engineers of 184 per cent. On leaving the nursing profession, one woman claimed, "I had dead-ended salary-wise at 27" (Bowers, 1990).

Nursing shortages are the result of women leaving the profession and, in some countries, of low rates of entry-level recruitment. Demographic trends, namely fewer young people, are causing a shortage of nursing candidates for recruitment. Women's entry into other health care occupations – which are highly skilled and have more professional autonomy, such as medicine, dentistry and pharmacy – has also contributed to the growing shortage of nurses across OECD countries. In France, for example, 24 per cent of all physicians are now women (*Le Journal d'Emploi/Service*, 1989).

Public sector policies, including privatisation, will have important consequences for the nursing profession and for the quality of health care. The nursing workforce, midwives included, forms the largest single group of health personnel in the European Communities, with a total of 2.5 million people. In the United Kingdom, nurses make up almost half of the workforce of the National Health Service, consume 45 per cent of the salary bill, and account for 34 per cent of the total expenditure on the service. Not surprisingly, plans to reorganise health care in the United Kingdom focus on managing the provision of nursing care.

Conclusion

The brief case study of nursing outlined above, suggests that, contrary to many of the myths that prevail about "women's work", many traditional female occupations require high levels of skill, long working hours, and high levels of professional responsibility. They are also differentiated, specialised and functionally flexible. This description applies to nursing but a similar case could be made for teaching and secretarial work. The evolving complexity of these jobs has not been reflected in a reworking of job classifications, career ladders or salary scales.

Internal labour markets and skills

Internal labour markets are predicated on the need for firm-specific skills and the relative importance of these compared to general, technical, or professional skills. They develop as a consequence of a visible employment ladder within a firm and are associated with social networks. People who have transaction-intensive jobs in an organisation are more visible to their superiors and have better opportunities for advancement. Internal labour markets have also been developed as an attempt to address problems associated with monitoring performance in large diverse organisations. When individual output is difficult to measure, bureaucratic structures emerge to distribute rewards and to encourage productivity through incentive structures such as career ladders.

The development of internal labour markets in service organisations has been limited by two factors. One is the nature of skills in services which are less firm-specific and more general, the other is increased emphasis on initial qualification, which means that priority is given to individual investment in training and education as a route to career mobility, rather than firm training and career ladders within firms. As a consequence, "the role of the firm as the principal locus of upward mobility is weakening... Increasingly mobility must be sought through job hopping and additional education" (Noyelle, 1987). In contemporary firms which rely more on general and specific skills obtained outside the workplace, internal labour markets have a stronger function with respect to employee monitoring (the uncertain output problem) than the need to retain employees who have firm-specific skills and in whom there has been a significant firm investment.

This pattern varies among national labour markets. It is much more characteristic of economies organised around external labour markets, such as the United States and the United Kingdom, than those organised around firms and firm hierarchies such as Japan. It also varies by sector, with internal labour markets operating in more mature sectors such as banking, but much less well developed in those sectors where there is no history of employment patterns such as information services.

In the United States, and to a lesser extent in France and Great Britain, many skilled service jobs, such as those in information, require industry- or occupation-specific skills rather than firm-specific skills. Work may even be designed to use workers with these kinds of externally-obtained skills rather than skills acquired in the firm. Many service jobs also require a broad, non-specialised qualification that prepares workers to be flexible and versatile (Carnevale et al., 1989). The availability on the external labour market of a large supply of such workers who have invested in their own basic qualification gives employers considerable latitude in how they compose their workforce. This system inherently promotes recruitment from the external rather than the internal labour market and benefits those with high levels of qualification, including younger women who have access to a wider range of jobs and can move into employment at various levels within a firm. It disadvantages less skilled women and older women who entered the firm at the bottom of the occupational hierarchy. Firms are less likely to provide women in this category with the kind of training which would allow them to be occupationally mobile within the firm.

In countries where skilled workers are recruited from the external labour market and skills are obtained largely through individual human capital investment, women's increased level of qualification has improved their access to jobs. However, there is some evidence, at least in the United States, that as women have become more qualified the returns to human capital investment beyond initial job access are deteriorating. That is, higher educational attainment does not translate into income improvements at the same rate as 20 years ago (Bluestone, 1990).

In broad contrast to this external labour-market-oriented system are those where skills are defined by and obtained within the firm. These exclusionary internal labour market systems are most prominent in Japan and Germany, but can be observed in specific industries everywhere. In this type of situation, the relationship between initial qualification, employment access and occupational mobility is quite different. German firms require a general qualification but also a technical qualification which is obtained through an apprenticeship. For instance, people intending to begin a managerial career in banking are likely to take an apprenticeship with a bank following completion of their *Abitur* (secondary school degree) and then remain with the bank in a part-time position while they complete a university degree. In effect, this system replaces the post-graduate business or management school. Following this extended educational preparation, during which the job "candidate" is already tied to the firm, promotion takes place within the firm.

Women are disadvantaged in several ways by this system which requires commitment to a particular career path at a young age, with few opportunities for reconsideration on the one hand, and lengthy preparation and personal investment given expected returns on the other (vertical occupational mobility for women is extremely limited in German firms) (Lane, 1990). Finally, women in Germany typically enter apprenticeships in traditionally female fields because employers implicitly or explicitly select apprentices on the basis of gender according to sector. At the end of the 1980s, 50 per cent of all apprenticeships were advertised for males, 25 per cent for females and only 25 per cent for either sex. The number of apprenticeships in "female" occupations was much greater than employment opportunities in these fields, so the link between apprenticeship and the expectation of long-term employment was not as strong for women as for men. To counteract this, the Federal Institute of Labour no longer accepts postings for apprenticeships citing a preference for male or female candidates. As a result of this initiative 90 per cent of apprenticeships are now open to either sex.

The Japanese system is similar to the German system in that the firm is the definer and arbiter of skills, but it differs in some other very significant respects. Vocational education and apprenticeships play a minor role in the Japanese approach to qualification. According to Schmid (1990), "Japanese employers prefer adaptable 'blank sheets' for whom they provide considerable internal training." New male employees receive extensive training within the firm and are rotated through a series of jobs which gradually broaden and deepen their skills base.

Women, on the contrary, are excluded from this training programme when joining the firm and relegated to routine and frequently unskilled work, whatever their level of initial qualification. This is highlighted in a study of the Japanese information technology industry which lays out the typical career path of the software engineer – from programmer, to system engineer, to project leader, to manager – and demonstrates the usual age cohorts in each of these "steps". Of the 20 per cent of software engineers who are female, approximately 40 per cent are programmers, 6 per cent are systems engineers and 1 per cent are managers. Clearly, a dual internal labour market is in operation with men in the management track and women in the more routine service track. This occurs despite the intense demand for more workers with engineering and managerial skills. One of the few alternatives for Japanese women is to circumvent this disadvantageous firm structure by using their externally-obtained qualifications in areas such as business services which do not follow the internal firm qualification practices. In these situations, although small in number, women are more likely to be hired on the basis of their already acquired skills and to be able to move into positions of authority and responsibility.

These examples point out that despite women's increased level of qualification across OECD countries, various institutional structures may inhibit the translation of these qualifications into successful career paths.

The role of firm structure

Although there is very little information available on women's employment by establishment and firm in service activities, a number of specific patterns are identifiable. Historically, much service activity across OECD countries was carried out in small firms (OECD/CERI, 1989). In many countries – Italy, France, Germany and Japan – family firms still dominate certain sectors, such as hotel and catering. In other industries, particularly tradeable international business services – such as auto rental, accounting, banking, insurance, and travel – work is carried out in small establishments near the market but away from firm headquarters. These establishments are frequently part of large transnational firms. The predominance of the large firm in the 1980s is a result of the increasing tradeability of some services and of international acquisitions, mergers and strategic alliances. In the United States, employment in retail and in some service industries (for example the hospital industry) has become more concentrated in large firms during the 1980s (Christopherson et al., 1990). In these firms, women carry out routine service functions in "branch" locations which are removed from the firm's headquarters. These firms employ large numbers of people but have no internal labour markets which link the branch or worksite location to the headquarters. Firm headquarters are concentrated in certain cities and increasingly recruit specialised employees from the external labour market, drawing on specialised business and professional services which tend to be based in the same urban centres.

Service sector employment is organised quite differently from one industry to another, depending on the nature of competition within that industry and the functions to be performed. In highly-skilled, information-based and transaction-intensive industries – such as advertising, media, and some types of financial services – activity is likely to be carried out by relatively small firms which may co-operate with one another on production projects. In other segments – such as insurance and banking – where a large-scale consumer service is provided, employment is both concentrated in very large firms and located in smaller establishments.

The way in which production is organised has important implications for women's access to employment and occupational mobility. Large firms with highly-developed internal labour markets are the most likely to invest in their employees and to promote from within because the proportion of firm-specific knowledge in their activities is very high. Large firms in some OECD countries, such as Sweden, Germany and Japan, are also those most likely to provide apprenticeships and train employees for a career. These firms, however, often develop highly-segmented labour markets in which women are relegated to more routine occupations, particularly clerical work. One reason for this segmentation is that in return for investment in the employee's training, the employer requires long-term, continuous employment.

In the 1980s, some large firms began to make greater use of the external market for hiring personnel and providing both routine (catering, building maintenance) and special-ised services. This breakdown of the internal labour market had both positive and negative consequences for women workers. It is now more difficult for a woman without educational credentials to be promoted gradually from within the firm. Moreover, with the subcontracting of some female-dominant activities such as food preparation, a secondary or peripheral labour market has been created. Women with few skills find themselves outside the benefit and wage bargaining structures available to employees of large firms, with few opportunities to cross the divide into those internal labour markets.

On the other hand, increased use of the external market and recognition of external credentials has dismantled some of the barriers inhibiting women's access to management positions. Women who have invested in higher education are more able to compete on an equal footing with men for management posts. Subcontracting specialised services also benefits women with specialised skills in fields such as graphic design, advertising and public relations.

SELF-EMPLOYMENT

Women increasingly see entrepreneurial activity and self-employment as alternative avenues for employment and advancement. For those facing obstacles in their career, self-employment may be a way of moving beyond occupational limitations. This is the case in traditional female occupations, such as nursing. In other instances, investment in higher education opens access to a professional field of self-employment, such as medicine or law.

Female self-employment has risen in countries with highly-educated women and with high levels of female labour force participation, particularly in France, the United Kingdom, the United States and Sweden (Table 4.5). In France, two-thirds of self-employed women have a *baccalauréat* degree and many of these have additional profes-sional degrees in fields such as law and architecture. In the United States, self-employ-ment in a professional field has become an alternative route to career advancement. The American Association of Nurse Attorneys is an example of this trend: it now comprises more than 500 members specialising in medical legal cases or health law, many of whom have set up on their own. These women left nursing and obtained a second professional degree in law in order to advance professionally (Bowers, 1990).

Another group of self-employed women appears at the opposite end of the skills spectrum. In this case, self-employment is seen as allowing the combination of domestic work and gainful employment. In Sweden, the fastest growing areas for female self-employment in the 1980s were in personal services and other traditional female service activities, such as health care and retail services.

There are thus two sides to self-employment: for highly-qualified women, it pro-vides an alternative to employment in large firms where gender-biased training and promotion systems limit their career prospects; for women with few qualifications, it

Table 4.5. Share of self-employment in total employment, by sex and activity

	All non-agricultural activities				Service activities (1990) both sexes			
	Share of female employment		Share of male employment		Wholesale and retail trade, restaurants and hotels (ISIC 6)	Transport, storage and communications (ISIC 7)	Financing, insurance, real estate and business services (ISIC 8)	Community, social and personal services (ISIC 9)
	1979	1990	1979	1990				
Australia	10.0	9.6	13.9	14.4	15.5	14.5	14.0	6.6
Austria	..	..	..	..	13.7	3.6	10.0	5.0
Belgium	8.8	10.3	12.6	16.7	36.0	5.5	21.7	8.2
Canada	6.0	6.4	7.2	8.3	7.2	6.4	10.4	8.5
Denmark	..	2.8	..	10.4	13.3	6.9	9.6	3.2
Finland	4.2	5.6	7.9	11.5	16.0	11.2	10.5	4.0
France	..	5.5	..	11.9	19.2	4.8	9.2	5.3
Germany	4.8	5.4	9.4	9.7	15.7	6.6	17.1	5.5
Greece	25.7	15.4	34.0	32.7	48.0	25.5	35.9	9.4
Ireland	..	6.1	..	16.8	24.4	13.7	13.6	6.8
Italy	12.8	15.1	21.7	25.8	45.8	14.1	8.9	15.5
Japan	12.9	9.3	14.6	12.1	15.0	4.8	8.1	12.0
Luxembourg	..	5.8	..	7.9	17.5	3.8	7.0	3.7
Netherlands	..	7.3	..	9.6	13.4	3.3	11.9	7.8
New Zealand	3.4	11.8	8.9	24.0	18.2	11.1	19.2	9.6
Norway	..	3.5	..	8.8	7.5	9.3	6.7	4.4
Portugal	..	12.3	..	18.3	38.3	8.6	13.7	4.6
Spain	12.5	13.9	17.1	19.2	34.0	26.8	13.7	6.0
Sweden	6.2	3.9	2.5	10.1	13.6	8.8	11.6	3.7
United Kingdom	3.2	7.0	9.0	16.6	15.9	10.5	14.2	7.8
United States	4.9	5.9	8.7	8.7	8.5	4.6	11.4	7.3

Sources: OECD, *Employment Outlook 1991*, Table 2.12; and *1992*, Tables 4.A.2 and 4.A.8.

provides a cost minimisation strategy, enabling them to do paid work while caring for their children or elderly dependants.

CHANGES IN EMPLOYMENT PATTERNS AND EQUALITY POLICIES

Patterns of sex segregation

Despite trends toward convergence throughout OECD countries, there are still significant differences in national service sector growth patterns, in the extent and nature of female labour force participation and in occupational segregation. Two sets of factors are important if we are to understand these differences. The first is the economic path taken by different countries as firms adjust to changing competitive conditions in the global economy. The second is the different role of regulation in shaping competitive conditions for services and employment practices.

Recent international data suggest that, at the highest level of occupational aggregation, sex segregation has decreased in some countries, most notably in the United States, Canada, and the United Kingdom (OECD, 1988). Nevertheless, disaggregated data suggest that the levels of segregation across OECD countries have declined only marginally.

Patterns of sex segregation relate to differences between OECD economies with still sizeable manufacturing workforces and those where the majority of workers, both men and women, are employed in service industries. Manufacturing-oriented economies tend to have many service jobs carried out within large firms or under firm hierarchies which utilise internal labour market structures. Occupational mobility is closely linked to work experience and firm-specific skills. In these situations, sex segregation and gender-based employment inequalities are a consequence of:

  i) women's discontinuous employment patterns;
  ii) inadequate access to firm-based training;
  iii) the "tracking" of women into separate internal labour markets because of expectations about their commitment to employment.

However, in order to avoid a situation where women are used to undercut negotiated wage levels, women employed in jobs similar to those of men are likely to be paid equivalent wages. Wage levels in these situations are a consequence of group rather than individual bargaining power. This system extends beyond manufacturing industries to service industries such as banking and insurance where wages, working hours and working conditions are nationally regulated.

In countries where a higher proportion of the total workforce, both male and female, is employed in services, the conditions are different. Internal labour markets tend to have less influence in wage structures and working conditions, employment bargaining is generally more individualised, vacancies are more often filled through the external market than from within the firm and external qualifications become more important in assessing a person's skills.

These two systems have very different implications for gender segregation and equal opportunities. In the first set of countries, inequality is associated with entrenched gender segregation, based on women's limited opportunities to acquire firm-specific skills, especially at higher levels of the occupational hierarchy. In the second set of countries, inequality is linked to educational achievement and individual bargaining power. In this case, a range of factors enter into the process of negotiating employment contracts which introduces potential bases for inequality. Today, gender-based earning disparities are as much the result of low earnings as of a worker's relative ability to secure paid bonuses, rewards such as non-taxed non-wage income benefits, or the opportunity to work overtime.

Despite near pay parity at entry level, fewer women advance in their professional careers than their male colleagues, which results in increased earnings disparities over time (OECD/CERI, 1989). As described above, women are more likely to be segregated through the types of work contracts they hold. "Non-standard" work contracts, including part-time and fixed-term contracts, distance women workers from the central mission of the firm and place them outside the internal labour market.

Although the emerging labour market picture is not all that clear, a pattern of "segregated integration" – which includes aspects of both dual labour market and core-periphery models – appears to be occurring across OECD countries. Women are being incorporated into the workforce but in ways that preserve male-dominated work domains while increasing competition among women. In times of economic downturn, rather than women replacing men, there is likely to be increased competition among women for female-dominated jobs. However, both dual labour market and core-periphery models may be inadequate to describe employment opportunities for women in services: labour market deregulation, positive action, women's increasingly continuous employment histories and higher qualification levels also need to be given due consideration.

Equal opportunity and labour market intervention

Labour market interventions to achieve equality of opportunity take a number of different forms. They can be legally constituted or appear as directives or official guidelines. They can be procedural regulations aimed at changing the institutional structures which mediate inequality, such as providing access to job training programmes. They can alternatively take the form of incentives, such as tax subsidies to employers to encourage them to offer training to workers with less access to higher-level jobs.

Measures to alleviate employment inequalities were originally directed at changing conditions in the public sector, and in large firms with internal labour markets. Large firms were thought to have a greater capacity to implement equal opportunity policies without endangering their market position. In addition, it was thought that if major firms took the lead in correcting inequities, a "trickle-down effect" would occur throughout the economy. It was hoped in particular that the public sector would offer an equal opportunity model which private sector employers would emulate.

In contemporary OECD economies, the "traditional" type of labour segmentation – constituted within a firm's internal labour market – coexists with new forms of segmentation and inequality. This is especially true in service economies where the external labour market is now a major factor in occupational mobility patterns. Nevertheless, interventions such as positive action and equal pay provisions are still largely directed at changing conditions within the firm. It is much more difficult to address problems arising from an employer's ability to discriminate between workers on the external labour market on the basis of individually negotiated contracts. One such criterion introducing new forms of inequality might be based on a worker's willingness to work very long hours. Women with family responsibilities are unable to fulfil the implicit terms of such a contract, and are therefore relegated to a second-rate career track with less earning potential – sometimes referred to as the "mommy" track. This type of inequality is much more difficult to tackle because it is attributed to individual choice rather than to institutional or regulatory structures.

Given the persistence of sex segregation practices, we can assume that they will continue without some forms of intervention to change patterns of employment and promotion. Thus far, most attention has been paid to supply characteristics under the assumption that the problem of women's competitiveness in labour markets is a consequence of their low qualification level and discontinuous labour force participation and lack of experience. At least some social welfare policies are predicated on the notion that women's propensity to enter the workforce is exclusively affected by their domestic responsibilities and can be resolved by providing for those responsibilities collectively. As we have seen, however, access to wage work is one thing and integration is another.

Notes

1. Two international classificatory systems are used in OECD countries: the General Industrial Classification of Economic Activities within the European Communities (NACE), and the United Nation's International Standard Industrial Classification System (ISIC). Although there is still national divergence from these schemes, the gradual acceptance of a national accounts-based classification of service activities based on output has enabled more accurate international comparisons.

2. The chapter draws extensively on an unpublished report to the OECD Working Party on the Role of Women in the Economy by C. Hagemann-White, "Women in the Service Sector: A Synthesis of Five Country Studies", 1990. The country studies were authored by: F. Audier and E. Varikas (France), C. Schiersmann (Germany), M. Osawa (Japan), A. Goransson (Sweden) and S. Christopherson (United States).

3. "Germany" refers to the Federal Republic of Germany prior to 1990.

4. The trend towards increasing variability in employment contracts is documented in an extensive literature. In addition to the analysis in Chapter 3 on part-time work, see: Economic Council of Canada (1991); Christopherson et al. (1990); Beechey and Perkins (1987); Standing (1989).

5. For an elaborated discussion of these questions, see Daniels (1990) and Gibbs and Hayashi (1989).

6. For example, new openings for women film directors in France and the United States may erode as media investment becomes concentrated in fewer television and film enterprises, and in bigger international projects (Christopherson, 1990).

7. For example, in the United States in 1965, a dramatic change in the regulations governing migration allowed greater numbers of skilled Asian workers to immigrate.

8. Research is being conducted on the demand for such workers and the working conditions they face. The International Labour Organisation, for instance, is currently conducting a study of the migration of domestic workers from Asia to Italy.

9. An analysis of women's employment in the public sector is presented in Chapter 5. It appears that qualified women are heavily concentrated in this sector, which, for some countries, is estimated to comprise 70 per cent of all professionally qualified women.

10. The same is true of productivity. It is relatively easy to measure productivity gains achieved through the application of technology or job skills in manufacturing. They increase the volume produced per hour. It is much more difficult to measure productivity in service industries where the quality of the service enters the equation. Airlines, health care institutions, schools, and retail stores can process large numbers of customers and clients but at the cost of quality of service. The insertion of quality into evaluation of service "skills" raises questions which are difficult to answer with traditional quantitative product-oriented measures.

Bibliography

BALL, R. (1990), "The Process of International Contract Labour Migration from the Philippines: The Case of Filipino Nurses", Sydney, Australia: unpublished PhD. dissertation, The University of Sydney.

BEECHEY, V. and PERKINS, T. (1987), *A Matter of Hours: Women, Part-time Work and the Labour Market,* Minneapolis: University of Minnesota Press.

BERTRAND, O. and NOYELLE, T. (1990), "Changing Employment and Skill Formation in Service Industries: A Comparison of Supermarkets, Department Stores, Hospitals and Software Firms in France, Japan, Sweden, and the United States", in *Technological Change and Human Resources Development: The Service Sector,* The Hague: Dutch Ministry of Education and Science, and Van Gocum.

BEYERS, W. (1990), "Contrasts in Producer Services in the US and UK", paper presented at the 1990 Fulbright Commission Colloquium, Cardiff, UK.

BLUESTONE, B. (1990), "The Impact of Schooling and Industrial Restructuring on Recent Trends in Wage Inequality in the United States", AEA Papers and Proceedings, May, pp. 303-307.

BOWERS, B. (1990), "Fed up with Low Pay, Enterprising Nurses Attempt to Change Face of US Healthcare", *The Wall Street Journal,* September 1.

BRAVERMAN, H. (1974), *Labor and Monopoly Capital: The Degradation of Work in the Twentieth Century,* New York: Monthly Review Press.

BUCHTEMANN, C. and SCHUPP, J. (1988), "Socio-Economic Aspects of Part-time Employment in the Federal Republic of Germany", Berlin: Wissenschaftszentrum Discussion Paper FS I 88-6.

CARNEVALE, A., GAINER, L. and MELTZER, A. (1989), "Workplace Basics: The Skills Employers Want", Virginia: The American Society for Training and Development.

CHRISTOPHERSON, S. (1990), "Emerging Industrial Relations in Media Industries", in L. Gray and R. Seeber (eds.), *Technological Change in the Arts, Entertainment and Electronic Media Industry: Impact on Labor Relations,* Ithaca: New York State School of Industrial and Labor Relations, Cornell University.

CHRISTOPHERSON, S., NOYELLE, T. and REDFIELD B. (1990), *Policies for the Flexible Workforce,* Report to the Employment and Training Administration of the Department of Labor, New York: Eisenhower Center for the Conservation of Human Resources.

COHEN, M. (1987), *Free Trade and the Future of Women's Work,* Toronto: Garamond Press and the Canadian Centre for Policy Alternatives.

COMMISSION OF THE EUROPEAN COMMUNITIES (1990) *Employment in Europe,* Brussels.

DANIELS, P. (1990), "Services in the International Economy", unpublished paper presented at the 1990 Fulbright Commission Colloquium, Cardiff, UK, 10-11 December.

ECONOMIC COUNCIL OF CANADA (1991), *Employment in the Service Economy,* Ottawa: Ministry of Supply and Services Canada.

FIGGE, K. and QUACK, S. (1990), *Die Auswirkungen des europäischen Binnenmarktes 1992 auf die Beschäftigung von Frauen in Kreditgewerbe der BRD,* Discussion Paper Nr FSI 90-15, Berlin: Wissenschaftszentrum für Sozialforschung Berlin.

GIBBS, M. and HAYASHI, M. (1989), "Sectoral Issues and the Multinational Framework for Trade in Services: An Overview", in UNCTAD, *Trade in Services: Sectoral Issues,* New York: United Nations.

HAKIM, C. (1990), "Core and Periphery in Employers' Workforce Strategies: Evidence from the 1987 ELUS Survey", *Work, Employment and Society,* Vol. 4, No. 2, pp. 157-188.

LANE, C. (1990), *Management and Labour in Europe,* Aldershot: Edward Elgar.

LE JOURNAL D'EMPLOI/SERVICE (1989), "Bref Social", 10418, 9 March.

NOYELLE, T. (1987), *Beyond Industrial Dualism Market and Job Segmentation in the New Economy,* Boulder: Westview Press.

OECD (1988), *Employment Outlook,* Paris.

OECD/CERI (1989), "Changes in Work Patterns, Synthesis of Five National Reports on the Service Sector", Paris: OECD.

SCHMID, G. (1990), "Institutions Regulating the Labor Market: Support or Impediments for Structural Change?", in Appelbaum, E. and Schettkat, R. (eds.), *Labor Market Adjustments to Structural Change and Technological Progress,* New York: Praeger.

SOCIAL AND LABOUR BULLETIN 3-4/1989, pp. 282-283.

STANDING, G. (1989) "Labour Flexibility in Western European Labour Markets", in Laflamme, G., Murray, G., Belanger, J. and Ferland, G. (eds.) *Flexibility and Labour in Canada and the United States,* Geneva: International Institute for Labour Studies, Research Series 94.

Chapter 5

WOMEN IN THE PUBLIC SECTOR*

The State influences women's employment in various ways. Government departments and agencies as well as state-owned firms and public corporations employ women directly while a range of other policies – from aggregate-demand management to industrial subsidies, temporary public work schemes, wage subsidies and other active labour market policies – affect women's employment in less direct ways. Regulation of the private sector – *i.e.* workplace health and safety, employment security, prohibition of discrimination, and social security obligations – also affect women's labour market opportunities. This chapter however will mainly focus on the role of the State as an employer.

The expansion of the public sector[1] has been one of the most significant features of structural adjustment in OECD countries over the last few decades, although there are remarkable differences from country to country. For example, while the public sector share of employment remained at an almost constant rate of 15 per cent in the United States, it increased to a level of almost one-third of total employment in Sweden. In most countries, growth in public employment was accompanied by a feminisation of the labour force. In the 1970s and 1980s a high correlation between the female-intensity of public employment and the size of the public sector could be observed. There was also a clear tendency for the public sector to become increasingly female-intensive over time (OECD, 1982).

Recently, however, this expansionary trend has undergone a change while the public sector has come to be seen as a target for, rather than an instrument of, structural reform. In a world of increasing globalisation and market liberalisation there is growing concern about the competitiveness and performance of national economies. The public sector and the inefficient provision of public services are often held responsible for deteriorating competitiveness.[2] Market pundits calling for privatisation, deregulation and cost containment – in short, for more market and less State – have had no trouble finding an audience. Privatisation of public activities has so far affected mainly the marketable services of public enterprises, which is not the major focus of this study. However, new public-private mixes and the rationalisation of all branches of the public sector are clearly on the structural adjustment agenda.[3]

---

* This chapter is an abridged and edited version of *Women and Employment Restructuring: Women in the Public Sector*, by Günther Schmid [OECD/GD(91)213].

As the position of women varies with the size and structure of the public sector, the implications of public sector reform for women's employment will also vary from country to country. The feminisation of the public sector, once seen as a panacea for equal opportunities, may limit women's opportunities in times of public sector rationalisation. On the other hand, modernisation of the public sector and a corresponding emphasis on efficiency may offer opportunities for a new balance of equality and efficiency.

Gender inequalities are an obvious target for structural reform in general. Gender-based occupational segregation, for example, is a source of labour market inefficiency, especially when the feedback or secondary effects are taken into account. If women are confined to a narrow range of public or menial service jobs, the economy misses out on a valuable resource (Blau and Ferber, 1986). Furthermore, discrimination discourages women from investing in their human capital, which in turn entrenches occupational segregation and results in further costly under-utilisation of women's skills and talents.

This chapter examines the impact of changes in the public sector on women's employment in the following manner:

   i) How did women's employment in the public sector develop in selected OECD countries? What patterns, in terms of branches, occupations, wages and working time, can be identified?
   ii) Which equal opportunities policies have been implemented in the public sector? Have they been effective? What are the main obstacles preventing their effectiveness? Is the assumption that public employers act as models for private employers with respect to equal opportunities correct?
   iii) What are the challenges facing the public sector in the 1990s and what are the likely effects on women's employment?

PATTERNS OF PUBLIC SECTOR EMPLOYMENT

The expansion of the public sector – notably in the areas of health, education and social welfare – has had a significant impact on women's employment. Unfortunately, there has been little research on the role of the Welfare State as employer, and even less so on the role of the State as an employer of women. In particular, there is a special dearth of cross-national and longitudinal studies. Due to a lack of comprehensive empirical evidence for the different OECD countries, the following discussion uses illustrative examples to highlight the most important dimensions of the public sector labour market.

Levels and structure of public employment

Government employment as a percentage of total employment in OECD countries increased from 11.3 to 15.1 per cent between 1960 and 1989 (weighted average). The pace of growth, however, has declined substantially: from an annual rate of around three per cent in the 1970s, to around 1 per cent in the 1980s. The trend has even been reversed in a few countries, most remarkably in the United Kingdom (OECD, 1990). Growth in public sector employment has not been uniform across OECD countries

(Statistical Annex, Table E). Three patterns or "models" can be identified which will be illustrated with reference to three countries: Germany, Sweden and the United States.

Three theoretical scenarios of public employment

Women's employment in the public sector is largely determined by an implicit social contract through which societies shape their Welfare State. By comparing wage formation determined by market forces to those determined by social forces, and job creation in the public sector versus job creation in the private sector, it is possible to distinguish three theoretical but empirically relevant scenarios (Graph 5.1).

In the first scenario – the "integrated free market model" – wages are paid according to productivity or market values. This model has two major characteristics in relation to the labour market. First, there is a tendency towards a dual labour market split into a market of "good" jobs – with high productivity and high wages – and a market of "bad" jobs – with low productivity (especially in services) and low wages which may even fall below a socially-defined minimum standard. This holds true for the public as well as for the private sector. Second, the Welfare State is not particularly engaged in creating additional employment, especially not in the low-productivity service sector. There are no particular implications for women's employment, except that low wages and the effects on overall household incomes eventually force more labour market participation, especially among women.

In the second scenario – the "integrated Welfare State model" – each job is intended to provide a social wage, that is, a decent wage independent of its productivity or market value. The creation of high-productivity jobs is indirectly subsidised by solidaristic wage policies and strong active labour market policies, especially in further

Graph 5.1. **Three theoretical scenarios of public sector employment (PSE)**

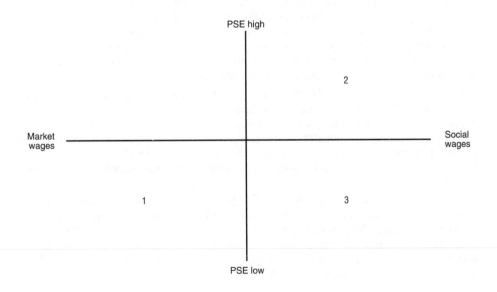

135

education and training. New jobs are created by the State or semi-public authorities (especially in low-productivity welfare services) and financed through taxes or other obligatory contributions. Welfare services provide employment opportunities both directly and indirectly – as a social infrastructure – in particular for women who formerly provided these types of services in the home. This model gives a high priority to full employment. The labour market is strongly segregated into a highly-productive private labour market, and a huge public labour market of welfare services with low productivity (or productivity that is difficult to measure). In this case, women's labour force participation increases through a self-reinforcing feedback loop of welfare services.[4]

In the third scenario – the "disintegrated Welfare State model" – each job is intended to provide a decent wage, independent of its market value. New jobs of high productivity are supported directly by industrial policies combined with public training and education and, to some extent, by moderate real wage policies. New jobs of low productivity (especially in services) are not subsidised. The provision of these services will be left mainly to the informal sector or to private individuals. Tasks such as care of the elderly are indirectly subsidised by generous transfer payments financed by the high-productivity sector. This high-productivity strategy creates a demand for skilled workers and favours those who work long hours and follow uninterrupted career paths. Those who are unable or unwilling to work in this manner are structurally disadvantaged. The labour market is strongly segmented into insiders and outsiders, and shows a tendency towards technological unemployment due to its low propensity to create new jobs. Rather than engaging in compensatory job creation, the Welfare State concentrates on transfer payments to the unemployed and to other reserves of potential labour, such as women with young children.

Three real scenarios of public employment: the United States, Sweden and Germany

Three countries come close to these theoretical Welfare State models; respectively, the United States, Sweden and Germany[5] (Graph 5.2 and Table 5.1).

The United States experienced a 15 percentage points increase in female labour force participation between 1973 and 1988. However, the government's share of total employment remained at the same level, and even decreased slightly in the 1980s. The bulk of new jobs for women was therefore created in the private sector, although women remain over-represented in the public sector. The majority of American women in government jobs are in positions related to education.

Sweden – and to a lesser extent the other Scandinavian countries – has an even higher female labour force participation than the United States: over the same 15-year period it grew from 63 to 80 per cent. Almost a third of Swedish workers, and a quarter of the total working-age population are government employees. Women are more concentrated in the public sector than in the United States. More than half of employed women have public sector jobs, mostly in welfare functions: health, care and social security.

Germany has followed a different track. Between 1973 and 1988 total labour force participation declined, and female labour force participation increased only slightly (from 50 to 54 per cent). Government employment doubled between 1960 and 1988, but the proportion of government employment as a percentage of the total working-age population remained almost constant and is inferior to the level attained by the United States free market model. Therefore, although the majority of new jobs for women have been

Graph 5.2. Women and public sector employment in three countries

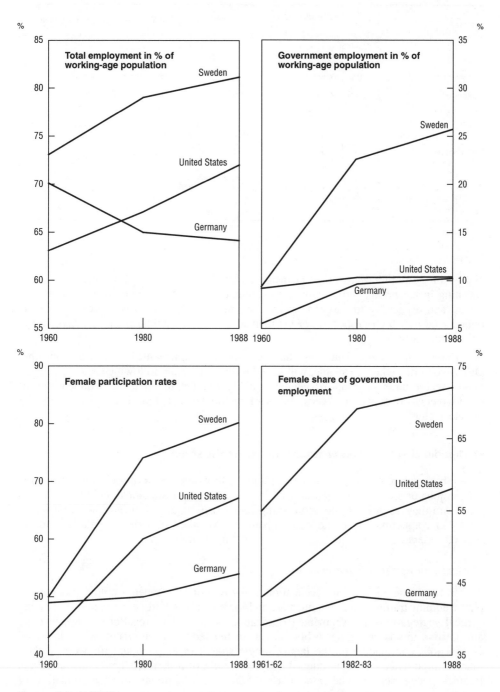

Total employment in % of working-age population

Sweden

United States

Germany

Government employment in % of working-age population

Sweden

United States

Germany

Female participation rates

Sweden

United States

Germany

Female share of government employment

Sweden

United States

Germany

Source: Schmid (1991).

Table 5.1.   **Women in general government employment, by function**

Country	Year	Total ('000)	Distribution of women by function[b] (per cent)				Women as per cent of function			
			Public admin.	Health	Educ.	Social security and care	Public admin.	Health	Educ.	Social security and care
Germany[a]	1961	710	11.8	23.2	21.5	24.2	27.6	60.2	42.7	57.7
	1982	1 813	10.3	29.1	29.0	16.1	30.1	66.4	53.0	62.1
Sweden	1964	365	12.7	32.4	24.4	66.1	33.3	83.9	66.1	79.6
	1983	1 046	8.8	32.0	19.6	27.6	44.0	84.8	69.0	91.0
United States	1962	3 302	26.5	16.5	53.1	0.5	30.5	61.7	61.5	71.0
	1983	7 565	24.9	14.0	52.5	4.7	39.9	71.4	64.7	71.0

a) Data refer to the public sector excluding public utilities, social security administration and some public enterprises.
b) The four functions do not total 100 per cent.
Source: Schmid (1991), Table 3.

created in the public sector, the expansion of this sector did not compensate for labour shedding in the private agriculture and manufacturing sectors. In contrast to the United States, and especially to Sweden, women are not significantly over-represented in the public sector. A high proportion of German women in the public sector are involved in educational services.

Empirical evidence from these three countries, complemented with data from other OECD countries where available, will serve to illustrate in the following sections how the public sector fares in terms of gender equality relative to three main dimensions of employment – occupation, wages and working time – and how it compares with the private sector.[6]

Occupational segregation of women in the public sector

Which public sector jobs do women hold? Do women perform only the menial and routine jobs or are they also represented in management, professional and highly-skilled jobs? Are they confined to non-competing (closed) occupations, or are they well represented in competing (open-ended) occupations? Are they promoted regularly, and are they considered on the same basis as men for further training?

Vertical and horizontal segregation

In the United States, the occupational distribution of women employed in general public administration at the federal, state and local levels is fairly compressed (indicating vertical segregation) and segmented (indicating horizontal segregation), although there are positive trends emerging in both cases. In the federal government, while low-paid clerical jobs continue to be the largest single source of employment for women, their relative importance has been reduced, and the weight of professional, administrative and technical categories has increased (Table 5.2). The traditional over-representation of women in administrative support jobs (85 per cent) is similar to that of other countries. In

Table 5.2.   **UNITED STATES**
Women in general government at federal level, by occupational category

Occupational category	Numbers ('000)		Distribution of women by category (per cent)		Women as per cent of category	
	1982	1988	1982	1988	1982	1988
Professional	91	128	11.6	14.3	25.9	30.8
Administrative	128	189	16.3	21.0	31.1	37.1
Technical	158	193	20.3	21.5	45.0	51.7
Clerical	363	341	46.1	38.0	84.6	85.0
Other white-collar	3	4	0.1	0.4	8.1	9.2
Blue-collar	44	46	5.5	4.7	10.4	11.0

Source: Schmid (1991), Table 6.

contrast to other countries, however, there seems to be a relatively high representation of women in professional (31 per cent) and technical jobs (51 per cent). Although true comparisons are impossible to make, American women seem also to be less compressed in the lower ranks of the public sector than in other countries. In 1988 the average grade for women in the federal government administration was seven (the highest grade being 15) which compares to an average grade of 10.1 for men.

According to the 1985 Swedish census, the vast majority of public sector employees in Sweden are women (67.2 per cent). Women appear to have taken over public employment, but more so at the municipal (72.4 per cent) and county level (83.5 per cent) – where jobs are mainly in direct service delivery – than at the central level (41.8 per cent) – where there are more influential positions. Overall, the proportion of women is higher among workers than in the white-collar category (73.1 versus 62.6 per cent). Vertical segregation is marked among workers in the public sector: the bulk of unskilled service workers are female, while women are very much under-represented among skilled workers in goods production (Table 5.3). Women in the Swedish public sector are concentrated in a few occupations: nearly 60 per cent are found in the 10 most common public sector occupations. The corresponding figure for men is less than 30 per cent.

Women made up approximately a third of the German public sector in 1988 (including public utilities and social security administration) but only 18 per cent of employees at the highest career step were found to be women. They were equally represented at the second highest level but over-represented at the lower intermediate level and under-represented at the lowest level and among blue-collar workers in public services. This situation remained relatively constant all through the 1980s (Table 5.4).

Horizontal occupational segregation has also persisted over the last decade. The bulk (75 per cent) of female employees (non-civil servants) in the public sector continued to work as either office employees (senior officials, secretaries, typists, clerical assistants) or in cleaning professions. In terms of skilled occupations, however, there have been some improvements. Women's relative share has increased (albeit from a low base level) in a number of occupations, including engineers and chemists (from 3 per cent in 1977 to almost 9 per cent in 1990), technicians (from 16 to 23 per cent), legal professions (from 13 to 26 per cent), and physicians (from 38 to 50 per cent).

Table 5.3. SWEDEN
Women's share of employment by sector and socio-economic status, 1985

Socio-economic status	All sectors	Public sector					Private sector
		Public enterpr.	Central State	Municipal	County	Total	
Production workers, total	**1 924 586**	**100 178**	**37 696**	**342 626**	**211 871**	**695 642**	**1 214 185**
Percentage of women in:							
Total	46.0	31.7	39.1	79.6	88.1	73.1	30.6
Unskilled, goods prod.	28.0	14.5	16.6	22.0	51.6	18.1	29.1
Unskilled, service prod.	68.9	46.1	62.7	85.6	90.5	81.1	54.6
Skilled, goods prod.	7.3	6.0	6.6	4.2	11.0	5.6	7.5
Skilled, services prod.	79.2	8.1	51.0	92.9	87.5	86.3	56.3
White collar, total	**1 700 148**	**60 189**	**191 177**	**364 894**	**176 030**	**816 306**	**874 447**
Percentage of women in:							
Total	51.2	47.1	42.5	67.0	79.1	62.6	40.7
Lower level I	77.0	81.9	71.6	60.7	67.1	69.9	81.2
Lower level II	59.1	57.7	59.1	80.7	92.5	74.9	47.5
Intermediate level	47.3	21.3	28.4	72.2	87.6	65.9	26.7
Higher level, top pos.	31.6	24.9	28.5	51.8	50.6	43.6	17.7
Self-employed, total	**265 787**	**168**	**460**	**1 622**	**331**	**2 600**	**262 853**
Percentage of women	26.3	29.8	19.8	43.5	57.7	40.4	26.2
Professions, total	**6 010**	–	–	–	–	–	**6 010**
Percentage of women	19.0	–	–	–	–	–	19.0
All status, total	**4 285 109**	**172 245**	**247 214**	**786 319**	**432 192**	**1 667 266**	**2 590 807**
Percentage of women	47.2	37.8	41.8	72.4	83.5	67.2	34.5

Source: Schmid (1991), Table 7.

Table 5.4. **GERMANY**
Women in public sector employment[a] by class level

Class level	Full-time				Part-time[b]			
	Total employment ('000)		Percentage of women		Total employment ('000)		Percentage of women	
	1980	1988	1980	1988	1980	1988	1980	1988
Civil servants and employees[c]								
Higher	410	429	18.3	18.4	27	59	74.1	62.7
Higher intermediate	861	857	31.9	31.0	79	145	88.6	91.0
Intermediate	1 486	1 534	43.5	45.6	153	244	98.0	97.5
Ordinary	234	200	22.2	24.0	13	14	92.3	92.9
Blue collar	811	790	18.2	17.0	181	192	95.6	94.3
Total	3 802	3 809	31.5	32.3	453	654	93.8	91.9

a) Including public utilities and social security administration; excluding army members.
b) With at least half of the regular working time in full-time employment.
c) *Higher* = "Höherer Dienst", academic degree; *higher intermediate* = "Gehobener Dienst", college degree; *intermediate* = "Mittlerer Dienst", secondary degree; *ordinary* = "Einfacher Dienst", primary degree.
Source: Schmid (1991), Table 8.

Women in the lower career steps are often over-qualified. In the civil service the average formal education of female civil servants is higher than that of their male colleagues, yet male employees are allocated positions with better career prospects and are more likely to be promoted. Moreover, male civil servants receive twice as much further training than their female counterparts (Gerigk *et al.,* 1986). Some very recent improvement may be related to a 1986 directive for the promotion of women in the federal public administration. The first monitoring report established that the proportion of women promoted or participating in further training in the civil service was higher than their representation in employment. Female recruitment also increased slightly. Given the relatively high representation of women in initial civil service training, a continuation of this positive trend can be expected (Bericht der Bundesregierung, 1990).

The situation in the three "model" countries can be compared with that of other OECD countries. A recent report on the situation of women in the federal public service in Canada suggests that women are highly concentrated in a small number of occupational groups. Three-quarters of the female labour force are found within four of the 72 occupational classifications: in clerical, secretarial, administrative and programme administration services. One group alone – the clerical and regulatory group – accounts for 44 per cent of all women in Canada's federal public service. In terms of vertical segregation, women occupy the lower levels of almost every occupational group. Significantly, they are vacating their posts in the federal public services at a higher rate than men; this applies to all categories except the "management" category. A simulation showed that – given the small numbers of women in the middle-through-upper levels of many occupational groups – the fact that women are vacating jobs at these levels plays an important role in preventing a better gender balance within a reasonable period of time *(Beneath the Veneer,* 1990).

In the United Kingdom an evaluation of progress towards achieving equal opportunities for women in the civil service (Cabinet Office, 1990) reflected the same concerns with respect to the higher overall level of women's resignation, high propensity of career breaks, and lower promotion rates, especially between the ages of 25 and 35, when the majority of women have children and when important decisions about careers are made (see also Fredman and Morris, 1989). However, the review also revealed that apart from the three highest grades – in which women are still absent – increases in female recruitment and promotion are a reason for some optimism.

Public/private comparisons

Only the Swedish source allows public/private sector comparisons in terms of occupational segregation and compression. It shows that, in general, when looking at socio-economic status, women fare better in the public rather than in the private sector. In the worker category, women's share of unskilled goods-producing jobs is lower in the public than in the private sector, while the female share of skilled service jobs is higher. In the white-collar category half of higher or top-level employees in municipalities and counties (51.8 and 50.6 per cent, respectively) are women. In the private sector women hold only 17.7 per cent of similar jobs. The proportion of women among low-level white-collar workers is also lower in the public sector. However, women remain significantly more represented at the lower levels in both the public and the private sectors. In central state employment, for instance, women make up 71.6 per cent of the lowest-level white-collar labour force, while they comprise only 28.5 per cent of top level employees.

Although the current lack of comparative research does not allow for any generalisation, the available evidence clearly shows that gender-specific occupational segregation in the public sector is common to all countries, albeit to different degrees. Occupational inequality also seems to be correlated to the size of the female labour force in the public sector. In addition, as the Swedish example shows, vertical segregation is associated with the level of government: women fare better – in terms of skills acquisition and seniority – at local or regional levels than at the central level.

Occupational segregation seems to be greater in the public than in the private sector. However, this observation must be qualified with respect to vertical segregation. Women occupy relatively more of the medium- and high-level positions at decentralised levels of the public sector.

The salaries of women in the public sector: wage inequalities

How well do state employers pay women? Do public sector jobs attract women by offering high wages or has public sector expansion occurred on the basis of low wages? Do wages differ between institutional levels of government or according to government function? How do women's and men's wages compare? Does the private sector pay comparatively higher wages? Here again the answers are limited by the paucity of empirical evidence and the lack of comparative research.[7]

Gender-specific wage differentials

In the United States in the early 1970s, the public sector male-female pay gap (the percentage by which male employees' earnings exceed those of female employees with equivalent personal characteristics) was about 29 per cent at the federal, 21 per cent at the state, and 18 per cent at the local level. The corresponding private sector pay gap was estimated at 28 to 36 per cent (Ehrenberg and Schwarz, 1986). A recent evaluation of comparable worth policy in Washington State shows that between 1983 and 1987, the female-to-male wage ratio rose from 80.2 to 85.6 per cent. Of this increase, 80 per cent was attributed to the re-evaluation of jobs according to comparable worth schemes (O'Neill et al., 1989). The wage ratio in non-state employment also rose, from 63 to 56 per cent.

In the Swedish public sector, gender pay differentials have narrowed more than in the United States. Among women employed full-time in the national civil service, average pay rose from 80 to 91 per cent of the average male salary between 1973 and 1985. Among women employed by municipal governments, average pay rose from 74 to 87 per cent of the male average over the same period. Women employed by county councils received 75 per cent of the average male pay in 1985; this wider differential is due largely to the fact that women and men in this segment of the labour market work in very different occupations (for example, women are nursing assistants while men are physicians).

A similar situation applies to white-collar categories in the private sector where the pay range is also wide. In 1985, women with white-collar jobs in the private sector earned only slightly more than 70 per cent of the salaries of males in the same category, although the relative level of women's pay had increased. The pay of female white-collar employees in industry rose from 63 per cent of men's average salaries in 1973 to 73 per cent in 1985. Among industrial workers, the ratio increased from 84 per cent in 1973 to 91 per cent in 1985 (Persson, 1990).

There has been no improvement in Swedish women's earnings relative to men's in any sector since 1984. Women may have even lost ground. One explanation for this downward trend is the movement away from solidaristic wages towards more competitive performance-based pay policies. For example, employees whose skills are in high demand in the private sector have been entitled to a "market supplement" at the central government level since 1985. Because most of those salary supplements have gone to men, they are sometimes referred to as the "men's supplement"[8] (Wise, 1990).

The predominant feature of public sector pay structures in Germany is the stability of differentials and relativities between the different groups of public sector employees. Germany has a single, all-encompassing salary structure for public sector employees which is almost completely status- rather than performance-based. Pay increases are proportionally the same; only lower-grade posts improved their position, and then only marginally. Given their concentration in the lower grades, women's relative pay improved slightly.

Public/private wage differentials

A recent international study (OECD, 1990) compares the evolution of public sector wages in the 1970s and 1980s for 17 OECD countries. The data suggest that real and relative public sector wages have grown very slowly in most countries since the mid-1970s. Aside from Austria, Finland, Japan, Switzerland and the United States, real wages have become static or decreased since the beginning of the 1980s. Comparisons show that for a wide range of countries, public sector wages have declined relative to the private sector.[9,10] There is, however, no breakdown of these data according to sex.

According to results available for the United States in the 1970s, the public(federal)/ private sector wage differential for this period remained positive but seemed to be diminishing. The differential appeared to be greater for females than for males. This may have reflected a lower level of gender discrimination in the federal government than in the private sector. The state and local sectors also showed public/private earnings differentials which were larger for females than for males, although the size of these differentials varied according to level of government. After controlling characteristics, males employed by local governments (and possibly also males employed by state governments) earned on average less than their private sector counterparts. At the state level women earned on average between 8 and 14 per cent more than their private sector counterparts, but their pay levels tended to equalise at the local level (Ehrenberg and Schwarz, 1986).

For Sweden, according to a dissertation calculating wage differentials standardized for personal characteristics, the 1974 wage rates for males were slightly higher in the private than in the public sector. By 1981 this private/public wage differential had increased markedly. The wage rates for white-collar males were 6 to 7 per cent higher in the private sector. The female pattern is different. As in the United States, the wage rates are higher for females employed by central government than for females in the private sector (around 8 per cent higher in 1974 and 5 per cent in 1981). However, while the 1974 female wage rates were higher in local government than in the private sector, by 1981 this sectoral wage differential had been reversed: the wage rate for women of given characteristics was found to be 5 per cent higher in the private sector (Zetterberg, 1990).

German data also indicate that women earn on average more in the core public sector (civil service) than in the private sector. Overall, however, public sector employees fell behind the private sector between 1980 and 1990, by 4.1 per cent in the case of white-collar staff and 3.8 per cent for blue-collar workers (Seglow, 1990).

Denmark offers an interesting comparison. Danish public employment growth has been one of the most rapid of all OECD countries over the last 30 years. Whereas average changes in annual wages in the public sector surpassed those of the private sector in the 1960s – when there was the fastest public sector growth – this relationship was reversed in the 1970s. Using longitudinal data covering the years 1976-1985, Pedersen *et al.* (1990) found a decrease in relative public sector wages even after correction for differences in relevant background factors and individual fixed effects such as education and experience. As well as confirming the existence of a gender-based pay gap, the study discovered differences between the public and private sectors in the rate of return on education: for men, 6 per cent in the public against 4 per cent in the private sector; for women, about 2 per cent in the public against zero in the private sector. Moreover, the rate of return on experience is only about 0.8 per cent for men and almost nil for women in both the public and private sectors. Women's low level of on-the-job training, part-time work with corresponding low promotion rates, and higher incidence of career interruption are mentioned as plausible reasons for these differences.

Conclusion

The gender-based pay gap in the public service is still found today in all OECD countries, to the disadvantage of women. It seems, however, to be diminishing, albeit slowly, in most countries. On the other hand, competition between the private and public sector and between men and women seems to have become more effective, especially at the local level (this is in contrast to the 1960s and early 1970s, a period of fast expansion); and the public sector and women appear to be losing in relative terms.

The evidence of a trade-off between wages and employment is not very clear. In the United States improvements in relative wages due to comparable worth implementation may have occurred at the expense of employment.[11] Denmark and Sweden show an opposite but consistent pattern; continuous employment gains in the public sector occurred alongside decreasing wages relative to the private sector. In Germany, women working full-time in the public sector do not appear to have lost ground relative to the private sector in terms of wages, but employment gains in terms of full-time jobs have been small compared to Denmark and Sweden.

Inequalities in relation to working time

Three dimensions with respect to working time are relevant in any qualitative evaluation of employment. Does the job provide enough income to enable economic independence (income dimension)? Does the job provide income security or is it precarious, that is, short-term or even "on call" (stability dimension)? Does the job allow adjustments in working hours to fit with family obligations or other activities such as educational sabbaticals (flexibility dimension)?

Comparable data for all OECD countries on these aspects are unavailable and the same applies to comparative data for the public and private sectors. The following therefore concentrates on country-specific insights, complemented by some information from the European Labour Force Survey (ELFS)[12] in relation to part-time and fixed-term employment.

Part-time employment

The development of part-time employment in the public sector is only one aspect of the development of part-time employment in society as a whole. This phenomenon should therefore be seen in the light of the analysis provided in Chapter 3.

In the United States, the proportion of part-time work in federal employment is very small – 2.4 per cent, 70 per cent of which is made up of women in spite of the part-time career employment act introduced in 1978. The proportion of part-timers in total employment at state and local government levels is much higher and not very distant from the 20 per cent of part-time employment in the overall economy.

The 1985 Swedish census revealed higher levels of female part-time work at the local government level than among white-collar workers in the private industrial sector. Excluding women aged 25-29 – who make up a slightly lower proportion of part-time employment – more than 60 per cent of women at the municipality level work part-time in Sweden. Women working at the central state level show working-time patterns that are similar to female white-collar private industrial sector employees: about 40 to 50 per cent of women work part-time, except for the youngest age group (fewer of whom work part-time) and the oldest age group (more of whom work part-time). The expansion and feminisation of the public sector in the Swedish example, therefore, is closely connected with reduced work time. A considerable number of men, especially at the local level of the public sector, also have reduced work schedules. Between 18 and 30 per cent of male municipal employees between the ages of 25 and 34 work part-time.

In Germany the growth of women's public sector employment in the 1980s was almost entirely connected with part-time work. In the governmental public sector, women's full-time employment increased only slightly, whereas, overall, part-time employment increased by 47 per cent (Table 5.4). In education, it increased by 52 per cent. The fact that full-time employment in education decreased at the same time suggests that more workers are job-sharing. Although the share of part-time employment increased from 12 to 16 per cent in the governmental public sector, part-time employment is considerably less common in the public sector than in the private sector. Part-time employment in the public sector is highly feminised (more than 90 per cent). In the higher service level, women's share of part-time work is lower and has declined; the fact that men's share has relatively increased may indicate that some more homework-sharing is occurring. It is worth noting that the higher civil service provides relatively more "long" part-time jobs, between 20 and 35 hours, than the private sector (Bericht der Bundesregierung, 1990).

Considering public administration only, the same pattern appears in European Community countries. With the exception of France, the public administration sector employs relatively fewer part-timers than the private sector. If part-time work is further qualified by distinguishing between "short" and "long" part-time work, a consistent pattern across countries emerges: two-thirds or more of part-time work in public administration is "long part-time work", which means more than 20 hours per week (in the United Kingdom, however, the proportion is lower) (Graph 5.3).

The increasing numbers of part-timers in the public sector raises questions related to the relative benefits of part-time work (see Chapter 3). There is no doubt that women working part-time enjoy greater economic independence than women outside the labour market, especially given that most public sector part-time jobs range between 20 and 34 hours and are therefore not marginal. There is, however, also a negative side, as part-time employment is associated with reinforced horizontal as well as vertical segregation. Moreover, the question of whether part-time work is freely chosen needs to be considered for both women and men, especially given the effects of part-time employment on family income.

Fixed-term employment

During the 1980s, the public sector increasingly turned to fixed-term employment as a means of relieving its payroll burden. In Germany, the proportion of fixed-term employees in the public sector doubled within only five years (1981-86) from 2.7 to 5.6 per cent (4.6 to 9.6 per cent if civil servants are excluded). This trend appears to be accelerating. A survey in 1987/88 revealed that 53 per cent of newly-hired persons in the public service were contracted for less than six months compared to 37 per cent in private industry. The same survey calculated a fixed-term ratio of 9.4 per cent in the public sector compared to 7.3 per cent in the private sector (Büchtemann and Höland, 1989). There is little difference between the proportions of men and women employed on fixed-term contracts.

As a comparison, in Canada fixed-term employment grew (as a proportion of all employment in the federal public service) from 11 per cent in 1983 to 14.3 per cent in 1988. Sixty per cent of those workers are women. Twenty per cent of all working women (and 10 per cent of men) are fixed-term employees. The majority of those women (57 per

Graph 5.3a. **Part-time female employment in general government**
1987

☐ "Short" part-time of 1-15 hours   ▨ Part-time in the range of 16-19 hours   ■ "Long" part-time of 20 hours +

Belgium

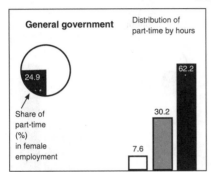

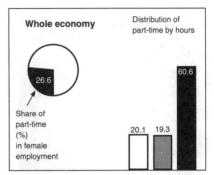

Germany

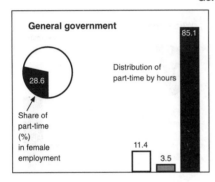

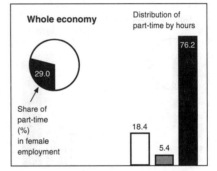

Denmark

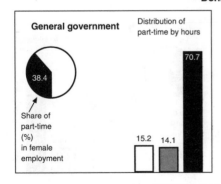

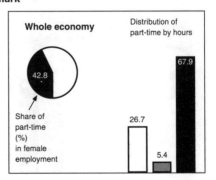

Source: Schmid (1991), Tables 14 and 15.

Graph 5.3b. **Part-time female employment in general government**
1987

☐ "Short" part-time of 1-15 hours   ▨ Part-time in the range of 16-19 hours   ■ "Long" part-time of 20 hours +

France

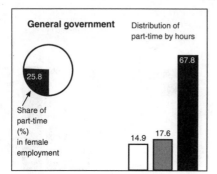

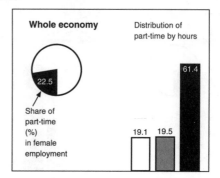

Netherlands

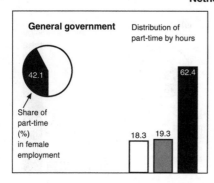

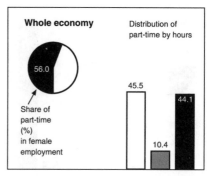

United Kingdom

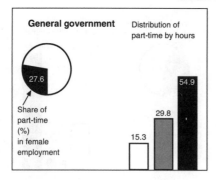

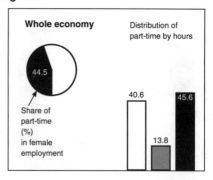

Source: Schmid (1991), Tables 14 and 15.

cent) are in fixed-term positions of less than six months (*Beneath the Veneer*, 1990, Vol. I).

Some countries report concerns about increasing numbers of fixed-term employees in the public sector, *i.e.* declining levels of stability. Social security benefits related to fixed-term employment are often non-existent or significantly inferior to those applied to other forms of employment. Further research is needed to identify the extent to which the increase in fixed-term positions is a result of the changing recruitment strategies used by public employers, or a result of supply-side factors, for example an increasing number of students looking for fixed-term employment.

EQUAL OPPORTUNITY POLICIES IN THE PUBLIC SECTOR

Equal opportunity policies rely mainly on four broad categories of instruments: equal rights legislation, positive action, incentives and infrastructural support. Within each category there are further differentiations. The degree of obligation imposed on employers varies according to the type of instruments; those bearing the highest degree of obligation do not however bear necessarily the greatest efficiency. In practice, the different types of policy instruments are most often interlinked. Table 5.5 shows the range of a comprehensive equal opportunity policy and gives one illustrative example of the application of each type of policy instrument to each of the three main dimensions of employment – occupation, wages and working time. Effective monitoring of this complex mix is obviously a most essential component of sound equal opportunity policies.

Equal rights legislation

The modern public sector is a prototype of an internal labour market, or, more specifically, of a bureaucratic organisation (Rose, 1985). It is predominantly characterised by impersonal entry rules (recruitment by merit and formal qualification), hierarchical exchange rules (salary by status and seniority), and stable exit rules (employment security). Until recently, women were openly discriminated against in all three aspects. Laws were in force that precluded married women's access to public service jobs, especially

Table 5.5. **A matrix of equal opportunities policies**

	Occupations	Wages	Working time
Equal rights legislation	Abolition of celibacy clause	Equal pay for equal work	Equal treatment of part-timers
Positive actions	Preferential hiring of equally qualified women	Equal pay for work of comparable worth	Entitlement to paid parental leave or working-time reduction
Incentives, infrastructure	Provision of public training centres	Wage subsidies for hiring women	Crèches and kindergartens in public agencies

high-level or civil service jobs. For example, various "celibacy" clauses applying exclusively to women existed in the majority of OECD countries until the 1940s or 1950s. Ireland was one of the last countries to remove this clause, in 1973, on joining the European Community. Other laws or regulations prevented the promotion of women who interrupted their career for family reasons; and there was no protection from discriminatory dismissal.

Today, direct sex discrimination with respect to entry, exchange and exit in public service employment appears to be largely eliminated (Wurster, 1989). In addition, equal pay for equal work has acquired a long tradition in the public sector. The enforcement of equal rights legislation, however, differs among countries. This can be illustrated from the three countries serving as examples. The United States puts high emphasis on sanctioning unequal treatment, whereas in Sweden and Germany there is much less active practice of enforcement of equal rights legislation.

Positive action

Despite legislation prohibiting unequal treatment, women still experience *de facto* discrimination in the public sector and their disadvantaged position persists. As a result, almost all OECD countries have introduced various equal opportunity laws, guidelines or directives making provision for positive action. This is aimed at supporting equal or preferential treatment of women on the labour market concerning in particular entry, or re-entry; it may also target the employment relationship, especially wage formation. The following gives a few selected examples, illustrating how positive action develops in practice.

Legal support of equal or preferential treatment: the case of Germany

In Germany, the most important positive action programmes have been initiated at the *Länder* level; most of these apply only to the public sector. This reflects both the pioneering role of the State as an equal opportunity employer, and the less complicated consensus between the industrial relations partners in the public sector. The Social Democratic Länder Governments in North Rhine-Westfalia (1989), Hamburg and Bremen (1990) and Berlin (1991) have all enacted equal opportunity or anti-discrimination laws, of which the latter is the most far-reaching.[13] This applies to the public administration only. A summary of the Berlin law demonstrates a range of positive action measures aimed at ensuring equal or preferential treatment (see box).

There are conflicts between traditional (male-biased) promotion rules and modern (gender-neutral or female-supporting) equal opportunity rules. Recently a civil servant in North Rhine-Westfalia went to court on the grounds that he was discriminated against by the new law.[14] The complainant argued successfully that – given the same qualification – he was eligible to be promoted because of seniority gained through military service. According to the old rule, seniority is decisive in case of same qualification. This obviously disadvantages women who usually have less seniority due to career interruption or later entry into the labour market. To promote women according to the equal opportunity laws violates the civil servants' skeleton law as well as Article 3 of the basic law that prohibits discrimination by sex. The judges stated that it was unacceptable for an individual man to suffer for past injustices against women. The case raised constitutional issues and was sent to the Supreme Court.

BERLIN ANTI-DISCRIMINATION LAW (1991): a summary of requirements

- The development of a woman's promotion plan for a period of six years with binding targets for two years;
- the obligation to advertise all vacancies internally as well as externally; where no women apply, external advertisements have to be repeated;
- any group of candidates to be considered by a selection committee shall comprise an equal number of men and women fulfilling the formal qualification requirements. Selection committees shall be composed equally of both genders;
- in areas where women are under-represented, at least 50 per cent of apprenticeship places shall be allocated to women;
- women trained in an occupation with less than 20 per cent of women have priority for jobs after training;
- in case of "same qualification" women have preferential recruitment until they make up 50 per cent of the respective occupation or career step and 50 per cent of the respective pay groups within an occupation or career step;
- training must be emphasized – including special training for personnel managers in equal opportunity policies; there is a need to compensate for additional costs arising from the care of children or other dependent family members;
- reduced work hours are explicitly recognised as compatible with the higher echelons of the public service; the return of workers to full-time positions shall be supported;
- government orders involving more than DM 10 000 shall be given to suppliers who can prove they operate an effective equal opportunity policy;
- administrative units must have a women's representative who shall be elected by female colleagues;
- administrative units must provide regular reports on progress made in implementing programmes and meeting targets.

The criteria of "same qualification" nurtures a controversial debate. It is criticised by some because it can be circumvented by changing definitions or is rendered ineffective by the lack of objective measurements of "qualifications". During the debate over the Berlin law, there was a proposal to replace "same qualification" with "required qualification", to allow women to compete with men who have more work experience or higher formal qualifications, but are not necessarily more suitable for the job. The proposal was overridden by the Berlin Parliament and the "same qualification" clause remained. The evaluation of qualification is probably impossible to define by law. Other positive action measures – such as fixing a proportional participation of women in promotion and hiring boards – may therefore be more effective in ensuring women's promotion (Raasch, 1988). However, as long as formal qualifications will keep playing the same major role in recruitment and promotion in the public sector, this also will have a limited effect.

Support of equal or preferential treatment: experiences from other countries

In Canada, the Charter of Rights and Freedoms entrenched equality between the sexes in the Constitution in 1982. A variety of positive action measures have been introduced over the past decade, aiming at developing employment equity in the federal public service and also in enterprises linked with the federal government. Of the latter, two are particularly interesting. The Federal Contractor's Program requires federal suppliers with 100 or more employees tendering for contracts worth over $200 000 to make a commitment to employment equity as a condition of bidding. Federally-regulated employers and Crown corporations must report annually to the government on equal opportunity progress. Those reports are made public and housed in libraries across the country. A report is also presented to Parliament each year in which those corporations are ranked according to level of female representation and rate of improvement in meeting equity objectives *(Beneath the Veneer,* 1990, Vol. I).

The Cabinet Office in the United Kingdom launched in 1984 a programme to achieve equal opportunities for women in the civil service. Emphasis was placed on encouraging women into the public service by changing recruitment literature and by adapting working arrangements to help staff combine work and family responsibilities. Each department was required to designate an equal opportunity officer, responsible for discrimination on the basis of race as well as sex. To enhance women's career development, the emphasis was laid on training, including specific courses to help women prepare for middle management positions. The establishment of childcare facilities was another focal point. Special unpaid leave (providing the employee returns to work within five years) will be counted in the calculation of length of service. It is also recommended that at least one woman be included in promotion boards, and that seniority as a criterion for promotion be dropped.

Comparable worth: the case of the United States[15]

Slow progress in closing the male-female earnings gap and persistent occupational segregation led to the idea of extending the notion of equal pay for equal work to the broader concept of equal pay for comparable worth. In the United States, this concept was pioneered in the public sector (Blau and Ferber, 1986). In the widely publicised case "County of Washington vs. Gunther" (1981), the Supreme Court opened the way for comparable worth litigation by ruling that it is not essential for a man and a woman to be doing "equal work" in order to establish pay discrimination. The plaintiffs were four women employed as matrons at the Washington County jail. The matrons guarded female inmates, while their male equivalents – correction officers – guarded male inmates. The matrons were paid about 30 per cent less than their male counterparts. The plaintiffs won the right to equal pay, but not on the basis of proved intentional sex discrimination. As a result the Supreme Court did not explicitly endorse the comparable worth approach.

In a later case between the American Federation of State, County, and Municipal Employees (AFSCME) vs. State of Washington, the judge ordered implementation of a salary schedule based on comparable worth and back-pay of up to $800 million. The Court of Appeals, however, rejected that decision by stating that the value of a job depends on factors other than just the actions performed on the job, including factors such as the availability of workers and the effectiveness of unions in negotiating wages. Moreover, the Court of Appeals stated that the legislative history of equal opportunity legislation should not suggest that Congress intended "to abrogate fundamental economic principles such as the laws of supply and demand." In other words: pay systems based on seniority, merit, quantity or quality of production or on "any factor other than sex" are legitimate sources of wage differentials (Twomey, 1990).

Because comparable worth did not gain a legal footing, pay-equity claims will be a continuing focus for litigation. Nevertheless, public employers at state, county and municipality level have developed their own mechanisms to deal with equal pay questions (Cook, 1985). By 1987, 12 states had begun to implement wage adjustments based on comparable worth studies. Several other states had implemented pay rises for some predominantly female jobs, usually through the collective bargaining process. New Mexico, for example, allocated $40 million (to be phased in over a number of years) to increase salaries in the lowest-paid job classifications. Women held 86 per cent of these positions. At the federal level, it has been proposed that a study of pay equity for federal employees should be designed and implemented (Koziara, 1987).

An evaluation of the Washington case revealed mixed results. Pay increased in the female-dominated occupations and the gender gap narrowed during the first round of comparable worth adjustments. The penalty for career breaks and for part-time work were both also reduced. Accompanying these developments, however, was a reduction of the share of employment in occupations receiving comparable worth pay adjustments. For male and female employees, returns on investment in education and work experience fell. The job evaluation procedure appeared to be somewhat capricious (O'Neill et al., 1989).

Comparable worth or pay equity is quite controversial in the United States.[16] Opponents refer to the high costs of equity plans and their negative employment effects. Others claim that wage increases interfere with the market allocation process; that higher wages in the public sector will put pressure on the private sector to offer higher wages, which will lead to unemployment. A counter to these arguments could be that comparable worth exercises can also identify areas where overpayment occurs, such as in male-dominated jobs.

Incentives

Equal opportunity incentives can be provided in different forms: tax credits, direct wage subsidies, exemption from social security contributions, and subsidisation of social security benefits, all of which can encourage employers to recruit from the target group. There can also be non-monetary incentives, such as special employment protection and options of flexible work arrangements, for example sabbaticals or parental leave, to attract candidates from the designated groups. Non-monetary incentives are specially relevant in the case of public employment.

The public sector's use of employment incentives has been dictated mainly by labour market rather than equity reasons. At the beginning of the 1970s, when labour was scarce, governments offered voluntary reductions in working time, unpaid leave of absence to care for children, training sabbaticals and other privileges to make public service jobs more attractive, or to assist retention of long-term and trained employees. Together with the general expansion of public sector employment, women profited from these policies. This, however, was a side effect and not the primary goal.

When unemployment rose in the 1970s and early 1980s, governments modified their objectives and used incentives to develop work-sharing or temporary public work to reduce unemployment. Although an overall systematic evaluation of this policy change is not available, there are indications that equality for women lost ground during this period (MacLennan and Weitzel, 1984). In recent times, equal opportunity objectives *per se* have gained momentum, and this coincides with rising concerns about potential shortages of skilled labour in the future. This resulted in particular in innovations in working-time regulations allowing for more flexibility.

No special incentive programme, in terms of modifications of working time, has been introduced in the United States. Sweden, on the contrary, has a long tradition of providing incentives (or at least financial compensation) for flexible working-time arrangements, especially parental leave and leave for the care of sick children.[17] In addition to the universal schemes, there are some special agreements in the Swedish public sector providing rights to reduced working hours for parents with young children.

Germany also has improved the options for flexible working time for public service employees. Access to part-time leave for personal or social reasons (childcare, health care or care of the elderly) has been extended from civil servants to all permanent employees. The allotted time frame within which it is possible to take childcare leave has also been extended from 9 to 15 years. However, the ability to work part-time (with the right to return to full-time) is limited because it is conditional on the employer's approval.

Belgium and France offer additional examples of countries having considerably extended the option to work part-time (with the right to return to full-time work) to public sector employees. In Belgium, all permanent employees in the public sector are now entitled to reduce their working time by 50 per cent for up to two years, without any further criteria. Special incentives for part-time employment of older workers have also been introduced. In France the option to work part-time is available to all public sector employees regardless of the nature of their contract. The working-time reduction is flexible, and part-time may vary from 50 to 90 per cent of the normal full-time duration. In contrast, the federal public service in Canada employs relatively few part-timers. This is attributed to the lack of pension entitlement for those working less than 30 hours per week.

Overall, the public sector has pioneered the provision of flexible working-time arrangements. However, it is too early, and the statistical basis is too weak to evaluate the long-term effects of these policies on women's employment in the public sector. Longitudinal data – especially mapping changes from full-time to part-time employment and vice versa – would be necessary for any comprehensive evaluation.

Infrastructure

The State as employer can provide infrastructural support to advance equal opportunities for women in a great variety of ways. First, it can introduce special and compensatory training measures for women returning to employment after a career interruption. Second, it can make public sector employment more accessible by decentralising the location of public services and reducing commuting time between home and work. Third, it can ensure that the social infrastructure – including opening hours of public service agencies – are compatible with family and work schedules, and that school schedules facilitate women's labour market participation by providing full-day supervision and midday meals for children. Fourth, it can provide childcare at or near the workplace.

OECD countries – including the three chosen "model countries" – show a great variety of individual measures with respect to this range of possibilities. However, a coordinated approach is missing in most cases and a synoptic evaluation is therefore not possible. Sweden is the "model" country showing the most consistent approach on all fronts. Its public schools offer day-long activities for children, and extensive public childcare is also available. The Swedish model consisting of drastically expanding public service employment and creating jobs for women relies in addition on the decentralised structure of the Swedish public sector. As noted earlier (Table 5.3), the majority of public sector jobs have been created at the local and regional level. Municipalities assume significant tax authority, and there is a conscious policy to locate central public agencies or offices outside the centre of agglomerations.

EQUALITY AND EFFICIENCY: THE FUTURE OF EQUAL OPPORTUNITY IN THE PUBLIC SECTOR

Challenges for the public sector in the 1990s

Cost containment in the public sector remains a major concern in most OECD countries. In 1989 twelve Member countries showed a public deficit; five of those had deficits of over 5 per cent of GDP. On the other hand, "a certain battle fatigue is appearing after almost a decade of restraint" (OECD, 1990). In the 1990s governments will find it even more difficult – for various reasons – to combine cost containment exigencies with new challenges or unresolved problems of the 1980s.

Public-sector wages fell relative to private-sector wages in most countries in the 1980s (see above). Further cost containment through reduction of wages appears highly problematic. If the public sector wants to compete with the private sector for skilled staff, it will have to pay competitive wages. Employment security offered by the public sector will not be enough to compensate for lower wages and attract skilled workers: private sector employers can also offer long-term employment. Competitiveness through low wages is in any case not a good strategy in the long term, whether in the public or the private sector. It may even trigger a vicious circle: lower wages $\rightarrow$ lower quality of services $\rightarrow$ lower willingness to pay for these services $\rightarrow$ higher cost pressure $\rightarrow$ further reduction of wages, and so on. It is recognised that the high rates at which employees in the public sector are vacating their posts are the result of deteriorating salary and employment conditions *(Beneath the Veneer,* 1990).

Cuts in public investment may have been too severe in the 1980s. In many countries the public infrastructure is literally cracking (OECD, 1990). Aschauer (1989) attributes as much as 60 per cent of the productivity slump in the United States to the neglect of core infrastructure, including streets and highways, mass transportation, airports, water and sewer systems and electrical and gas utilities.

There is increasing concern about the deteriorating quality of public services, especially in education. Quality of education systems at all levels (primary, secondary, vocational, academic, and further training) is a determining factor in a country's ability to produce high-quality goods and services and maintain international competitiveness (Schmid, 1990).

Social and demographic changes present new challenges to government. As populations age throughout the OECD, extra pressure will be put on public budgets for health care and pensions. The demand for childcare will intensify in relation to female labour force participation and the increase in single-parent households. It has been argued that the availability of subsidised childcare is necessary to encourage certain groups, such as single parents receiving income support, to re-enter the labour market (Fuchs, 1988; Moller Okin, 1989; OECD, 1990). Moreover, the recognition that early childhood education influences the future social and educational performance of young people has raised the issue of the quality of childcare and led to calls for an expansion of public sector kindergarten and pre-school systems, and for some regulation of private sector childcare institutions.

The combination of persisting pressures to contain costs further while answering new needs and demands will necessitate further public sector reform. This need not necessarily take the form of privatisation or decentralisation. What is important is to create a competitive environment for public action. This can be achieved for instance by linking budget allocation to performance and outcome quality; or by establishing effective public/private mixes through vouchers, contracting out, or charging for services. The only common direction for public sector reform across OECD countries is likely to be a reorientation away from crude overall budgetary cuts to specific efficiency-enhancing measures that are compatible and, if possible, complementary to equality or equity objectives.

The three scenarios

As shown above, there are marked differences in public sectors from one OECD country to the other and this has implications for the policy priorities which will be elaborated to meet the challenges facing the public sector in the 1990s. It will also affect approaches to equal employment opportunities. The three model countries used earlier help to illustrate possible scenarios. Specific problems identified in these countries may offer insights to countries with similar characteristics.

The case of the United States illustrates the ''integrated free market model'', displaying an overall low productivity together with low social security and public job creation. Apart from unionised areas (which play a minor and decreasing role), wage formation is basically left to the market, thus establishing relatively high wage differentials. This strategy has a double impact on women: it forces many into ''fuller'' employment because of precarious economic conditions (large pockets of poverty), while another substantial group of women enjoys better opportunities (less segregation, more upward mobility) than may be the case in the other model countries.

Such a strategy lends itself to positive action and comparable worth policy rather than public job creation, active labour market policies or hard line quotas. However, increasing numbers of working poor and non-working able-bodied persons (including single parents) depending on welfare payments are creating pressure for the public services to enhance their economic self-sufficiency (Ellwood, 1988).

In addition, declines in productivity are of increasing concern in the face of intensified international competition. Improving public infrastructure and an educational offensive appear as preconditions for redressing the situation. If policy goes in this direction, it is likely that employment opportunities in the public sector will increase and that women will benefit. Public infrastructure developments such as the extension of quality childcare services and expansion of educational provision would contribute to brighter employment perspectives for women across the whole economy.

Sweden, an example of the ''integrated Welfare State model'', has given priority to full employment. It has engaged in an overall low productivity track by creating additional employment for women and other relatively disadvantaged groups, but almost exclusively in the public sector. Sweden has been largely successful in providing economic independence for women, albeit in the context of an extremely segregated labour market. Given this institutional framework, equal opportunity policies are likely to continue to emphasize active labour market measures, job creation, childcare provision and individual taxation, rather than a regulatory approach.

Wage drift, inflation, low productivity, and the reappearance of a balance of payment deficit are signs that Swedish competitiveness has been gradually weakened in the 1980s. The large public sector no longer seems to support economic growth and efficiency. There are also indications that inequalities may be increasing and that the marginal costs (in terms of output lost) of raising public funds are on the rise (Persson, 1990). Women appear *a priori* fairly vulnerable in the event of pressure for public sector rationalisation, especially given the segmented labour market.

Future structural change will likely set a premium on intelligent or flexible public/ private mixes. This will call for de-segregation and improving the competitiveness – not necessarily reducing the size – of the public sector as priority objectives. In a situation where an infrastructure favourable to women's employment is already well developed, it seems that equal opportunity efforts will have to be directed more towards dismantling vertical segregation – by ensuring women's access to higher positions – and enhancing training to allow more women into non-traditional occupations. The Swedish system has already allowed substantive gains in terms of women's economic independence and relatively strong political representation (Hernes, 1987). This gives reasons for some optimism that reactions to new challenges will bring favourable outcomes for women.

Germany – an example of the ''disintegrated Welfare State model'' – has engaged in a high productivity track with few aspirations to full employment. Public sector employment and female labour force participation are low. There is a high degree of redistribution through generous transfer payments. Equal opportunity policies will more likely focus on entry regulation – such as anti-discrimination laws, quotas, equal opportunity offices or ombudsmen/women – than on wage equalisation. However, high legal or *de facto* minimum wages and moderate wage differentials (lower than in the United States, higher than in Sweden) tend to reduce the potential range of wage discrimination.

Such a strategy is unlikely to remain unchanged given new challenges in the 1990s. According to OECD projections, Germany is facing an especially unfavourable dependency ratio.[18] Policies involving generous transfer payments for able-bodied people of working age remaining out of the labour market (passive measures) will become too costly. Moreover, the extremely low labour force participation of women (in the western part of Germany) amounts to a serious waste of productive human resources. Political pressure for an extension of public services will come from two sides: from West German non-employed women who wish to gain more economic independence, and from East German women wanting to maintain their previously established (albeit under politically and economically difficult conditions) economic independence. Furthermore, extensive public investment and temporary public job-creation programmes will be required to ease the problems of German unification.

CONCLUSIONS

In spite of the differences which have been outlined in this chapter, employment characteristics and perspectives concerning women in the public sector show enough common features across all OECD countries to allow for some broad general conclusions, in particular as relates to equal opportunity objectives.

Empirical evidence reveals a picture made of successes and failures, and also a possible reversal or at least discontinuation of past trends. In most countries the public sector has come to employ women in a relatively greater proportion than the private sector. Over the years where it was expanding fast, the public sector offered women jobs providing greater employment protection and social security and higher wages than did the private sector.

To the extent that persistent gender-based earnings differentials in the public sector can be interpreted as an indicator of labour market discrimination, it has to be recognised that the public sector has not been particularly effective in implementing equal employment opportunity programmes directed at its own employees. This should not imply, however, that government employment has not reduced labour market discrimination overall. Evidence collected so far suggests that gender differentials are smaller in the public sector than in the private one. Given that women generally earn more in the public than in the private sector (at least at the higher institutional levels of government) and that women's rate of entry into the public sector is higher than that of men, public sector employment seems to have caused the average female wage to rise relative to the average male wage. But there are signs that this equalising effect on the overall economy has been exhausted or even reversed.

Horizontal and vertical occupational segregation is as much a feature of the public sector as of the private sector. Women's representation in top public service positions is very low and only slowly improving. At current rates – and there is evidence that some occupations or sectors are becoming more rather than less gender-segmented – it would take at least 25 years to achieve numerical gender equality.

Although empirical evidence for the public sector remains sketchy, it appears that men are more often in open or competing occupations or positions, and are more likely to move inter-occupationally. In contrast, women are confined to non-competing occupational groups and are thereby limited to intra-occupational mobility; as these groups provide almost no upward mobility, possibilities to compete for higher classifications are extremely limited in the case of women. Thus, enhancing flexibility in occupational classifications, and opening job categories especially for upward competition seem to be one of the most urgent equal opportunities strategy needed within the public sector.

Women's relative lack of geographical mobility is often cited as a reason for the discrepancy between near gender equality at recruitment and increasing vertical inequality during the occupational career. Family responsibilities do affect women's ability to participate in long-term training courses outside the local area, and they may force women to decline promotions (or not apply for them) if this implies relocation, which is often the case in higher civil service jobs. The same constraints would apply to men who assume significant family responsibilities. Decentralisation of employment and training facilities in the public sector, therefore, may prove to be an important equal opportunities strategy. All policies facilitating compatibility between career and family can also contribute to a redistribution of domestic responsibilities.

Increased access to part-time work in the public sector has developed in most countries. When combined with adequate employment protection, social security and the right to return to full-time work, part-time work can constitute a real "equal opportunity bridge". Making this option widely available could well be one of the most important positive action measures for the 1990s. Specific incentives may be needed to increase the attraction of part-time work for men as well as women; counting part-time work as full-time service with respect to seniority rights, pension entitlements and workers' representation is an example of such incentives.

Progress in equal opportunities is currently inhibited by the generally high ratio of women to men resigning. Policies referred to above are all likely to reduce the rate at which women are vacating their jobs. New forms of work organisation that involve less hierarchy and a more co-operative decision-making style also seem promising. They would make the workplace more "woman-friendly" and make it easier for women to take on more responsibilities and subsequently have access to promotion.

Laws prohibiting open discrimination in terms of recruitment, pay, promotion and dismissal in the public sector have been well developed in most OECD countries for many years. Rigorous implementation of those laws as well as the development of improved management techniques, flexible organisation of work, and institutional incentives are now needed to fully operationalise equal opportunity policies. The public sector appears more innovative in that respect than the private sector, which can be illustrated by the great number of positive action initiatives which have been introduced. There are however clear indications that public sector employment growth will at best be slow in the coming years. It will therefore be crucial to enhance the role of public employers as "model" equal opportunities employers and to find ways to translate good public sector practices into the private sector.

Notes

1. The public sector is defined here, if not mentioned otherwise, as the range of activities covered by general government. As defined in the System of National Accounts (SNA), this covers the various departments and agencies at central, state, provincial and local levels which produce non-market goods and services. The main exclusions from a comprehensive coverage of the public sector are government-owned firms and public corporations which produce and sell goods and services in a market, plus a range of non-profit-making organisations which are close substitutes for public-sector activities.

2. Choices about how much and what sort of government intervention are as related to national preferences and cultures as they are to economic considerations. Even from an economic perspective, there is no clear-cut correlation between the size of the public sector and efficiency. While a number of earlier cross-country studies pointed towards a negative relationship between the size of the public sector and economic growth, several recent contributions to comparative public policy have found evidence that institutional factors – such as stable industrial relations, the provision of training and education, well-functioning financial systems, and the provision of social services – actually enhance economic performance. The Welfare State if not necessary for economic efficiency, is at least compatible with it (Saunders and Klau, 1985; Castles and Dowrick, 1990; Mosley and Schmid, 1991).

3. Privatisation *per se* is no guarantee of more competition; yet those advocating a comprehensive public sector should be very concerned about efficiency. A competitive environment is achievable in the public sector, and various public/private mixes can also be effective. "Public versus private matters, but competitive versus non-competitive usually matters more" (Donahue, 1989).

4. For example, the provision of family services such as childcare provides employment for women and also frees women to participate in the labour market.

5. Germany refers to West Germany, *i.e.* to the former Federal Republic of Germany before the unification in October 1990.

6. The concept of equality is a complex one and a methodology to analyse important distinctions can be useful. In his seminal work on *Equalities,* Douglas Rae (1981) distinguishes five dimensions of equality: subject, domain, approach, value and distribution criteria. The "subject" dimension – which is relevant here – has three sub-categories: simple equality, segmental equality and bloc equality. The two first ones relate to equality at individual level, the third one at class level. Ideally all three types of equality should be checked in relation to the three domains of the labour market under investigation (occupation, wages, working time). However, given that the comparative data on equality-related questions are so poor, specially concerning class inequalities, most of the observations in the chapter relate to individual-level inequalities. Only class inequalities related to the public/private cleavage are illustrated separately where possible.

7. International comparative studies on gender-related wages between the public and private sectors or within the public sector seem to be non-existent. Even on a national basis, there are only a few very good studies available, such as the overview by Ehrenberg and Schwarz

(1986) for the United States based mainly on the extensive work by Smith (1977), Zetterberg (1990) for Sweden, Pedersen *et al.* (1990) for Denmark, and Meron (1991) for France.

8. A recent Finnish study found gender-specific wage differentials smallest in the most female-dominated occupations and largest in the most male-dominated occupations. Systematic variation appears also with respect to "openness" of the sectors: the more the sectors are exposed to competition, the higher the wage differentials between men and women. These patterns also hold true for subsections of the public sector: the ratio of average female to male earnings (standardized according to educational background) was 86 per cent in 1985 in central government services, 80.8 per cent in local government services, 75 per cent in local administration, 70.5 per cent in private export industry, and 69.7 per cent in government enterprises (Allen *et al.*, 1990).

9. The authors of the study warn that conclusions should be drawn carefully and hint at the main problem: the general government wage rate is calculated as the general government wage bill divided by government employment, thus not taking into account the changing composition of public sector employment, especially increasing part-time work. OECD conclusions can be compared with those of national studies. Guilhamon (1989) suggests that public sector wages in France grew in line with the private sector over the period 1978 to 1986; Bailey (1989) and Pedersen *et al.* (1990) confirm OECD findings for the United Kingdom and Denmark, that is, they found relative wage decline. Moulton (1990) found a similar narrowing in the differentials for the federal service in the United States.

10. Another major flaw of this type of studies (often acknowledged by the authors) is their focus on measures of earnings rather than total compensation which would include fringe benefits; there are indications that fringe benefits are higher in the public than in the private sector.

11. In a simulation, Ehrenberg and Smith (1987) found a negative effect, albeit small, of comparable worth wage adjustments on employment. They warn, however, against drawing any policy conclusions because of uncalculated side-effects. In addition they doubt if women as a group would benefit: "the higher wages for women employed in the public sector may be at least partially offset by resulting lower wages for women in the private sector."

12. The European Labour Force Survey (ELFS) provides harmonized data for all European Community countries. Information on employment is available using the General Industrial Classification of Economic Activities within the European Communities (NACE). Public administration appears as a specific activity. It leaves out, however, the core of public welfare employment in health and education.

13. We do not report here about the implementation of "equal opportunity units" in various organisational forms and at various levels of public administration. Their function relates often both to the private and the public sectors. They also play a pilot role for the private sector.

14. To date about a dozen men have taken legal action against the NRW law (according to *Frankfurter Rundschau*, 8.3.1991, p. 16).

15. Other countries practising comparable worth on a legally-supported basis are Australia, Canada and the United Kingdom; it remains, however, a matter of academic debate in Scandinavia and other European countries.

16. There are indications that opposition to private sector legislation will be even more determined. In fact, some opponents of pay-equity legislation in the public sector are employers concerned that the legislation will have spill-over effects into the private sector (Koziara, 1987).

17. Parental leave pay has gradually been extended and in 1989 was granted for 450 days, 360 days with normal sick pay (about 90 per cent of wages), and 90 days with a minimum payment. In 1989 it was decided that parental leave with full payment would gradually be extended to 18 months and that the leave could be used until the child was eight years old. Since 1980 pay for care of a sick child has been granted until the child is 12 years old and during a total of 60 days per child per year. That is to be extended to 90 days and until the child is 16. Data from the National Social Insurance Board show that about 92 per cent of the days

of parental leave are used by women. The take-up of short-term leave to care for sick children, however, is distributed relatively equally between Swedish parents (Persson, 1990).

18. The ''dependency ratio'' is defined as the ratio of the number of young and old dependants to the working-age population. The OECD predicts a change in the ratios of +7.4 compared to –4.8 in the United States and –2.8 in Sweden (OECD, 1990, Table 13).

Bibliography

ALLEN, T. *et al.* (1990), *Palkkaa työstä ja sukupuolesta* (Wage from Work and Gender), Studies No. 169, Central Statistical Office of Finland, Helsinki.

ASCHAUER, David A. (1989), "Is Public Expenditure Productive?", *Journal of Monetary Economics,* Vol. 23, 177-200.

BAILEY, Rachel (1989), "Pay and Industrial Relations in the UK Public Sector", *Labour* 3 (2), 31-56.

BENDA, Ernst (1986), *Notwendigkeit und Möglichkeit positiver Aktionen zugunsten von Frauen im öffentlichen Dienst,* Rechtsgutachten erstattet im Auftrag der Senatskanzlei - Leitstelle Gleichstellung der Frau - der Freien und Hansestadt Hamburg, Freiburg.

BENEATH THE VENEER (1990), The Report of the Task Force on Barriers to Women in the Public Service, Ottawa, Canadian Government Publishing Centre, Vol. I-IV.

BERICHT DER BUNDESREGIERUNG (1990), Bericht der Bundesregierung zur Umsetzung der "Richtlinie zur beruflichen Förderung von Frauen in der Bundesverwaltung" -Berichtzeitraum 1986 bis 1988, Bundestagsdrucksache 11/8129.

BLAU, Francine D. and FERBER, Marianne A. (1986), *The Economics of Women, Men, and Work,* Englewood Cliffs, N.J., Prentice Hall.

BRAUN, Rachel Eisenberg (1984), "Equal Opportunity and the Law in the United States", in Günther Schmid, Renate Weitzel, eds., *Sex Discrimination and Equal Opportunity,* Aldershot, Gower, 92-106.

BROWN, Charles and WILCHER, Shirley J. (1987), "Sex-Based Employment Quotas in Sweden", in Claire Brown and Joseph A. Pechman, eds., *Gender in the Workplace,* Washington D.C., The Brookings Institution, 271-298.

BÜCHTEMANN, Christoph F. and HÖLAND Arnim (1989), *Befristete Arbeitsverträge nach dem Beschäftigungsförderungsgesetz 1985,* Reihe Forschungsberichte (ed.), Federal Ministry of Labour, Bonn.

BULMAHN, Edelgard *et al.* (1990), *Frauenförderung in der kommunalen Verwaltung,* Bonn, Verlag Friedrich Ebert Stiftung.

CABINET OFFICE (1990), *Equal Opportunities for Women in the Civil Service,* Progress Report, HMSO, London.

COMMISSION OF THE EUROPEAN COMMUNITIES (1990), *Equal Opportunities for Women and Men,* The Third Medium-Term Community Action Programme 1991-1995, Brussels, COM (90) 449 final.

COOK, Alice H. (1985), *Comparable Worth: A Casebook of State and Local Experiences,* Honolulu: Industrial Relations Center, University of Hawai.

CORNELIEN, Waltraud (1989), "Strukturen von Gleichstellungsorganen in den Mitgliedstaaten der EG", *Informationen für die Frau,* 10, 11-16; 11/12, 20-22.

DONAHUE, John D. (1989), *The Privatization Decision. Public Ends, Private Means,* New York, Basic Books.

EHRENBERG, Ronald G. and SCHWARZ, Joshua L. (1986), "Public-Sector Labor Markets", in O. Ashenfelter and R. Layard, eds., *Handbook of Labor Economics,* Vol. II, Amsterdam, New York, Oxford, Tokyo, North Holland, 1219-1268.

EHRENBERG, Ronald G. and SMITH, Robert S. (1987), "Comparable-Worth Wage Adjustments and Female Employment in the State and Local Sector", *Journal of Labor Economics,* Vol. 5, No. 1, 43-62.

ELLWOOD, David T. (1988), *Poor Support. Poverty in the American Family,* New York, Basic Books.

ESPING-ANDERSEN, Gösta (1990), *The Three Worlds of Welfare Capitalism,* Oxford, Polity Press.

FREDMAN, Sandra and MORRIS, Gillian S. (1989), *The State as Employer: Labour Law in the Public Services,* London and New York, Mansell Publ. Lim.

FUCHS, Victor R. (1988), *Women's Quest for Economic Equality,* Cambridge, Mass., London, Harvard University Press.

GERIGK, Mechthild, HOCKAUF-SCHNEIDER, Reinhilde and SCHULZ, Reiner (1986), *Frauen im öffentlichen Dienst - Charakteristika beamteter Frauen,* Stuttgart, Verlag Kohlhammer (Schriftenreihe des Bundesministeriums des Innern, Bd. 18).

GUILHAMON, J. (1989), *Les négociations salariales dans la fonction publique.* Rapport au ministre de la Fonction publique et des Réformes administratives, Paris, La documentation francaise.

HERNES, Helga (1987), *Welfare State and Women Power: Essays in State Feminism,* London, Norwegian University Press, Oxford University Press.

ILO (1988), Joint Committee on the Public Service, Report I. *General Report,* Geneva, International Labour Office.

JOHNSON, Roberta Ann (1990), "Affirmative Action Policy in the United States. Its Impact on Women", *Policy and Politics,* 18, 2 77-90.

KOZIARA, Karen Shallcross (1987), "Women and Work: The Evolving Policy", in Karen Shallcross Koziara *et al.,* eds., *Working Women. Past, Present, Future,* Washington D.C., The Bureau of National Affairs, 374-408.

LANGKAU-HERRMANN, M. *et al.* (1983), *Frauen im öffentlichen Dienst,* Bonn, Friedrich Ebert Stiftung.

LANGKAU-HERRMANN, M. *et al.* (1988), *Frauenförderung in der öffentlichen Verwaltung. Ergebnisse einer Pilotstudie,* Bonn, Friedrich Ebert Stiftung.

MacLENNAN, Emma and WEITZEL, Renate (1984), "Labour Market Policy in Four Countries. Are Women Adequately Represented?", in Günther Schmid, Renate Weitzel, eds., *Sex Discrimination and Equal Opportunity,* Aldershot, Gower, 202-248.

McRAE, Susan and DANIEL, W.W. (1991), "Maternity Rights. The Experience of Women and Employers. First Findings", London, Policy Studies Institute.

MERON, Monique (1991), "La dispersion des salaires de l'État 1982-1986", *Économie et Statistique,* No. 239, 37 ff.

MOLLER OKIN, Susan (1989), *Justice, Gender, and the Family,* New York, Basic Books.

MOSLEY, Hugh and SCHMID, Günther (1991), "Public Services and Competitiveness", Paper prepared for the Workshop on European Competitiveness, Wissenschaftszentrum Berlin, June 14th-15th.

MOULTON, B.R. (1990), "A Re-Examination of the Federal-Private Wage Differential in the United States", *Journal of Labor Economics,* Vol. 2, No. 2.

MUSGRAVE, Richard A. and MUSGRAVE, Peggy B. (1968), *Public Finance in Theory and Practice*, London, McGraw-Hill.

OECD (1982), *Employment in the Public Sector*, Paris.

OECD (1990), *The Public Sector: Issues for the 1990s*, Economics and Statistics Department Working Papers, OCDE/GD(90)9.

O'NEILL, June, BRIEN, Michael and CUNNINGHAM, James (1989), "Effects of Comparable Worth Policy: Evidence from Washington State", *American Economic Review* (AEA Papers and Proceedings), Vol. 79, No. 2, 305-309.

PEDERSEN, P.J., SCHMIDT-SORENSEN, J.B., SMITH, M. and WESTERGARD-NIELSEN, N. (1990), "Wage Differentials Between the Public and Private Sectors", *Journal of Public Economics*, Vol. 41, 125-145.

PERSSON, Inga (1990), "The Third Dimension - Equal Status between Swedish Women and Men", in Inga Persson (ed.), *Generating Equality in the Welfare State. The Swedish Experience*, Oslo, Norwegian University Press, 223-244.

PFARR, Heide M. and EITEL, Ludwig (1984), "Equal Opportunity Policies for Women in the Federal Republic of Germany", Günther Schmid and Renate Weitzel, eds., *Sex Discrimination and Equal Opportunity*, Aldershot, Gower 155-187.

RAASCH, Sybille (1988), "Gleichstellung per Gesetz?", in Marianne Weg and Otti Stein, eds., *Macht macht Frauen stark*, Hamburg, 154-165.

RADFORD, Gail (1990), "EEO For Women in the 1990s". Paper presented to the National Women's Conference in Canberra on 30 September 1990, Australian Public Service Commission, mimeo.

RAE, Douglas (1981), *Equalities*, Cambridge, Mass., and London, Harvard University Press.

REIN, Martin (1985), *Women in the Social Welfare Labor Market*, Discussion Paper IIM/LMP 85-18, Wissenschaftszentrum Berlin.

ROSE, Richard (1985), *Public Employment in Western Nations*, Cambridge, Cambridge University Press.

SCHMID, Günther (1990), "Institutions Regulating the Labor Market: Support or Impediments for Structural Change?", in E. Appelbaum, R. Schettkat, eds., *Labor Market Adjustments to Structural Change and Technological Progress*, New York, Praeger.

SCHMID, Günther (1991), *Women in the Public Sector*, OCDE/GD(91)213.

SCHMID Günther, WEITZEL Renate, eds. (1984), *Sex Discrimination and Equal Opportunity. The Labour Market and Employment Policy*, Aldershot, Gower.

SEGLOW, Peter (1990), "Pay Regulation of Government Employees in Germany", Paper given to the Public Finance Foundation - International Conference on Pay Policies, Brunel University (mimeo).

SHAW, Josephine (1990), "Equal Opportunities for Women in the Federal Republic of Germany: Institutional Developments", *Equal Opportunities International*, 9, 6, 15-21.

SKINNER, Jane (1988), "Who's Changing Whom? Women, Management and Work Organisation", in Angela Coyle and Jane Skinner, eds., *Women and Work. Positive Action for Change*, Houndmills, Macmillan, 152-158.

SMITH, Sharon P. (1977), *Equal Pay in the Public Sector: Fact or Fantasy?*, Princeton University Press, Princeton, NJ.

STEINBERG, Ronnie J., HEIGNERE, Lois and CHERTOS, Czynthia H. (1990), "Managerial Promotions in the Public Sector. The Impact of Eligibility Requirements on Women and Minorities", *Work and Occupations*, 17, 3, 284-301.

TWOMEY, David P. (1990), *Equal Employment Opportunity Law*, 2nd ed., South Western Publishing Co., Cincinnati, Ohio.

WISE, Lois Rescacino (1990), "Social Equity in Civil Service Systems", Bloomington, Indiana University (mimeo).

WURSTER, Barbara, ed. (1989), *Women in the Higher Public Service: Recruitment and Career Planning,* European Institute of Public Administration, Maastricht.

ZETTERBERG, Johnny (1990), *Essays on Inter-Sectoral Wage Differentials,* Uppsala University, Department of Economics.

Chapter 6

EQUAL OPPORTUNITIES POLICIES
ON THE LABOUR MARKET IN THE 1980s

The previous chapters showed the extent to which the profound structural changes that have reshaped overall employment patterns in the OECD countries in the 1980s have also modified the characteristics of women's employment. At the same time the 1980s were also a relatively active period in terms of equal opportunity policies for women.[1]

In general, these policies seem to have moved in much the same direction in all countries during the course of the decade. In 1980, the Declaration on policies in favour of the employment of women, adopted by a high-level OECD conference, identified 14 points as the primary objectives for equal opportunities (OECD, 1980). In retrospect, ten years later, the policies implemented during the 1980s may be based on the following considerations:

i) a growing awareness that policies that merely guarantee equal rights and treatment can at best only perpetuate existing inequalities. A genuine equal opportunities policy must do away with the inequalities generated by past discrimination as well as dismantle structural barriers; it must hence include specific measures in favour of women *(positive actions)*;

ii) an ongoing effort to reduce occupational segregation according to sex (through *diversification of vocational orientation and occupational choices*) and to find ways to counter its most harmful effects *(applying the principle of "equal pay for work of comparable worth")*;

iii) a recognition of the special needs of workers with family responsibilities *(flexible working time, parental leave)* and that action to promote equal opportunities in this respect should be oriented towards men as well as women;

iv) a commitment to *include equal opportunities as one of the aims in all policy areas* in order to do away with any adverse effects of these policies and to reinforce the potential for global implementation of equal opportunity.

Among the measures adopted in the 1980s in line with equal opportunities policies, only those taken on the labour market will be considered here.[2] These include:

– legislation on employment equity;
– labour market programmes;
– flexibility of working time.

The question of whether or not these measures have been effective given the structural developments in employment analysed in the previous chapters will also be examined.

Developments in legislation in the 1980s

Equal rights for men and women and prohibition of discrimination based on gender are usually enshrined in the constitutions of OECD Member countries. The law spells out the concept of equality of the sexes for specific areas; as regards employment, legislation mainly encompasses two aspects: *equal pay* and *equal opportunities*. While legislative activity in this field started in general much earlier than the 1980s, the main developments took place in the course of the decade (ILO, 1986, 1988).

Equal pay: the principle of comparable worth

Equal pay for women has been guaranteed by law for a long time in most OECD countries. The ILO Convention on equal remuneration which dates back to 1951 (Convention No. 100) certainly had a strong influence on the development of national legislation;[3] but the Directive on equal pay adopted by the European Economic Community in 1975 (Directive No. 117) had an even stronger impact due to its binding character for member countries.

Both the ILO Convention No. 100 and the EEC Directive refer to "equal pay for work of equal value", but until the 1970s, the concept of equal pay was interpreted in a restrictive fashion to mean "equal pay for equal work". However, during the 1980s, the concept of "equal pay for work of comparable worth" started to prevail in legislation (OECD, 1991).

The concept of work of comparable worth should make it possible to compare men and women's wages even if they are not performing the same job. This concept is especially useful where there is occupational segregation on the grounds of sex. In this way equal pay legislation has been extended to cover not only direct discrimination but also the indirect discrimination which consists in undervaluing work done by women.

The main substantive problem of equal pay legislation concerns how to determine the worth of work.[4] Methods for evaluating work objectively and without sexual bias have been devised and recommended in the context of the implementation of this legislation. In general these methods recognise that worth is determined by a combination of factors, *i.e.* qualifications, effort, responsibility and working conditions. In reality, salary scales and job classifications are rarely established according to such methods. Thus, pay equity legislation can challenge the very system of setting and ranking wages which is central to labour/management relations.[5] In fact, the social partners can have an important role to play with respect to equal pay.

The United Kingdom may be cited as an example of the type of developments in legislation which became manifest during the 1980s. The law on equal pay, dating from 1970, was amended in 1983 in order to change the basis according to which comparisons may be established; whereas before comparisons could only be made concerning "like work", from 1983 onwards the concept of work "rated as equivalent" could also be applied.

The increasing inclusion of the concept of equal pay within the framework of general employment equity legislation is another tendency which became apparent in the 1980s. Thus new laws on equality adopted during the course of the decade in Canada,

Finland, France and Greece specifically cover remuneration conditions (Table 6.1). Implicit in these laws is the recognition that equal pay and the right to all elements of remuneration cannot be obtained in a general context of inequality and that discrimination pertaining to aspects of employment other than wages result, in fact, in creating wage inequalities.

Equal opportunity: positive action

Throughout the 1970s and 1980s there was an unremitting effort in OECD countries to enact legislation guaranteeing women's right to equality in all fundamental aspects of employment: recruitment, access to training, promotion, working conditions (including remuneration), dismissal, and retirement[6] (Table 6.1). Several international instruments covering the same aspects were also adopted during this period, such as the EEC Directive 76/207 on equal treatment of men and women and the 1980 United Nations Convention on the elimination of all forms of discrimination against women.[7]

These laws are aimed at employers' policies and practices in terms of recruitment and personnel management. Lately there has been a noticeable change in the orientation of the legislation: just as legislation on equal pay evolved from the principle of "equal pay for equal work" to that of "equal pay for work of comparable worth", so legislation on employment equity is progressively replacing the concept of "equal treatment" with the concept of "equal opportunities" (OECD, 1988).

A prerequisite for equality of the sexes with regard to employment is the elimination of all forms of discrimination, direct, indirect or even systemic.[8] In addition, since women are in a much less favourable situation than men, because of the accumulated weight of past discrimination, equality of opportunity can only be attained if remedial and compensatory measures are taken.

This is increasingly recognised today in some legislation on employment equity which allows a preferential treatment for women through positive action.[9] In some countries – including Australia, Belgium, Canada, France and the United States – legislation is directly binding on employers.[10] In other countries, such as the Scandinavian countries, it is intended more as a framework for collective bargaining.

The enforcement of equity legislation and its limits

The intention of the legislator – "the spirit of the law" – is, in all cases and without any doubt, to establish equity for women in employment; there is, however, a considerable discrepancy between the intention and the effect, the law and reality. This may be due in part to the presence of imperfections in the laws that have been adopted. It is also due to the fact that, as a means of bringing about change, the law is a blunt instrument.

There are significant differences from one country to another in the legislation in relation to employment equity: in its scope, in the terms according to which the laws are formulated and in the available means of activating a legal procedure. Unfortunately, national legislations generally suffer from basic flaws in conception which risk jeopardizing their actual implementation. Experience is however being accumulated rapidly in this field – including at the international level.

Employment equity legislation generally applies to all employers.[11] The laws which aim to promote equal opportunities through positive action are generally much more restricted in scope than those limited to equality of treatment: they only apply to larger

Table 6.1. **Recent developments in employment equality legislation applicable to the private sector**

Australia
  1986 Affirmative Action Act
  1984 Sex Discrimination Act

Austria
  1990 Amendment of the 1979 Act
  1979 Equal treatment in employment for men and women

Belgium
  1987 Promotion of equal opportunity for men and women
  1978 Economic Reorientation Act. Title V: Equal treatment for men and women
  1975 Royal Decree on CCT No. 25

Canada
  1986 Employment Equity Act
  1978 Human Rights Act

Denmark
  1989 New Equal Treatment Act
  1989 Consolidation of the 1976 Act
  1984 Amendment of the 1978 Act
  1978 Equal treatment for men and women concerning employment
  1976 Equal pay for men and women

Finland
  1987 Equality between men and women

France
  1983 Equality in employment
  1972 Equal pay

Germany
  1980 EC Labour Law Adjustment Act (equal treatment)

Greece
  1984 Equality concerning employment

Iceland
  1985 Equal status and equal rights of women and men

Ireland
  1985 Amendment of 1977 Act
  1977 Employment Equality Act
  1974 Anti-Discrimination (Pay) Act

Italy
  1991 Positive action for equality between men and women at work
  1977 Equal treatment for men and women concerning employment

Japan
  1985 Equal opportunity and treatment for men and women in employment

Luxembourg
  1981 Equal treatment for men and women concerning employment
  1974 Equal remuneration

Netherlands
  1980 Equal treatment for men and women
  1975 Equal pay for men and women

Table 6.1. *cont'd* **Recent developments in employment equality legislation
applicable to the private sector**

New Zealand	
1972	Equal pay
Norway	
1978	Equal Status between the Sexes Act
Portugal	
1979	Equality between women and men in employment and at the workplace
Spain	
1989	Procedural principles in work-related matters
1989	Change in Workers' Statute
1988	Infringements and sanctions in social matters
1980	Basic law on employment
Sweden	
1992	Equal Opportunities Act
1991	Amendment of the 1979 Act
1979	Equality between women and men in working life
Switzerland	
1981	Equality for men and women
United Kingdom	
1986, 87, 89	Amendment of the 1975 Act
1984, 87	Amendment of 1970 Act
1975	Sex Discrimination Act
1970	Equal Pay Act
United States	
1990	Amendment of the 1964 Civil Rights Act
1978	Pregnancy Discrimination Act
1972	Equal opportunity in employment

firms, or, as in the United States, to firms which have secured public contracts. Public sector employment is often covered by separate rules, but these always guarantee at least the same rights for women as the private sector. The obligation to develop positive actions is also more frequent in the public sector.

In general, the laws are activated when a complaint is lodged. The complaint may be lodged either by the individual concerned or by a third qualified party (a trade union or the commission responsible for enforcement of the law). In some cases, it may also be possible to lodge a complaint collectively.[12] Patently, the case of complaints lodged by third parties or on behalf of an entire group of women offers a better prospect for activating the law. A single individual will almost always find the complexity of the legislation on equal treatment and of the legal system itself an insurmountable barrier.

The question of the burden of proof also plays an important role in activating the law. Up to now the burden has almost always rested on the complainant. The European Commission has put forward a proposal for the reversal of the burden of proof in the context of the two equality Directives. This initiative represented a remarkable attempt to change the current situation. If this tendency were to spread, it would make legal recourse much easier for the complainant.

The results of grievance procedures are somewhat disappointing. In many countries the number of complaints lodged is small and shows no sign of increasing; the time lapse between lodging a complaint and settlement is long and getting longer; in addition, many complaints are never dealt with or, if they are, do not result in compensatory adjustment.[13]

ONTARIO (CANADA): PAY EQUITY ACT

Date: January 1, 1988
(phased-in implementation over the period 1990-94)

Coverage:
all organisations of more than 10 employees
(public and private sector)

Implementation:
comparison of job groups where 60 per cent or more of the employees are female to job groups where 60 per cent or more are male

evaluation of jobs using a job evaluation plan free of gender bias and measuring skill, effort, responsibility and working conditions

comparison of total compensation of equally valued jobs

Pay equity plan:
must be posted in the workplace

must identify: the relative value of positions affected
the gender-neutral evaluation system
the pay for performance criteria
the schedule of wage-rate adjustments
(payroll increase can be limited to 1 per cent a year until the wage gap is closed).

A complaints system is usually based on the assumption that infringements are the exception rather than the rule. But if systemic discrimination against women is assumed, then this type of remedy is unlikely to produce significant results. Because of the shortcomings of the complaints system, some countries such as Australia, Canada, Finland and France have enacted laws obliging employers to adopt practices that do not discriminate against women and in some cases even introduce positive action plans. By way of example, the main provisions of the law on pay equity enacted in 1988, by the Canadian Province of Ontario are set out below (see Box). There is much potential in this new type of legislation for the identification and elimination of discrimination. Furthermore, this system has the advantage of avoiding individual confrontations between employees and their employer. It is unlikely, however, that this type of legislation will be rapidly generalised in all OECD countries, due to the scope of the task imposed on employers and the costs involved in ensuring that the law is respected.

Equality commissions

In many countries the enforcement of equal rights legislation is entrusted to a commission set up for this purpose.[14] This is the case in Australia, Canada, the United States, Ireland and the United Kingdom. In Nordic countries the Ombudsman plays a similar mediating role. These commissions are management and control organisations which act as an independent public authority. Their actual powers in terms of activating the law are generally limited to conducting preparatory enquiries and arbitration procedures. These commissions thus work closely with the courts which are the only institutions entitled to make enforceable decisions.

Certain commissions also have an important role to play when it comes to informing and educating the public. The Equal Opportunities Commission in the United Kingdom, for example, publishes practical handbooks for employers and employees, organises conferences and publicity campaigns, and promotes research into and awareness of all aspects of discrimination against women. Finally, equality commissions may provide counselling and training services to firms intending to set up positive action schemes.

Such organisations are extremely useful in promoting equal opportunities; unfortunately, their influence is often limited because they tend to be underfunded and understaffed.

Collective bargaining and the law: a necessary complementarity

Pay equity and equal employment opportunities legislation touch upon matters which are central to collective bargaining – wages, training, conditions of work, job security. This legislation challenges long-term established practices and attempts to replace them by new ones whose technical difficulties are not yet fully mastered. The effective implementation of the law therefore depends on whether the principle of equality between the sexes becomes an integral part of collective bargaining and whether the social partners give themselves the means and determination necessary to make this principle a reality.

Legislation and collective bargaining are clearly complementary: the law establishes a general framework and sets out broad principles, and collective agreements fill in the details of how these principles are to be applied in a specific sector or activity. The respective roles of legislation and collective bargaining depend to a large extent on the structures and institutional practices specific to each country.

In the Nordic countries, for example, central government hardly intervenes in the collective bargaining process and all questions pertaining to it are left entirely to trade unions and management. In these countries, equity legislation was enacted once equal treatment of men and women had been written into the collective bargaining process, the aim being to ensure the same rights for those women not covered by a collective bargaining agreement.

Systems in which collective bargaining is both very centralised and generalised seem to have been more successful at introducing equality into working conditions. In Australia and New Zealand, for example, all wages are negotiated at the central level and unions have been able to fight wage discriminations within this framework. It is also most efficient to define actions and policies in favour of disadvantaged workers at the central level. On the contrary, defending the interests of women in bargaining at a decentralised level is difficult because unions hold relatively weak positions in sectors employing a majority of women.

In countries where collective bargaining does not operate to any great extent, or is for the most part decentralised, legislation plays a different and none less important role. In the United Kingdom, where collective bargaining takes place at enterprise or even shopfloor level, reference to equality laws serves as a lever in the bargaining process and a way of making the social partners take account of equity matters.

In most countries collective agreements which do not conform to equity legislation run the risk of being invalidated.[15] Thus the Portugese government, in virtue of its right to decree the extension of a collective agreement to an entire branch or region, can refuse to extend the agreement if it does not respect equality of pay. The law can also make equal opportunity and positive action a subject of the collective bargaining procedure. Nevertheless, in France and Sweden where this is the case, the number of agreements which include clauses on equal opportunity remains very limited.

There seems to be an increasing trend towards decentralisation in the collective bargaining procedures. This could form an obstacle to their integration of equity matters in the collective bargaining process. These matters, however, seem to be eliciting more interest on the part of unions and of some employers. A major problem remains: how to ensure that the required competences are available at the level where bargaining will develop in the future.

Evaluation and future prospects

As mentioned earlier, the number of complaints lodged on the basis of discrimination in employment is not indicative of a very high degree of activation of equity legislation. Nevertheless, it is generally believed that the very existence of such laws does induce employers to abandon their most discriminatory practices, if only to avoid legal proceedings which they know can be long and costly, with the possibility of heavy penalties and damage to the firm's reputation. Laws which advocate positive action are generally too recent to be evaluated systematically.

Evaluation of the impact of sex equality legislation on the employment situation of women may appear as a rather hazardous and difficult endeavour; for this reason the usefulness of such an exercise is sometimes called into question. So many variables have a simultaneous bearing on the developments occurring in employment that it is impossible to single out any one in particular. Moreover, the impact of legislation cannot be properly assessed until some time after its enactment when all the expected effects have had time to materialise. The period that has to elapse before some effects become apparent may be quite long; for instance, the rate at which women are promoted will not improve until they have been better trained. It is generally agreed that only after five or ten years can the full effects of legislation be measured. In most OECD countries national legislation has not yet been on the statute books for this long.

The potential effectiveness of the legislation should be considered with regard to the changes in women's employment. A recent Canadian study (Bakker, 1992) notes that some of the on-going structural changes in employment may well make Ontario's pay equity law less effective. Among the changes cited are: more women employed in small and medium-sized enterprises, more women self-employed, declining trade union membership, more part-time work and more precarious jobs. All of these changes translate into lower wages and reduced opportunities to access internal labour markets. New forms of employment are developing outside the scope of pay equity legislation; therefore, they cannot benefit from any form of protection against discrimination.

Moreover, job classifications for different sectors are currently being revised in many countries. The new classifications introduced as an element of modernisation strategies are the product of a different approach and do not apply the same criteria as the old methods. It is extremely important that the relative worth of the new employment categories be determined according to methods which will not allow discrimination on the basis of sex. But the evaluation methods, devised in the context of pay equity legislation, may not be applicable to employment categories which can no longer be defined in terms of simple tasks and job descriptions. Furthermore, new pay systems with their highly individualised approach render equal-pay legislation largely inoperative.

Thus, as another author has pointed out (Standing, 1989), the intense legislative activity may be quite illusory, because of an implicit deregulation process due to the failure to activate the legislation and, also, the possibility for systematic bypassing due to the structural developments of employment. Hence there are many who think equality legislation is not the most effective way of redressing inequalities. They maintain that other initiatives could have better results, such as, for instance, raising the minimum wage or low wages in general to reduce gender wage differentials rather than applying the principle of "equal pay for work of equal worth".

EQUAL OPPORTUNITIES THROUGH LABOUR MARKET PROGRAMMES

Labour market policies have an important role to play if women are to attain their full productivity potential. The development of labour market policies over the last decades in the different countries is analysed in a recent OECD publication, *Labour Market Policies for the 1990s*. It is stated that the conditions women face on the labour market represent "one of the broad areas where policy innovation is needed" (OECD, 1990b). A brief survey of the policies implemented in the 1980s points out which direction these policies should take in the future in order to make a more useful contribution to equal opportunities.

The general orientation of labour market policy in the 1980s

In the early 1980s the labour market in most OECD countries was characterised by the emergence and rapid increase of unemployment due to a variety of factors – a sharp and prolonged economic recession, economic restructuring and a growing labour force. Unemployment persisted even once the recovery had been firmly established.

The first – and most obvious – consequence of the emergence of large-scale and lasting unemployment on labour market programmes was almost automatic: the costs of financing unemployment benefits rose sharply. To the extent that these expenses have to be met out of public funds, and because the expansion of public expenses is severely limited at a time of economic crisis, especially when attempts are being made to bring public finances into balance, the provision of unemployment benefits (a "passive" measure) absorbed funds that could not be allocated to such activities as training, job creation, and employment services ("active" measures). Table G in the Statistical Annex gives the level and structure of labour market budgets in OECD countries at the end of the 1980s.

Budget restrictions also prompted a more careful targeting of active labour market measures. Unemployed workers receiving benefits constitute an obvious target for budgetary economies.[16] As a matter of fact, this category is often the one to benefit most from active measures. Women job-seekers for numerous reasons[17] have less access to unemployment benefits; a system in which assistance in finding employment is conditional on benefit entitlement acts as a double penalty for many of those women.

Other categories on which active measures were increasingly centered in the 1980s were young people and workers made redundant, or under threat of redundancy, due to economic restructuring. Young people seeking their first job are usually treated in the same way, regardless of gender. As many girls as boys take part in labour market programmes. However, participation varies according to the type of programme; unemployed girls are less likely to take part in programmes giving them access to marketable skills or a steady job (this is also true of older unemployed women).

Programmes for workers made redundant or threatened with redundancy have had little to offer women because these were either designed for predominantly male sectors (except for textile industry programmes in some countries) or because women were less likely to be eligible. In addition, programmes were not on a sufficiently large scale to cater to all workers concerned.

More recently the long-term unemployed have been targeted as a priority group for labour market programmes.[18] In general, long-term unemployment is defined according to a minimum period of continuous unemployment. Recurrent unemployment is not given as much attention as long-term unemployment, although the risks for being deskilled, marginalised or definitely excluded from the labour market are just as real. In the same way, the needs of "discouraged" workers (those giving up looking for work because they feel they have no chance of finding it) and of workers who have been inactive for a long time, could in all likelihood be dealt with by the same programmes as those directed at the long-term unemployed.

Recurrent unemployment is affecting more and more adult women because jobs being offered are increasingly fixed-term jobs and because women are over-represented among job-seekers. Moreover, women leave the labour market more easily than men because they become discouraged after job-loss and by doing so they lose access to programmes aimed at the long-term unemployed. Women who have stayed away from the labour market for a number of years are not considered to be long-term unemployed when they try to return, in spite of the fact that they experience very similar problems of integration into employment.

As a rule, women benefit from general measures on the labour market in a limited fashion because these measures are not designed to take account of occupational segregation by gender or of the specific labour market situation of women. In order to offset these shortcomings, measures aimed specifically at women have been introduced in most OECD countries. They vary a great deal and reflect different philosophies but their basic objective is always the same: to promote equal opportunity for women on the labour market.

Specific measures for women

Three types of labour market programmes specifically designed for women may be seen in almost every OECD country in the 1980s:
- programmes to integrate women into non-traditional occupations;
- programmes to promote entrepreneurship;
- programmes aimed at lone mothers.

Measures to assist women who return to work after having been absent from the labour market for several years and encourage employers to set up positive action programmes have not been developed in the same systematic way, despite the considerable potential impact.

Integrating women into non-traditional occupations

Labour market schemes aiming to integrate women into non-traditional occupations are based on a double observation:
- i) inequalities between men and women on the labour market are largely due to occupational segregation according to gender;
- ii) general labour market training programmes have tended as a rule to reproduce occupational segregation.[19]

Such schemes were quite common in the 1980s and the programmes running today have benefited greatly from previous experience.

At first programmes focused only on training, the aim being to diversify employment for women. The mechanism was to reserve a certain number of places for women in training courses preparing for professions in which they were under-represented.[20] But this approach met with several difficulties: in recruiting women for the courses, in finding jobs for them after they had qualified, and finally in helping them maintain their jobs. Maintaining a job may be a purely economic matter: it is often the case that a sector which loses its attraction to men because it is undergoing a crisis becomes accessible to women; when an employer has to lay off personnel, women find themselves protected by no seniority whether in their post or in the profession. Remaining in the job can also be difficult as women tend to feel vulnerable in a predominantly male environment that may be unwelcoming and sometimes even hostile with possible sexual harassment.

Today, schemes to encourage women to train for and work in non-traditional occupations are organised differently, according to what has been learnt from earlier experiences. Their aim has been redefined to promote women in occupations that are most in demand rather than in non-traditional occupations. This puts a particular focus on new occupations and occupations based on new technologies. Preparatory training is available for women who want to participate in the programme but do not possess the requisite level to engage in qualifying training. Courses are specially arranged to suit the needs of female trainees, and attempts are made to bring the number of women taking part in each training session above a critical threshold. A job is more often guaranteed on completion of the training programme. Financial incentives are offered to employers in order to encourage them not only to hire trained women but also to join in training activities and to facilitate the transition process at the enterprise level. Finally, provision is made for individual follow-up of the women over a certain period after training or recruitment.

In spite of these improvements, schemes to promote the training and employment of women in non-traditional occupations remain marginal in relation to the labour market measures in general and even more so in relation to overall employment. Their impact on occupational segregation is therefore minimal. A lot more could probably be achieved in this respect through a policy aimed at overcoming segregation in student orientation and reforming educational paths particularly as far as apprenticeship is concerned.

Assistance to entrepreneurship

Women are still largely under-represented among entrepreneurs, and yet starting up one's own business is deemed to be one way of escaping unemployment as well as the discrimination women are faced with as dependent workers. Women who do decide to start their own business, however, encounter specific difficulties and forms of discrimination. Many attempts fail, either at the project stage or once the business has been created.

Very few women were able to take advantage of the schemes to help the unemployed set up their own business which were introduced in many countries in the 1980s, either because they were not eligible, or because existing programmes did not meet their needs. Over the past few years governments have therefore set up specific schemes to help women who wish to become entrepreneurs. The goal of these programmes is to inform, train and advise women who engage in enterprise creation, while they design and launch their project. Some of these programmes address another important obstacle which women entrepreneurs face: obtaining bank credit (OECD, 1990a). While relatively few women are likely to start up their own business, assistance to women entrepreneurs can be especially useful under certain circumstances as, for example, in rural zones where the local labour market is relatively undeveloped.

A primary target group: lone mothers

During the 1980s lone mothers became a primary target group for labour market measures everywhere. While this is of course attributable to the large increase in the numbers of lone parents, it denotes, too, a shift in the direction of government policy. As in the case of the unemployed receiving benefit, there is now a realisation that income support alone cannot adequately deal with the problems of lone mothers, especially in the medium or long term. In this larger perspective, the cost of helping lone mothers into employment, though fairly high, seems easily affordable when compared with the costs likely to be incurred if they remain excluded from the labour market and dependent on welfare payments for a very long time.

Labour market programmes aimed at this group present a rather innovative approach on several counts. The coverage rates of the group are relatively high. Attaining economic autonomy is a medium-term objective which supposes a relatively long and continuous period of participation in the programme. Finally, these programmes take specific account of constraints outside the labour market met by the target group (constraints in relation to time, childcare, and travel).

The Australian programme "Jobs, Employment and Training" (JET), aimed at recipients of lone parent benefits, provides a very good illustration of these new trends. This programme relies on the co-ordinated action of three ministries: social security, employment and training, and social services and health. Participation is voluntary. After an initial interview with an official of the social security services delegated to the programme, the candidate is oriented towards employment services which help her examine different possibilities for training and employment. Childcare is guaranteed for the first three months of training or employment. Other needs, pertaining to other social services, are also taken into account. In addition, employment subsidies may be attributed to the employer. Allowances are structured in such a way that there is always a financial incentive for women to engage in employment or training. After an experimental phase, additional resources had to be attributed to the JET programme in order to fully meet demand. *popular.*

Re-entering the labour market: a neglected problem

Unlike lone mothers, women returning to the labour market after a particularly long absence (usually to look after their children) tend not to benefit from any specific labour market policies.[21] These women fall into none of the categories of unemployed to which priority is being given. Their needs are not met by nor do they fulfill conditions of eligibility. Childcare problems or expenses incurred in participating in a programme (*e.g.* transportation, childcare) may constitute a real obstacle for returning women.

Many of these women have long years ahead of them on the labour market. Specific integration or reintegration programmes – preparing for professionnal life, training, follow-up counselling – would certainly be most useful. Returning to working life may well provide a second professional chance: women returning to the labour market should have the possibility of making a new career choice which could lead them to making full use of their potential capacities. In order to achieve this, they must be able to benefit from prolonged training or retraining programmes. Some countries now acknowledge the identity of these women when they return to the labour market. In some cases, they are assimilated to the long-term unemployed but more often, specific programmes are set up for them.

Measures aimed at employers

As mentioned above, programmes for the insertion of women into non-traditional occupations or programmes targeting lone mothers sometimes include financial incentives for potential employers. More recently, programmes aiming to encourage and assist employers in setting up positive actions for their female staff have been organised in a number of countries, either as part of the implementation of equal opportunity legislation or in the framework of labour market measures. These programmes include financial incentives, but also information, training and counselling activities. They are still not very widespread and the results of their evaluations are not known at present.

The promotion of equal opportunities through public employment offices

Equality legislation related to employment does not, in most cases, apply only to employers but also to all institutions active on the labour market. As in the case of legislation, the concept of equality in labour market programmes has evolved from a concept of equal rights and treatment to a concept of equal opportunities and to the implementation of positive actions. This evolution has brought a certain number of new practices into the activities of the public services responsible for labour market programmes.

Numerical targets for female participation in labour market programmes

The very first step in order to evaluate equal opportunities in labour market programmes is to compile and publish statistics on participation broken down according to gender. This practice is increasingly widespread. Such statistics make it possible to measure the gap remaining to be filled in order to attain a satisfactory female representation for each programme. The overall objective is to arrive at a proportion of female participants equivalent to the proportion of women found – depending on the case – among the active population, the unemployed or the population as a whole.[22] In Ireland, for example, yearly targets have been set since 1990 for the participation of women in programmes organised by the employment and training authority (FAS) within the framework of the positive action programme in favour of women.

Positive action in employment offices

Employment services can make an important contribution to equal opportunities on the labour market through their different functions: information, counselling, placement, enrolment in training and employment programmes. It is essential that the role of these services in each of these functions be explicitly defined and that appropriate means be placed at their disposal. This implies employment offices staffed with properly trained personnel.[23]

Equal opportunity counsellors were introduced in public employment offices during the 1980s. They have a crucial role in implementing the equal opportunity policies defined by employment services. The case of Denmark is representative of a trend which has been detected elsewhere. Equal opportunity counsellors were established in regional employment offices on an experimental basis in 1981; they became a permanent feature in 1986. There are now two equal opportunity counsellors in each regional employment office and four in Copenhagen. Counsellors sit on the Labour Market Commission for their region and draw up annual plans and activity reports which they submit to the Commission for its approval. The 30 or so counsellors constitute a network whose activities are co-ordinated by the Ministry of Labour.[24]

Several countries also established special employment offices for women during the 1980s. Sometimes, these offices are a sub-branch of the general employment offices, and in any case their activity is always organised in close co-operation with the general office. Six of Canada's main cities, for example, have Women's Employment Counselling Centres. In 1988, France opened experimental information centres for women in 13 départements. In 1979 Japan introduced Women's Employment Assistance Centres, subsidised and supervised by the Ministry of Labour. These centres are now present in 45 prefectures.

The publication and distribution of documents for the information of women and employers remains however one of the most common ways of promoting equal opportunities through employment offices. There is everywhere both an abundance and variety of literature – reference cards, guides, directives, directories, etc. – on all sorts of programmes and subjects related to equal opportunities.

Equal opportunities for women as a priority objective in general employment measures

According to the available quantitative results, specific measures in favour of women seem, up to now, to have had only a limited effect on their labour market situation; the fact that most of these are still at the pilot scheme stage makes it difficult to assess their potential effects on women's employment or unemployment. Wherever a significant reduction in unemployment among women has been achieved, this is usually ascribable to general measures (schemes to assist disadvantaged groups, job creation in the social economy sector). However, there has been more significant success in reducing unemployment in the short term than in improving prospects for the employment of women in the longer term (Lévy, 1983).

Since women represent half the human resources available in a given country, and occupational segregation by gender subsists, it would make sense to take explicit account of the specific conditions women face when designing general labour market measures. This would certainly bring better results, from the point of view of maintaining, developing and mobilising the skills required on the labour market than the current practice of trying to reach a proportional representation of women in each programme.

Some countries have already chosen this path. The French government's Second Employment Plan, adopted in September 1989, made the reduction of unemployment among women one of its priority aims. It was argued that women job-seekers had not benefited from the fall in unemployment in general because they were disadvantaged by labour market selectivity (Circular DE/DFP No. 89/54). Of the policy directions recommended for remedying the exclusion of women, the most innovative consisted in taking greater account of women's specific problems when implementing overall employment measures. It would be particularly interesting to evaluate the results of this initiative, as well as those of any other initiative aiming, in a similar fashion, to make general measures more directly responsive to women's specific problems and needs.

FLEXIBLE WORKING TIME

The high activity rates in most OECD Member countries today, for both women and men, mean that reconciling work and family responsibilities is an increasingly important problem. The stakes are high as far as equality between the sexes is concerned and striking a better balance between work and family life has become central to equality strategies.

The scope of this problem goes far beyond the labour market and measures undertaken only in the field of employment will, of course, not be sufficient; adjustments in the private sphere and in the organisation of society as a whole are just as necessary. Nevertheless, the present employment and career system constitutes an obstacle to achieving a harmonious balance between the world of work and family life and it needs to be redesigned. Adjustments were introduced in the 1980s, bearing essentially on the flexibility of working time. This flexibility seems to have developed almost everywhere in the two areas of:

– parental leave; and

– part-time work.

Parental leave

The development of leave entitlement

For a long time policies to reconcile working life with family responsibilities were mainly confined to the protection of pregnant women at work and the development of the entitlement to maternity leave. Today, the prohibition of discrimination based on pregnancy and the entitlement to maternity leave have become an integral part of minimum protective standards for workers in most OECD countries,[25] although there is considerable variation in legal provision for maternity leave from one country to another as regards eligibility, length of leave, payment of allowances and their funding.

Entitlement to maternity leave further developed during the 1980s and the nature of the leave itself started changing. Spain may be cited as an example of the type of evolution which occurred during this period. In this country, the length of time allotted for maternity leave was extended in 1989 from 14 to 16 weeks, and the last four weeks may now be taken by the father. Thus a new form of leave developed: parental leave. Beyond a certain length of time, the object of maternity leave is no longer to help the mother recover after the birth but to let her look after her baby. Increasingly, the period of maternity leave remaining once the mother has had time to recover may be taken by either parent. In some countries, parental leave was introduced separately; its conditions, like those relative to maternal leave, vary a great deal from country to country (Table 6.2).

Collective bargaining has an important role to play if the leave entitlement enshrined in law is to become a reality; it is usually through collective bargaining that the specific conditions and arrangements for parental leave are set. In some cases, for instance, the law only institutes the entitlement to request leave; under these circumstances, the employer is under the obligation of granting the request only if this has been the object of collective bargaining. This is the case in particular in Belgium, where employees are entitled to request career break leave and an increasing number of employers have accepted to write this entitlement into collective agreements. Career break leave is most often being used as parental leave, and there is a rapid increase of the number of employees availing themselves of this right (in 80 per cent of cases, they are women).

In countries where the law does not provide for parental leave, certain employers voluntarily introduce schemes whereby employees may be entitled to a career break. Their objective is to attract qualified women and retain their female staff who would otherwise simply have left the labour market after a pregnancy. Several big firms in the United Kingdom have taken this approach. Their programmes are generally available only to employees who have been with the firm for several years, have reached a certain position and show good potential. While they are by no means available to all, these schemes at least have the merit of enabling a number of women to leave the labour market for a few years and later be reinstated in their former job (or an equivalent position) without major problems. During their absence these women must either participate in training sessions or replace a colleague for a few weeks (the purpose being to maintain permanent contact with the firm).

Table 6.2. **Legislated maternity and parental leave**[a]

	Maternity leave		Parental leave[b]	
	Maximum duration	Replacement rate	Maximum duration	Replacement rate
Australia	52	–	24th month	Flat rate allowance[c]
Austria	16	100%	–	–
Belgium	15	100% to 79.5%	–	–
Canada	17 or 18[d]	Up to 60%[e]	–	–
Denmark	28	90%	10 weeks	–
Finland	17.5	80%	36th month	Flat rate allowance
France	16-28[g]	84%	36th month	80% during 28 weeks
Germany	14	100%	18th month	Flat rate allowance[h]
Greece	14	100%	30th month[i]	Flat rate allowance
Iceland	13	Flat rate allowance	–	–
Ireland	14	60%	–	–
Italy	20	80%	36th month	–
Japan	14	60%	12th month	–
Luxembourg	16	100%	–	–
Netherlands	16	100%	–	–
New Zealand	14	–	–	–
Norway	28	100%	1 year[j]	80% up to 35th week
Portugal	13	100%	12th month	Flat rate allowance[c]
Spain	16	90%	36th month	–
Sweden	m	m	1 year	90% then flat rate allowance[m]
United Kingdom	40[k]	90% then flat rate allowance[l]	65 weeks	–
United States[f]	–	–	–	–

a) This table describes the general provisions in each country's labour legislation at 31.12.1991. Workers may have additional benefits under collective agreement provisions (longer leave, higher replacement rates).
b) When leave is expressed as a number of weeks, it is in addition to maternity leave.
c) Only in some cases.
d) According to the province.
e) Benefits are not paid during the two first weeks.
f) There is no provision at national level. Several states grant unpaid maternity leave, or parental leave, or both.
g) According to the rank of the child.
h) For third child and over.
i) In enterprises with more than 100 employees.
j) Does not apply to women with less than one year's employment with the same employer and those working less than 10 hours per week.
k) Does not apply to women with less than two year's employment with the same employer and those working less than 16 hours per week.
l) Six weeks with 90% of earnings, flat rate thereafter up to 18 weeks.
m) Parental leave can be used at any time between 60 days before birth until child's eighth birthday. The first 52 weeks are compensated at 90% of earnings.
Source: Information provided by the national authorities.

Effects of maternity and parental leave on equal opportunities in employment

What concrete effects do maternity and parental leave have on the general employment situation of women? Even if they are entitled to it, parents do not necessarily take or wish to take leave. The combined effect of the different conditions of implementation – eligibility, length, and replacement rate – may limit the participation of certain categories of male and female workers. If long leave with high pay is made available, it may be presumed that parents will return to work later rather than sooner (and vice versa). On the other hand, a prolonged absence from the workplace will most likely have a negative impact on earnings, career development and, more generally, on competitiveness on the labour market.

Although no thorough or systematic surveys are available, the few existing data do point to a number of observations. First of all, leave entitlements are not systematically taken up.[26] A survey carried out in Australia showed that for every 100 women who had had a baby in 1984, 44 had both requested and obtained maternity leave, 32 who could have obtained leave had not applied for it, and 24 were not entitled to it (Glezer, 1988). The survey covered all sectors, and the take-up rate was three times higher in the public sector than in the private. In Germany, on the other hand, approximately 98 per cent of the women who were entitled to take maternity leave in 1988 did so, and 94 per cent of those entitled took the maximum length of time allotted (18 months).

Second, it has been observed that when maternity leave is granted, this is associated with a rapid return to work following a birth. From the surveys which look at the reasons why a woman with a new-born baby returns quickly to the labour market, or leaves it altogether, it appears that maternity leave entitlement which guarantees reinstatement in one's former (or comparable) job, or some similar arrangement offered by the employer, makes a very positive contribution to the labour force attachment. Thus, the Australian survey showed that in Australia mothers who had obtained leave returned to work earlier than others. This situation is also noted in the United States (O'Connell, 1990).

Of central interest in relation to parental leave is the extent to which parents avail themselves of the possibility of sharing the leave. In theory, the fact that fathers may take such leave should promote equal opportunities on the labour market: the mother can return to the labour market earlier if the father takes some time off. In reality, this is not what happens and data indicate that, in the very great majority of cases, women are still the ones who avail themselves of this right. The case of Sweden is particularly enlightening. When parental leave was first introduced in 1974, only 3 per cent of fathers availed themselves of the possibility. In 1981, 22 per cent of fathers took leave. On the average, men took parental leave for an average of 47 days whereas mothers were absent from work for an average of 288 days (maternity leave included). Figures available for 1988 show much the same picture.

Sharing parental leave is difficult for many reasons. The first is, of course, the persistence of the traditional view according to which young children should be looked after by the mother. The fact that attitudes are slow to change constitutes a very serious obstacle. The other difficulties involved in the implementation of parental leave are of a different sort and are due, for the main part, to the fact that such leave can have drawbacks even for women. Thus, the benefit allocated is a determining factor in deciding whether or not to take leave. When no benefit is allocated, the take-up rate is very low; many women simply do not have the financial means to do without an income for a relatively long period of time. Furthermore, if the benefit is low, this serves as an disincentive to sharing parental leave: the man's wages being almost always higher than those of the woman, the family suffers a heavier financial loss if it is the father who takes leave rather than the mother.

On the other hand, it has been observed that women with high earnings and good career prospects are disinclined to avail themselves of parental leave, even if an allowance is allocated, because any prolonged absence from the workplace during a crucial career phase can cause irreparable damage. Given these difficulties, the tendency in certain countries is now to make parental leave increasingly flexible in order to ensure continuous contact with the workplace. In France, for instance, the possibility of working half-time while on parental leave has now been extended to the possibility of choosing to work any amount of time between 16 and 32 hours a week. As for career progression, the assurance of either a retraining or refresher training programme at the end of the leave can ensure at least that reintegration will be at the same level of employment.

With regard to equal opportunities for women on the labour market, parental leave policies are certainly a positive element. Leave with a guaranteed return to employment means that temporary breaks in activity do not necessarily turn into major breaks in career path. But these measures are efficient only insofar as they trigger the interest of mothers and fathers. This in itself is a direct result of the kind of impact they have on both income and career.

Lastly, however much parental leave can contribute to equal opportunities for women, all its benefits will come to nothing if, once the leave is finished, the parents find themselves confronted by insurmountable problems of childcare. Parental leave is only one element in an overall system which should include other adjustments in order to make employment less constraining as well as childcare services. Greater flexibility in working hours thus appears to be an essential complement to leave entitlement for family reasons.

Part-time work

Of all the ways in which working time can be made more flexible, the only one to have developed significantly is part-time work. In fact, part-time work has become a major structural feature of the employment systems within the OECD. Job-sharing and flexitime, though no longer experimental as they were in the 1970s, have not developed to the same extent.

The spread of part-time work in the 1980s and its implications have been considered in some detail in Chapter 3. Some of the findings set out previously might be pertinent to the question under scrutiny: in what respect has the development of part-time work made it easier to combine working life with family life and in what respect has it contributed to equal opportunities for women?

A harmonious combination of working life and family life is based on two conditions: a balanced distribution of the time spent in each area and compatible hours for the exercise of the different activities which have to be undertaken. While these two conditions are generally more easily attainable within the context of part-time work, it would be erroneous to believe that this is always the case.

As stated in Chapter 3, there is a great variety in the number of hours required in a part-time job. Some part-time workers work very short hours. But, a certain number of part-time workers work longer hours than full-time workers in certain sectors or occupations. Neither do part-time work schedules necessarily make working life and family life compatible. Quite frequently, the working day begins and ends at times that are incompatible with the schedules of schools or day care centres. The fact that employers increasingly resort to part-time employment as a way of organising shift-work results in working hours that are staggered in comparison to a normal working day. If working life and family responsibilities appear more compatible in this case, it is only to the extent that it is possible for one of the partners in a couple to be at home while the other is at work, which is hardly conducive to successful married life.

So far, women have been practically the only ones to use part-time work to reconcile working life with family responsibilities. In this sense, part-time work has contributed to maintaining traditional role-sharing in couples, since it is virtually always the woman who "chooses" to work part-time – for lack of a better alternative – while continuing to take on all the responsibilities of domestic and family life.

Furthermore, if "working life" is understood as the pursuit of a career, the compatibility between working life and family life derived from part-time work seems at present fairly illusory. This is because today part-time work is usually limited to unskilled and deskilling jobs. Most of these jobs are concentrated in the secondary labour market and are considered as a kind of ghetto. Some part-time jobs offer so few work hours that the concept of employment does not seem to apply significantly.

The redefinition of part-time work should be sought in such a way that it becomes compatible with career development. The alternatives chosen by certain countries serve as pointers. In Japan, for example, the possibility of working part-time now applies to certain managerial positions, making such positions more accessible to women. In Nordic countries workers have the possibility of reducing their working time under certain circumstances: in Sweden, for example, parents of children under 8 years old have been allowed to reduce their daily working time by 2 hours since 1976.

The considerable expansion of part-time work seems to have pre-empted all other attempts to develop other forms of time flexibility. Any other measure introducing more flexibility in the employment and career system and in the organisation of work in order to attain a greater compatibility between working life and family life should lead to a greater continuity in the course of women's careers. Employers today are increasingly aware that maintaining a position in an increasingly competitive market depends on whether they can rely on a qualified and committed workforce. Some are ready to grant their employees greater flexibility in exchange for this commitment and are taking initiatives in this direction. These initiatives should be strongly encouraged and their results widely circulated.

CONCLUSIONS

Today, most OECD countries have a relatively extensive legislative framework concerning equality between women and men in employment, especially in terms of wages. Moreover, legislation has developed from the notion of "forbidding" (fighting discrimination) to "obliging" (affirmative or positive action), becoming in the process more complex and difficult to implement.

The situation of women in employment has, itself, become more complex. Since so many women are now present on the labour market, the problem of access to employment has become relatively less important than such issues as working conditions and the situation at the workplace. Within that perspective, collective bargaining appears as a highly promising, although greatly under-utilised, means of promoting equal opportunity.

Labour market policies are of great potential interest for female workers but they do not seem to be fully responsive to structural developments. Because women are at the very heart of these developments (in the service sector, in new forms of employment), they do not benefit to a great extent from general labour market measures. Measures aimed specifically at women do address the needs of certain categories, but their scope remains limited and they do not have any significant impact on labour market structures.

The interface between working life and family and private life is giving rise to extremely acute problems for a growing number of both women and men. The adjustments that have been made to release the constraints of working life – parental leave, part-time work – have not, so far, concerned men and in most cases, the pursuit of a career remains incompatible with a balanced family life. If women, as well as men, are to lead working and family lives that are both full and harmonious, much more fundamental changes in the working world and society as a whole will have to be implemented.

Notes

1. This chapter relies to a great extent on the unpublished work by a group of national experts on equal employment opportunities programmes and policies.

2. Labour market measures represent, of course, only one element of an overall strategy aiming at equity which must cover virtually all policy areas.

3. By the end of the 1960s, the ILO Convention No. 100 had been ratified by 15 of the 24 OECD Member countries. It was ratified by seven other countries in the 1970s and by New Zealand in 1983. To this day, it has not been ratified by the United States.

4. Using a male worker as a basis for comparison calls forth another type of problem: legislation seems limited as far as entirely feminised institutions are concerned.

5. Actual systems often bear traces of indirect discrimination against women, especially when wages are to a large extent determined by seniority.

6. Turkey is the only OECD country which has not adopted a specific law guaranteeing gender equality in relation to employment. However, this principle is enshrined in the Constitution.

7. ILO Convention No. 111 on discrimination in employment and profession is much older, since it dates from 1958.

8. *Direct discrimination* may be defined as treating women differently from men (for example, allowing men, but not women, to work at night). *Indirect discrimination* occurs when the consequences of a seemingly neutral condition or practice are not the same for women as for men (for example, a minimum height requirement for certain occupations). *Systemic* or *structural discrimination* stems from social custom which handicaps or restricts women more than men (for example, the fact that women are responsible for looking after children when no childcare facilities are available).

9. The purpose, of course, is to offset the effects of past discrimination against women, which means that the measures will be of an exceptional and provisional nature.

10. In Australia and Canada, the law applies to firms of more than 100 employees and in France to firms of more than 50 employees. In the United States the law applies to firms of more than 50 employees holding public works contracts superior to US$ 50 000.

11. In countries with a federal structure, federal legislation only applies in the area of federal jurisdiction. A state or province may have its own laws (in some cases more progressive than federal law and in other cases less so). As a matter of example, in Canada, federal and provincial legislation pertaining to equal pay covers approximately a third of the active population.

12. This procedure has been used repeatedly in some countries to claim compensatory wage adjustments for whole categories of women workers.

13. National legislations differ widely from one country to another as to what is required of employers. In some rare cases the question of sanctioning employers for failing to comply with the law does not even arise. In most cases the employer is called upon to do no more than right the situation complained of and compensate the complainant(s) for any prejudice suffered.

Finally, in some countries an employer may be required to take positive action to improve the general position of his female staff as well as righting the particular situation originally complained of.

14. In other countries this is the responsibility of the Ministry of Labour, in particular labour inspectors.

15. This does not however apply universally, and Finland is for example an exception.

16. Especially those for whom it is relatively easy to find a new job.

17. See *Employment Outlook,* OECD, September 1988, Chapter 4.

18. The OECD has evaluated the measures aimed at the unemployed who were victims of employment restructuring and the long-term unemployed. However, the possibility that these measures would have a different impact according to gender was not brought up.

19. A study by the Economic Council of Canada reported that in 1986 more than half the total number of women taking part in vocational training were learning secretarial skills (D. Boothby, 1986).

20. The level defining under-representation may vary considerably. Canada has applied a 10 per cent threshold for this type of programme. In the United States the 1991 Non-Traditional Employment for Women refers to occupations in which there are less than 25 per cent of women. In Nordic countries the aim is to set a minimum for both sexes at approximately 40 per cent in all professions. In Spain, employers can obtain subsidies to hire women workers when they represent less than 50 per cent of all workers.

21. The scope of the problem varies from country to country. In certain countries, there is no longer a massive withdrawal of women from the labour market at a particular stage in their life cycle. If this trend towards continuous professional activity becomes generalised in other countries, the problem of re-entering the labour market will become less important in the future.

22. Thus, to counter the rapid increase of unemployment among women in the new German *Länder,* the target for their participation in employment promotion programmes (employment creation and training) has been set at the level of their share of unemployment in 1990 (55 per cent).

23. In Australia, for example, the Ministry for Employment, Education and Training launched "Action for Women" in 1989, to assist the Central Employment Services in its activities related to women.

24. The Francophone Training Office, linked to the Belgian Employment Office, is another example of a public institution comprising an equal opportunity counsellors network.

25. In 1992, the European Economic Community also adopted a directive establishing entitlement to paid maternity leave of at least 14 weeks in all its member countries.

26. A distinction must be made between take-up and eligibility. For example, in the United Kingdom in 1980, only about half the women who had had a baby were eligible for leave (Daniel, 1980).

Bibliography

BAKKER, I. (1992), "Pay equity and economic restructuring: the polarization of policy?" in Fudge, J. and Mc Dermott, P. (eds.), *The Politics of Pay Equity: Putting Feminism to Work,* Toronto: University of Toront Press.

BOOTHBY, D. (1986), *Women Re-entering the Labour Force and Training Programmes. Evidence from Canada,* Ottawa: Canadian Government Publishing Centre.

DANIEL, W.W. (1980), *Maternity Rights: The Experience of Women,* PSI Report No. 588, London: Policy Studies Institute.

GLEZER, H. (1988), *Maternity Leave in Australia: Employee and Employer Experiences,* Monograph No. 7, Melbourne: Australian Institute of Family Studies.

ILO (1986), *Equal Remuneration,* Geneva: ILO.

ILO (1988), *Equality in Employment and Occupation,* Geneva: ILO.

LEVY, (1983), "Women's Unemployment in the Community", European Community Commission, DGV. Document No. 37, April.

O'CONNELL, M. (1990), "Maternity Leave Arrangements: 1961-85", in *Work and Family Patterns of American Women, Current Population Reports,* Special Studies Series P-23, No. 165.

OECD (1980), *Women and Employment. Policies for Equal Opportunities,* Paris.

OECD (1988), "Women's Activity, Employment and Earnings: A Review of Recent Developments", *Employment Outlook,* Chapter 5, Paris.

OECD (1990a), *Enterprising Women,* Paris.

OECD (1990b), *Labour Market Policies for the 1990s,* Paris.

OECD (1991), "Equal Pay for Work of Comparable Worth: The Experience of Industrialised Countries", Labour Market and Social Policy, Occasional Papers No. 6, Paris.

STANDING, G. (1989) "Global Feminization through Flexible Labor", *World Development,* Vol. 17, No. 7.

STATISTICAL ANNEX

Table A. **Labour force participation rates by sex**

Percentages

	Men						Women					
	1973	1979	1989	1990	1991	1992	1973	1979	1989	1990	1991	1992
Australia	91.1	87.6	I85.7	85.9	85.6	85.3	47.7	50.3	I60.8	62.1	62.2	62.4
Austria	83.0	81.6	80.0	80.1	80.5	81.3	48.5	49.1	54.3	55.4	56.3	58.3
Belgium	83.2	79.3	72.4	72.7	72.8	..	41.3	46.3	51.6	52.4	53.2	..
Canada	86.1	86.3	85.6	84.9	83.9	83.4	47.2	55.5	67.3	68.1	68.1	67.9
Denmark	89.6	I89.6	89.5	89.6	88.5	..	61.9	I69.9	77.3	78.4	78.9	..
Finland	80.0	I82.2	80.9	80.6	79.6	78.5	63.6	I68.9	73.3	72.9	71.8	70.6
France	85.2	82.6	74.8	74.6	74.5	74.0	50.1	54.2	55.8	56.1	56.8	57.3
Germany	89.6	84.9	I81.5	80.8	80.6	80.1	50.3	52.2	I56.0	57.0	58.1	59.0
Greece	83.2	79.0	78.6	82.1	..	..	32.1	32.8	41.7	39.9	..	..
Ireland	92.3	88.7	82.7	82.2	81.9	..	34.1	35.2	37.5	38.9	39.9	..
Italy	85.1	82.6	78.5	78.9	79.4	79.2	33.7	38.7	44.3	44.9	45.8	46.3
Japan	90.1	89.2	87.3	87.8	88.9	89.3	54.0	54.7	59.3	60.4	61.5	61.7
Luxembourg	93.1	88.9	91.8	..	77.7	..	35.9	39.8	49.2	..	44.8	..
Netherlands	85.6	79.0	79.6	79.9	80.3	..	29.2	33.4	51.0	53.0	54.5	..
New Zealand	89.2	87.3	I82.8	82.2	82.3	..	39.2	45.0	I61.0	62.4	62.8	..
Norway	86.5	89.2	85.9	84.5	82.9	83.0	50.6	61.7	71.2	71.2	71.1	70.9
Portugal	100.8	I90.9	I86.7	86.1	85.9	79.8	32.1	I57.3	I59.4	60.4	62.8	59.2
Spain	92.9	I83.1	77.4	76.8	76.0	74.9	33.4	I32.6	39.9	40.9	41.2	42.1
Sweden	88.1	87.9	85.0	85.3	84.5	82.7	62.6	72.8	80.6	81.1	80.3	78.7
Switzerland	100.6	94.6	96.3	96.2	95.3	94.5	54.1	53.0	58.8	59.6	59.8	59.2
United Kingdom	93.0	90.5	I86.9	86.5	86.1	85.6	53.2	58.0	I64.8	65.3	64.5	64.5
United States	86.2	85.7	86.0	85.8	84.7	85.0	51.1	58.9	68.0	68.6	68.4	68.9
North America	86.2	85.8	85.9	85.7	84.6	84.8	50.7	58.6	68.0	68.5	68.4	68.8
OECD Europe	88.7	84.8	80.6	80.6	78.3	..	44.7	48.6	54.1	54.8	54.0	..
Total OECD	88.2	85.9	83.7	83.7	82.4	..	48.3	53.1	60.0	60.7	60.5	..

.. Not available.
I Break in series.
Source: OECD Labour Force Statistics.

Table B. Unemployment rates in the OECD countries

	Unemployment rates (in percentage of labour force)						Long-term unemployment (12 months or more) in percentage of total unemployment	
	Total		Women		Men		Women	Men
	1989	1979	1989	1979	1989	1979	1989	
Australia	5.7	5.8	6.2	7.7	5.3	4.7	16.9	28.0
Austria	3.1	2.1	3.6	3.1	2.8	1.5	..	..
Belgium	9.3	7.5	13.7	12.8	6.1	4.4	77.2	74.7
Canada	7.5	7.4	7.9	8.7	7.2	6.5	5.3	8.0
Denmark	8.1	6.0	8.9	8.3	7.5	4.2	29.0	22.6
Finland	3.4	5.9	3.4	5.5	3.5	6.2	5.9	7.9
France	9.4	5.9	12.6	8.5	7.0	4.1	45.6	41.6
Germany	6.8	3.2	8.1	4.3	6.0	2.5	45.9	52.3
Greece	7.5	1.9	12.3	3.2	4.6	1.3	58.8	42.2
Iceland	1.6	0.4	..	..	..	..	..	..
Ireland	15.6	7.1	11.3	6.4	17.5	7.4	58.2	71.9
Italy	11.8	7.6	18.6	13.1	7.9	4.8	71.9	68.2
Japan	2.3	2.1	2.3	2.0	2.2	2.2	12.5	23.3
Luxembourg	1.2	0.7	1.6	1.0	1.1	0.5	18.2	50.0
Netherlands	8.3	5.4	11.5	6.7	6.3	4.8	44.0	56.3
New Zealand	7.1	1.9	7.2	2.3	7.1	1.7	10.9	17.3
Norway	4.9	2.0	4.7	2.4	5.1	1.6	10.0	13.0
Portugal	5.0	8.0	7.2	12.9	3.3	4.8	51.7	43.0
Spain	16.9	8.4	25.2	9.6	12.6	7.9	65.5	51.3
Sweden	1.3	2.1	1.4	2.3	1.3	1.9	5.4	7.6
Switzerland	0.5	0.3	0.6	0.4	0.4	0.3	..	..
Turkey	8.3	9.4	9.5	..	7.8	..	..	..
United Kingdom	6.1	4.6	4.0	3.3	7.7	5.5	28.5	49.3
United States	5.2	5.7	5.3	6.8	5.0	5.0	3.7	7.4

Sources: OECD Labour Force Statistics: 1972-1992, OECD, Paris, 1993; Employment Outlook, OECD, Paris, July 1993.

Table C. Size and composition of part-time employment, 1973-1992
Percentages

	Part-time employment as a proportion of employment											
	Men						Women					
	1973	1979	1989	1990	1991	1992	1973	1979	1989	1990	1991	1992
Australia	3.7	5.2	7.8	8.0	9.2	10.5	28.2	35.2	40.1	40.1	40.9	43.3
Austria	1.4	1.5	1.6	1.6	1.5	..	15.6	18.0	20.0	20.2	20.1	..
Belgium	1.0	1.0	1.7	2.0	2.1	..	10.2	16.5	25.0	25.8	27.4	..
Canada	4.7	5.7	7.7	8.1	8.8	9.3	19.4	23.3	24.5	24.4	25.5	25.9
Denmark	..	5.2	9.4	10.4	10.5	..	..	46.3	40.1	38.4	37.8	..
Finland	..	3.2	4.6	4.4	5.1	5.5	..	10.6	10.4	10.2	10.2	10.4
France	1.7	2.4	3.5	3.3	3.4	3.6	12.9	16.9	23.7	23.6	23.5	24.5
Germany	1.8	1.5	2.3	2.6	2.7	..	24.4	27.6	30.7	33.8	34.3	..
Greece	..	..	2.4	2.2	2.2	..	..	..	8.0	7.6	7.2	..
Ireland	..	2.1	3.1	3.4	3.6	..	..	13.1	16.6	17.6	17.8	..
Italy	3.7	3.0	3.1	2.4	2.9	2.7	14.0	10.6	10.9	9.6	10.4	10.5
Japan	6.8	7.5	8.0	9.5	10.1	10.6	25.1	27.8	31.9	33.4	34.3	34.8
Luxembourg	1.0	1.0	2.0	1.9	1.9	..	18.4	17.1	17.0	16.7	17.9	..
Netherlands a	..	5.5 |	15.6	15.8	16.7	13.4	..	44.0 |	61.5	61.7	62.2	62.9
New Zealand	4.6	4.9	7.7	8.4	9.7	10.3	24.6	29.1	33.7	35.0	35.7	35.9
Norway	5.9	7.3	8.3	8.8	9.1	9.8	46.5	50.9	9.8	48.2	47.6	47.1
Portugal	..	2.5	3.3	3.6	4.0	4.2	..	16.5	9.9	10.1	10.5	11.0
Spain	..	..	1.6	1.6	1.5	2.0	..	..	11.9	11.8	11.2	13.7
Sweden b	..	5.4 |	7.3	7.3	7.6	8.4	..	46.0 |	42.1	40.9	41.0	41.3
United Kingdom	2.3	1.9	5.0	5.3	5.5	6.1	39.1	39.0	43.6	43.2	43.7	44.6
United States	8.6	9.0	10.0	10.0	10.5	10.8	26.8	26.7	25.5	25.2	25.6	25.4

	Part-time employment as a proportion of total employment						Women's share in part-time employment					
	1973	1979	1989	1990	1991	1992	1973	1979	1989	1990	1991	1992
Australia	11.9	15.9	20.9	21.3	22.5	24.4	79.4	78.7	78.1	78.1	76.3	75.1
Austria	6.4	7.6	8.8	9.0	8.9	..	85.8	87.8	88.8	89.1	89.7	..
Belgium	3.8	6.0	10.2	10.9	11.8	..	82.4	88.9	89.6	88.6	89.3	..
Canada	9.7	12.5	15.1	15.4	16.4	16.8	68.4	72.1	71.6	71.0	70.5	70.0
Denmark	..	22.7	23.4	23.3	23.1	..	..	86.9	78.0	75.7	75.5	..
Finland	..	6.7	7.4	7.2	7.6	7.9	..	74.7	67.0	67.8	65.2	64.3
France	5.9	8.2	12.0	12.0	12.0	12.7	82.3	82.2	83.2	83.9	84.0	83.7
Germany	10.1	11.4	13.4	15.2	15.5	..	89.0	91.6	89.6	89.7	89.6	..
Greece	..	..	4.4	4.1	3.9	..	..	..	64.4	64.9	62.9	..
Ireland	..	5.1	7.6	8.1	8.4	..	..	71.2	72.3	71.7	71.6	..
Italy	6.4	5.3	5.7	4.9	5.5	5.4	58.3	61.4	64.7	67.2	65.4	67.9
Japan	13.9	15.4	17.6	19.2	20.0	20.5	70.0	70.1	73.0	70.7	69.9	69.3
Luxembourg	5.8	5.8	7.2	7.0	7.5	..	87.5	87.5	81.8	81.8	83.3	..
Netherlands a	..	16.6 |	32.6	33.2	34.3	32.8	..	76.4 |	69.9	70.4	70.1	75.0
New Zealand	11.2	13.9	18.8	20.0	21.1	21.6	72.3	77.7	76.7	76.4	74.2	73.3
Norway	20.8	25.3	26.4	26.6	26.7	26.9	82.3	83.0	82.5	81.8	81.4	80.1
Portugal	..	7.8	6.0	6.4	6.8	7.2	..	80.4	68.4	66.9	66.7	67.4
Spain	..	..	4.8	4.8	4.6	5.9	..	..	77.2	78.0	78.0	76.8
Sweden b	..	23.6 |	24.0	23.3	23.7	24.3	..	87.5 |	84.2	83.6	83.4	82.3
United Kingdom	16.0	16.4	21.7	21.7	22.2	23.2	90.9	92.8	87.0	86.2	86.1	85.4
United States	15.6	16.4	17.0	16.9	17.4	17.5	66.0	68.0	67.8	67.6	67.2	66.4

.. Data not available.
a) Break in series after 1985.
b) Break in series after 1986.
See Table D, Statistical Annex, *OECD Employment Outlook*, July 1993, for notes, sources and definitions which refer to this table.

Table D. Sectoral contributions to employment and GDP

	Contribution to civil employment – %						Contribution to GDP – %					
	Agriculture		Industry		Services		Agriculture		Industry		Services[1]	
	1989	1979	1991	1981	1991	1981	1991	1981	1991	1981	1991	1981
Australia	5.5	6.5	24.2	30.6	70.4	62.8	3.3a	4.9	31.4a,f	36.1f	65.3a,f	58.9f
Austria	7.4	10.3	36.9	40.0	55.8	49.8	2.8	4.1	36.3	38.9	60.9	57.0
Belgium	2.6	3.2	28.1	33.3	69.3	63.6	1.8a	2.3	30.1a	31.5	68.1a	66.2
Canada	4.5	5.5	23.2	28.3	72.3	66.3	2.4b	3.7	29.1b	32.1	68.5b	64.2
Denmark	5.7	7.3	27.7	29.3	66.6	63.3	3.9a	5.1	24.4a	23.4	71.7a	71.4
Finland	8.5	13.0	29.2	35.0	62.3	51.9	4.8	8.0	27.0	34.8	68.3	57.2
France	5.8	8.4	29.5	35.2	64.8	56.4	3.1	4.1	28.7	32.5	68.2	63.3
Germany	3.4	5.2	39.2	43.0	57.4	51.9	1.5a	2.1	38.7a,g	41.6g	59.8a,g	56.4g
Greece	23.9a	30.7	27.7a	29.0	48.4a	40.4	13.5a	16.1	24.1a	27.8	62.5a	56.1
Iceland	10.7	12.4	26.4	34.5	62.9	53.1	10.1a	9.4	23.4a	25.0	66.5a	65.6
Ireland	13.8	17.3	28.9	32.1	57.2	50.6	9.0a	10.1	33.4a	32.3	57.6a	57.7
Italy	8.5	13.4	32.3	37.6	59.2	49.0	3.3	5.3	32.1	37.6	64.6	57.0
Japan	6.7	10.0	34.4	35.3	58.9	54.7	2.5a	3.5	41.8a	41.9	55.7a	54.6
Luxembourg	3.3a	5.1	30.5a	37.2	66.2a	57.7	1.4	2.6	33.7	37.9	64.9	59.5
Netherlands	4.5	4.9	25.5	29.9	69.9	65.2	4.2a	4.1	31.5a	32.9	64.2a	63.0
New Zealand	10.8	11.4	23.5	32.7	65.7	56.0	8.6b	9.4	26.7b	32.9	64.7b	57.7
Norway	5.9	8.4	23.7	29.3	70.4	62.4	2.9a	4.0	35.5a	39.5	61.6a	56.5
Portugal	17.3	26.0	33.9	37.0	48.7	37.0	5.8a	9.0	37.8a	39.9	56.4a	51.1
Spain	10.7	18.8	33.1	35.3	56.3	45.9	5.3c	5.9e	35.0c	37.3e	59.7c	56.8e
Sweden	3.2	5.6	28.2	31.3	68.5	63.1	2.6a	3.4	29.5a	29.6	67.9a	67.0
Switzerland	5.5	6.6	34.4	37.9	60.1	55.6	..	3.6e	..	35.5e	..	60.9e
Turkey	46.6	54.4	20.3	19.1	33.1	26.5	16.6a	21.1	35.4a	32.2	48.0a	46.8
United Kingdom	2.2	2.7	27.8	35.8	70.0	61.5	1.3c	1.9	30.0c,h	35.7h	68.7c,h	62.4h
United States	2.9	3.5	25.3	30.1	71.8	66.4	2.0d	2.8	29.2d,j	33.7j	68.8a,j,k	63.5j,k

.. Not available.
1. Including import duties and other adjustment, and excluding imputed bank service charge.
a) 1990.
b) 1989.
c) 1988.
d) 1987.
e) 1985.
f) Sewerage services included under industry.
g) Publishing included under services.
h) Repair services of consumer durables other than clothing included under services.
j) Sanitary and similar services included under industry.
k) Includes government entreprises.
Source: OECD in Figures, 1993 edition, pp. 26-27.

Table E. Service activities contribution to employment

Contribution to employment – % of total employment

	Wholesale and retail trade, restaurants, and hotels (I)		Transport, storage and communication (II)		Finance, insurance, real estate and business services (III)		Community, social and personal services [1] (IV)		Producers of government services (V)	
	1991	1981	1991	1981	1991	1981	1991	1981	1991	1981
Australia	24.3[a]	20.0[c]	7.0[a]	7.7	11.5[a]	8.8	22.1[a,m]	22.2[c,m]	4.7[a,s]	4.5[s]
Austria	..	..	..	..	..	..	..	..	..	..
Belgium	19.7[a,b]	19.2[b]	6.2[a]	7.2	4.0[a,h]	3.3[h]	20.7[a,b,h]	16.2[b,h]	19.5[a]	19.5
Canada	23.8	22.5	6.3	7.1	11.9	9.5	23.6	20.3	6.7	7.0
Denmark	12.8[a]	13.5	7.3[a]	7.0	10.0[a]	8.1	6.6[a]	6.6	30.5[a]	29.8
Finland	14.8	14.3	7.3	6.9	7.1	5.3	8.6	8.1	23.8	18.4
France	17.9	17.0	5.9	5.5	17.0[j]	13.2[j]	..	..	25.4[t]	22.4[t]
Germany	16.3[a]	15.8	5.6[a]	5.7	3.1[a,h]	2.8[h]	16.7[a,h,n]	13.1[h,n]	15.1[a]	14.8
Greece	..	15.9[f]	..	6.9[f]	..	3.7[f]	..	17.2[f,p]	..	..
Iceland	14.4[a]	13.1	6.4[a]	7.1	8.0[a]	5.9	12.0[a]	9.9	18.4[a]	17.1
Ireland	..	..	..	..	..	..	..	..	..	..
Italy	21.6[b]	19.4[b]	6.4	5.9	15.2[j]	9.9[j]	2.8[j]	2.1[j]	15.5	14.8
Japan	17.9[a,c]	17.9[c]	5.6[a]	5.6	4.8[a]	4.2	23.3[a,c]	18.5[c]	6.0[a]	6.7
Luxembourg	20.6	21.2	6.8	6.9	9.0[h]	5.5[h]	20.3[h]	13.4[h]	10.8	10.8
Netherlands	19.0[a]	18.0	7.1[a]	6.7	8.8[a]	7.8	17.5[a,q]	16.4[q]	14.7[a]	15.4
New Zealand	17.6	15.7[g]	5.5	6.2[g]	9.0	6.2[g]	24.3	19.6[g]	22.1	24.1[g]
Norway	16.7[a]	16.6	8.9[a]	9.2	7.5[a]	5.3	9.0[a]	8.4	27.6[a]	23.9
Portugal	17.2[a]	13.6	4.4[a]	4.5	3.2[a]	2.7	6.9[a]	6.5	13.6[a]	10.3
Spain	22.2[d]	20.4[f]	5.6[d]	6.2[f]	4.7[d,k]	4.3[f,k]	5.6[d,k]	5.4[f,k]	17.6[d]	16.8[f]
Sweden	14.1[a]	13.7	6.6[a]	6.6	8.4[a]	5.6	6.9[a]	6.8	31.7[a]	31.1
Switzerland	..	..	..	..	..	..	..	..	..	..
Turkey	..	..	..	..	..	..	..	..	..	..
United Kingdom	19.5[a]	19.3	5.6[a]	6.3	11.9[a]	7.8	11.8[a]	6.8	19.2[a,u]	21.8[u]
United States	23.1[e]	21.7	4.2[e]	4.5	14.6[e]	11.4	15.3[e,r]	14.0[r]	14.4[e]	15.3

.. Not available.
1. Including other producers.
a) 1990.
b) Recovery and repair services included under I.
c) Restaurants and hotels included under IV.
d) 1988.
e) 1989.
f) 1985.
g) 1983.
h) Real estate and business services included under IV.
Source: OECD in Figures, 1993 edition.

j) IV included under III.
k) Business services included under IV.
m) Excludes sewerage services.
n) Publishing included under IV.
p) V included under IV.
q) Repair services included in IV.
r) Excludes sanitary and similar services.
s) Refers to public administration and defence.
t) Other producers included under V.
u) Industries of general government included under V.

Table F. Government employment as a percentage of total employment[1]

	1960	1968	1974	1980	1981	1982	1983	1984	1985	1986	1987	1988	1989	1990	Average				
															60-67	68-73	74-79	80-90	60-90
United States	14.7	17.0	16.1	15.4	15.3	15.4	15.3	14.8	14.8	14.8	14.6	14.4	14.4	..	15.8	16.7	16.0	..	..
Japan	..	..	6.3	6.7	6.7	6.7	6.6	6.6	6.4	6.4	6.4	6.3	6.1	6.0	..	..	6.5	6.4	..
Germany	8.0	10.9	13.0	14.6	14.8	15.1	15.4	15.5	15.5	15.6	15.6	15.6	15.5	15.1	9.4	11.5	14.0	15.3	12.8
France	..	..	..	20.0	20.5	21.0	21.6	22.1	22.8	23.1	23.1	23.0	22.8	22.6	..	..	..	..	..
United Kingdom	14.8	17.5	19.6	21.1	21.8	22.0	22.4	22.0	21.7	21.8	21.4	20.8	19.6	19.2	15.6	18.5	20.9	21.3	19.2
Italy	..	..	13.4	14.5	14.8	14.9	14.9	15.1	15.2	15.2	15.5	15.6	15.7	15.5	..	..	14.1	15.2	..
Canada	..	18.6	19.8	18.8	18.9	19.9	20.2	20.0	19.9	19.7	19.8	19.4	19.4	19.7	..	19.6	19.9	19.6	19.5
Total of above countries	11.4	13.3	14.0	14.4	14.4	14.6	14.6	14.5	14.5	14.5	14.4	14.3	14.1	14.0	12.2	13.6	14.4	14.4	13.7
Austria	10.6	12.8	15.0	17.3	17.7	18.3	18.8	19.3	19.6	20.0	20.4	20.6	20.7	20.6	11.3	13.6	16.3	19.4	15.6
Belgium	12.2	14.0	14.7	18.9	19.5	19.9	19.9	20.2	20.4	20.8	20.1	20.2	19.9	19.5	12.9	14.2	16.6	19.9	16.3
Denmark	..	15.2	22.2	28.3	29.8	30.8	31.0	30.2	29.7	29.2	29.1	29.4	30.2	30.5	..	18.0	24.6	29.8	24.4
Finland	7.7	11.0	13.8	17.8	18.4	18.9	19.4	19.7	20.3	20.7	21.3	21.7	21.9	22.4	8.9	12.0	16.0	20.2	14.9
Greece	..	..	..	..	..	..	..	..	..	..	..	..	..	..	..	..	..	..	..
Iceland	..	11.6	11.6	15.7	17.1	16.8	17.0	16.4	16.5	16.8	16.9	17.4	17.6	13.7	..	12.4	14.6	15.3	..
Ireland	..	..	12.6	14.5	15.1	15.8	15.8	15.9	15.9	15.9	15.7	15.2	14.3	10.9	..	..	13.7	11.1	..
Luxembourg	..	..	9.5	10.8	10.8	11.0	11.1	11.3	11.5	11.4	11.3	11.4	11.1	14.7	..	..	10.0	11.1	..
Netherlands	11.7	11.9	13.3	14.9	15.4	15.9	16.2	16.1	16.0	15.8	15.7	15.4	15.1	14.7	11.6	12.4	14.1	15.6	13.7
Norway	..	15.4	19.0	23.2	23.9	24.4	25.1	25.2	25.2	24.8	25.1	25.7	26.9	27.7	..	17.0	21.0	25.2	19.8
Portugal	3.9	6.1	8.0	10.0	10.3	11.0	11.5	11.9	12.2	12.8	12.9	13.1	13.2	14.1	..	7.1	..	..	..
Spain	..	6.5	9.3	11.9	12.0	12.6	13.2	13.5	14.3	14.6	13.2	13.4	13.9	14.1	..	..	..	..	..
Sweden	12.8	18.4	24.8	30.3	31.1	31.7	32.1	32.6	32.5	32.2	31.6	31.5	31.6	31.7	14.6	21.2	27.3	31.7	24.4
Switzerland	6.4	7.4	8.9	10.7	10.7	10.9	11.1	11.3	11.2	10.7	10.7	10.9	11.0	11.0	6.6	8.0	10.0	10.9	9.1
Turkey	..	..	..	..	..	..	..	..	..	..	..	..	..	..	..	..	..	..	..
Smaller European	8.9	10.6	13.4	16.7	17.2	17.7	18.2	18.5	18.8	18.8	18.3	18.4	18.5	18.5	9.5	11.7	14.9	18.1	14.0
Australia[2]	23.0	23.8	24.3	26.0	25.8	26.0	27.0	26.8	26.7	25.8	25.3	24.1	23.0	22.8	23.3	23.8	25.9	25.4	24.6
New Zealand	17.9	18.4	17.9	19.2	19.3	19.0	19.1	18.9	18.1	18.6	18.6	19.2	19.2	19.1	17.8	18.4	18.6	19.1	..
Total smaller	10.4	12.2	14.8	17.9	18.3	18.8	19.3	19.6	19.8	19.7	19.3	19.2	19.2	19.1	11.1	13.2	16.3	19.1	15.4
Total EEC	11.1	13.0	15.1	16.9	17.3	17.6	18.0	18.1	18.2	18.3	18.2	18.1	17.8	17.6	11.8	13.8	16.1	17.8	15.2
Total OECD-Europe	11.0	13.0	15.3	17.3	17.7	18.0	18.4	18.5	18.7	18.8	18.6	18.5	18.3	18.1	11.8	13.9	16.4	18.3	15.4
Total OECD less USA	10.0	11.6	13.3	14.7	15.0	15.2	15.4	15.5	15.6	15.6	15.5	15.4	15.1	15.0	10.6	12.3	14.2	15.3	13.3
Total OECD	11.2	13.1	14.1	15.1	15.1	15.3	15.4	15.3	15.3	15.3	15.2	15.0	14.9	14.8	12.0	13.5	14.7	15.1	13.9

1. Figures for the majority of countries are based on the OECD annual publication *National Accounts*. For the remaining countries (Canada, Australia, New Zealand, France, Ireland, Spain and Switzerland) data are from national sources. They are a close approximation to the institutional sector "General Government" as defined in the SNA. Figures for Iceland, the Netherlands and Norway refer to man-years.
2. Including public enterprises
Source: OECD, *Historical Statistics*, Table 1.13.

Table G. Public expenditure[1] and participant inflows[2] in labour market programmes in OECD countries – 1990

Programme categories	Australia	Austria	Belgium	Canada	Denmark	Finland	France	Germany	Greece	Ireland	Italy	Japan	Luxembourg
1. Public employment services and administration													
• Public expenditures	0.09	0.11	0.18	0.23	0.09	0.11	0.13	0.22	0.08	0.13	..	0.02	0.03
2. Labour market training													
• Public expenditures	0.07	0.10	0.14	0.27	0.27.	0.24	0.33	0.38	0.24	0.49	..	0.03	0.01
• *Participant inflows*	*1.09*	*1.30*	*1.90*	*2.00*	*6.10*	*1.40*	*..*	*2.5*	*1.00*	*2.50*	*..*		
3. Youth measures													
• Public expenditures	0.04	0.01	–	0.02	0.26	0.05	0.21	0.04	0.03	0.46	..	–	0.12
• *Participant inflows*	*0.70*	*0.20*	*–*	*0.50*	*1.60*	*0.20*	*3.00*	*0.60*	*0.30*	*2.90*	*..*	*–*	
4. Subsidised employment													
• Public expenditures	0.03	0.05	0.58	0.02	0.30	0.45	0.07	0.17	0.14	0.28	..	0.07	0.06
• *Participant inflows*	*0.50*	*0.50*	*3.10*	*0.10*	*1.70*	*2.90*	*1.00*	*0.40*	*1.00*	*1.30*	*..*		
5. Measures for the disabled													
• Public expenditures	0.04	0.05	0.16	–	0.34	0.13	0.06	0.23	0.01	0.14	..	0.01	0.13
• *Participant inflows*	*0.10*	*0.50*	*..*	*–*	*2.10*	*0.60*	*..*	*0.30*	*–*	*–*	*..*		*–*
6. Unemployment compensation													
• Public expenditures	1.11	0.86	1.96	1.92	3.17	0.63	1.31	1.09	0.43	2.83	0.55	0.32	0.17
7. Early retirement for labour market reasons													
• Public expenditures	–	0.11	0.75	–	1.21	0.50	0.56	0.02	–	0.05	0.29	–	0.56
TOTAL													
• Public expenditures	1.38	1.29	3.78	2.46	5.64	2.11	2.66	2.14	0.93	4.39	..	0.45	1.09

Table G. *cont'd* **Public expenditure[1] and participant inflows[2] in labour market programmes in OECD countries – 1990**

Programme categories	Netherlands	New Zealand	Norway	Portugal	Spain	Sweden	Switzerland	United Kingdom	United States
1. Public employment services and administration									
• Public expenditures	0.09	0.16	0.14	0.11	0.13	0.21	0.06	0.15	0.08
2. Labour market training									
• Public expenditures	0.21	0.39	0.36	0.14	0.10	0.53	0.01	0.23	0.11
• *Participant inflows*	*1.40*	*5.10*	*2.70*	*2.00*	*1.20*	*2.20*	*0.20*	*1.10*	*0.90*
3. Youth measures									
• Public expenditures	0.07	0.03	0.13	0.25	0.07	0.07	0.04	0.19	0.03
• *Participant inflows*	*0.90*	*0.30*	*..*	*2.70*	*0.70*	*0.30*	*0.60*	*0.80*	*0.50*
4. Subsidised employment									
• Public expenditures	0.05	0.19	0.18	0.07	0.45	0.13	–	0.02	0.01
• *Participant inflows*	*0.30*	*1.60*	*..*	*1.00*	*5.40*	*0.60*	–	*0.10*	*0.40*
5. Measures for the disabled									
• Public expenditures	0.63	0.06	0.20	0.06	–	0.75	0.14	0.03	0.04
• *Participant inflows*	*0.10*	*..*	*..*	*0.10*	–	*0.60*	*..*	*0.10*	*0.80*
6. Unemployment compensation									
• Public expenditures	2.17	1.90	1.17	0.31	2.42	0.80	0.14	0.95	0.50
7. Early retirement for labour market reasons									
• Public expenditures	–	–	–	0.11	–	0.08	–	–	–
TOTAL									
• Public expenditures	3.22	2.73	2.18	1.05	3.17	2.57	0.39	1.56	0.76

1. Public expenditures as percentages of GDP.
2. Participant inflows as percentages of the labour force.
.. Data not available.
– Nil or less than half of the last digit used.
Source : OECD *Employment Outlook*, July 1993, Paris, Table 2.B.1.

MAIN SALES OUTLETS OF OECD PUBLICATIONS
PRINCIPAUX POINTS DE VENTE DES PUBLICATIONS DE L'OCDE

ARGENTINA – ARGENTINE
Carlos Hirsch S.R.L.
Galería Güemes, Florida 165, 4° Piso
1333 Buenos Aires   Tel. (1) 331.1787 y 331.2391
                     Telefax: (1) 331.1787

AUSTRALIA – AUSTRALIE
D.A. Information Services
648 Whitehorse Road, P.O.B 163
Mitcham, Victoria 3132   Tel. (03) 873.4411
                          Telefax: (03) 873.5679

AUSTRIA – AUTRICHE
Gerold & Co.
Graben 31
Wien I   Tel. (0222) 533.50.14

BELGIUM – BELGIQUE
Jean De Lannoy
Avenue du Roi 202
B-1060 Bruxelles   Tel. (02) 538.51.69/538.08.41
                    Telefax: (02) 538.08.41

CANADA
Renouf Publishing Company Ltd.
1294 Algoma Road
Ottawa, ON K1B 3W8   Tel. (613) 741.4333
                      Telefax: (613) 741.5439
Stores:
61 Sparks Street
Ottawa, ON K1P 5R1   Tel. (613) 238.8985
211 Yonge Street
Toronto, ON M5B 1M4   Tel. (416) 363.3171
                       Telefax: (416)363.59.63

Les Éditions La Liberté Inc.
3020 Chemin Sainte-Foy
Sainte-Foy, PQ G1X 3V6   Tel. (418) 658.3763
                          Telefax: (418) 658.3763

Federal Publications Inc.
165 University Avenue, Suite 701
Toronto, ON M5H 3B8   Tel. (416) 860.1611
                       Telefax: (416) 860.1608

Les Publications Fédérales
1185 Université
Montréal, QC H3B 3A7   Tel. (514) 954.1633
                        Telefax : (514) 954.1635

CHINA – CHINE
China National Publications Import
Export Corporation (CNPIEC)
16 Gongti E. Road, Chaoyang District
P.O. Box 88 or 50
Beijing 100704 PR   Tel. (01) 506.6688
                     Telefax: (01) 506.3101

DENMARK – DANEMARK
Munksgaard Book and Subscription Service
35, Nørre Søgade, P.O. Box 2148
DK-1016 København K   Tel. (33) 12.85.70
                       Telefax: (33) 12.93.87

FINLAND – FINLANDE
Akateeminen Kirjakauppa
Keskuskatu 1, P.O. Box 128
00100 Helsinki
Subscription Services/Agence d'abonnements :
P.O. Box 23
00371 Helsinki   Tel. (358 0) 12141
                  Telefax: (358 0) 121.4450

FRANCE
OECD/OCDE
Mail Orders/Commandes par correspondance:
2, rue André-Pascal
75775 Paris Cedex 16   Tel. (33-1) 45.24.82.00
                        Telefax: (33-1) 49.10.42.76
                        Telex: 640048 OCDE

OECD Bookshop/Librairie de l'OCDE :
33, rue Octave-Feuillet
75016 Paris   Tel. (33-1) 45.24.81.67
               (33-1) 45.24.81.81
Documentation Française
29, quai Voltaire
75007 Paris   Tel. 40.15.70.00
Gibert Jeune (Droit-Économie)
6, place Saint-Michel
75006 Paris   Tel. 43.25.91.19
Librairie du Commerce International
10, avenue d'Iéna
75016 Paris   Tel. 40.73.34.60
Librairie Dunod
Université Paris-Dauphine
Place du Maréchal de Lattre de Tassigny
75016 Paris   Tel. (1) 44.05.40.13
Librairie Lavoisier
11, rue Lavoisier
75008 Paris   Tel. 42.65.39.95
Librairie L.G.D.J. - Montchrestien
20, rue Soufflot
75005 Paris   Tel. 46.33.89.85
Librairie des Sciences Politiques
30, rue Saint-Guillaume
75007 Paris   Tel. 45.48.36.02
P.U.F.
49, boulevard Saint-Michel
75005 Paris   Tel. 43.25.83.40
Librairie de l'Université
12a, rue Nazareth
13100 Aix-en-Provence   Tel. (16) 42.26.18.08
Documentation Française
165, rue Garibaldi
69003 Lyon   Tel. (16) 78.63.32.23
Librairie Decitre
29, place Bellecour
69002 Lyon   Tel. (16) 72.40.54.54

GERMANY – ALLEMAGNE
OECD Publications and Information Centre
August-Bebel-Allee 6
D-53175 Bonn 2   Tel. (0228) 959.120
                  Telefax: (0228) 959.12.17

GREECE – GRÈCE
Librairie Kauffmann
Mavrokordatou 9
106 78 Athens   Tel. (01) 32.55.321
                 Telefax: (01) 36.33.967

HONG-KONG
Swindon Book Co. Ltd.
13–15 Lock Road
Kowloon, Hong Kong   Tel. 366.80.31
                      Telefax: 739.49.75

HUNGARY – HONGRIE
Euro Info Service
POB 1271
1464 Budapest   Tel. (1) 111.62.16
                 Telefax : (1) 111.60.61

ICELAND – ISLANDE
Mál Mog Menning
Laugavegi 18, Pósthólf 392
121 Reykjavik   Tel. 162.35.23

INDIA – INDE
Oxford Book and Stationery Co.
Scindia House
New Delhi 110001   Tel.(11) 331.5896/5308
                    Telefax: (11) 332.5993
17 Park Street
Calcutta 700016   Tel. 240832

INDONESIA – INDONÉSIE
Pdii-Lipi
P.O. Box 269/JKSMG/88
Jakarta 12790   Tel. 583467
                 Telex: 62 875

IRELAND – IRLANDE
TDC Publishers – Library Suppliers
12 North Frederick Street
Dublin 1   Tel. (01) 874.48.35
            Telefax: (01) 874.84.16

ISRAEL
Electronic Publications only
Publications électroniques seulement
Praedicta
5 Shatna Street
P.O. Box 34030
Jerusalem 91340   Tel. (2) 52.84.90/1/2
                   Telefax: (2) 52.84.93

ITALY – ITALIE
Libreria Commissionaria Sansoni
Via Duca di Calabria 1/1
50125 Firenze   Tel. (055) 64.54.15
                 Telefax: (055) 64.12.57
Via Bartolini 29
20155 Milano   Tel. (02) 36.50.83
Editrice e Libreria Herder
Piazza Montecitorio 120
00186 Roma   Tel. 679.46.28
              Telefax: 678.47.51
Libreria Hoepli
Via Hoepli 5
20121 Milano   Tel. (02) 86.54.46
                Telefax: (02) 805.28.86
Libreria Scientifica
Dott. Lucio de Biasio 'Aeiou'
Via Coronelli, 6
20146 Milano   Tel. (02) 48.95.45.52
                Telefax: (02) 48.95.45.48

JAPAN – JAPON
OECD Publications and Information Centre
Landic Akasaka Building
2-3-4 Akasaka, Minato-ku
Tokyo 107   Tel. (81.3) 3586.2016
             Telefax: (81.3) 3584.7929

KOREA – CORÉE
Kyobo Book Centre Co. Ltd.
P.O. Box 1658, Kwang Hwa Moon
Seoul   Tel. 730.78.91
         Telefax: 735.00.30

MALAYSIA – MALAISIE
Co-operative Bookshop Ltd.
University of Malaya
P.O. Box 1127, Jalan Pantai Baru
59700 Kuala Lumpur
Malaysia   Tel. 756.5000/756.5425
            Telefax: 757.3661

MEXICO – MEXIQUE
Revistas y Periodicos Internacionales S.A. de C.V.
Florencia 57 - 1004
Mexico, D.F. 06600   Tel. 207.81.00
                      Telefax : 208.39.79

NETHERLANDS – PAYS-BAS
SDU Uitgeverij Plantijnstraat
Externe Fondsen
Postbus 20014
2500 EA's-Gravenhage   Tel. (070) 37.89.880
Voor bestellingen: Telefax: (070) 34.75.778

NEW ZEALAND
NOUVELLE-ZÉLANDE
Legislation Services
P.O. Box 12418
Thorndon, Wellington   Tel. (04) 496.5652
                              Telefax: (04) 496.5698

NORWAY – NORVÈGE
Narvesen Info Center – NIC
Bertrand Narvesens vei 2
P.O. Box 6125 Etterstad
0602 Oslo 6   Tel. (022) 57.33.00
                              Telefax: (022) 68.19.01

PAKISTAN
Mirza Book Agency
65 Shahrah Quaid-E-Azam
Lahore 54000   Tel. (42) 353.601
                              Telefax: (42) 231.730

PHILIPPINE – PHILIPPINES
International Book Center
5th Floor, Filipinas Life Bldg.
Ayala Avenue
Metro Manila   Tel. 81.96.76
                              Telex 23312 RHP PH

PORTUGAL
Livraria Portugal
Rua do Carmo 70-74
Apart. 2681
1200 Lisboa   Tel.: (01) 347.49.82/5
                              Telefax: (01) 347.02.64

SINGAPORE – SINGAPOUR
Gower Asia Pacific Pte Ltd.
Golden Wheel Building
41, Kallang Pudding Road, No. 04-03
Singapore 1334   Tel. 741.5166
                              Telefax: 742.9356

SPAIN – ESPAGNE
Mundi-Prensa Libros S.A.
Castelló 37, Apartado 1223
Madrid 28001   Tel. (91) 431.33.99
                              Telefax: (91) 575.39.98

Libreria Internacional AEDOS
Consejo de Ciento 391
08009 – Barcelona   Tel. (93) 488.30.09
                              Telefax: (93) 487.76.59
Llibreria de la Generalitat
Palau Moja
Rambla dels Estudis, 118
08002 – Barcelona
                    (Subscripcions) Tel. (93) 318.80.12
                    (Publicacions) Tel. (93) 302.67.23
                         Telefax: (93) 412.18.54

SRI LANKA
Centre for Policy Research
c/o Colombo Agencies Ltd.
No. 300-304, Galle Road
Colombo 3   Tel. (1) 574240, 573551-2
                      Telefax: (1) 575394, 510711

SWEDEN – SUÈDE
Fritzes Information Center
Box 16356
Regeringsgatan 12
106 47 Stockholm   Tel. (08) 690.90.90
                              Telefax: (08) 20.50.21

Subscription Agency/Agence d'abonnements :
Wennergren-Williams Info AB
P.O. Box 1305
171 25 Solna   Tel. (08) 705.97.50
                              Téléfax : (08) 27.00.71

SWITZERLAND – SUISSE
Maditec S.A. (Books and Periodicals - Livres
et périodiques)
Chemin des Palettes 4
Case postale 266
1020 Renens   Tel. (021) 635.08.65
                              Telefax: (021) 635.07.80

Librairie Payot S.A.
4, place Pépinet
CP 3212
1002 Lausanne   Tel. (021) 341.33.48
                              Telefax: (021) 341.33.45

Librairie Unilivres
6, rue de Candolle
1205 Genève   Tel. (022) 320.26.23
                              Telefax: (022) 329.73.18

Subscription Agency/Agence d'abonnements :
Dynapresse Marketing S.A.
38 avenue Vibert
1227 Carouge   Tel.: (022) 308.07.89
                              Telefax : (022) 308.07.99

See also – Voir aussi :
OECD Publications and Information Centre
August-Bebel-Allee 6
D-53175 Bonn 2 (Germany)   Tel. (0228) 959.120
                              Telefax: (0228) 959.12.17

TAIWAN – FORMOSE
Good Faith Worldwide Int'l. Co. Ltd.
9th Floor, No. 118, Sec. 2
Chung Hsiao E. Road
Taipei   Tel. (02) 391.7396/391.7397
                              Telefax: (02) 394.9176

THAILAND – THAÏLANDE
Suksit Siam Co. Ltd.
113, 115 Fuang Nakhon Rd.
Opp. Wat Rajbopith
Bangkok 10200   Tel. (662) 225.9531/2
                              Telefax: (662) 222.5188

TURKEY – TURQUIE
Kültür Yayinlari Is-Türk Ltd. Sti.
Atatürk Bulvari No. 191/Kat 13
Kavaklidere/Ankara   Tel. 428.11.40 Ext. 2458
Dolmabahce Cad. No. 29
Besiktas/Istanbul   Tel. 260.71.88
                              Telex: 43482B

UNITED KINGDOM – ROYAUME-UNI
HMSO
Gen. enquiries   Tel. (071) 873 0011
Postal orders only:
P.O. Box 276, London SW8 5DT
Personal Callers HMSO Bookshop
49 High Holborn, London WC1V 6HB
                         Telefax: (071) 873 8200
Branches at: Belfast, Birmingham, Bristol, Edin-
burgh, Manchester

UNITED STATES – ÉTATS-UNIS
OECD Publications and Information Centre
2001 L Street N.W., Suite 700
Washington, D.C. 20036-4910 Tel. (202) 785.6323
                              Telefax: (202) 785.0350

VENEZUELA
Libreria del Este
Avda F. Miranda 52, Aptdo. 60337
Edificio Galipán
Caracas 106   Tel. 951.1705/951.2307/951.1297
                       Telegram: Libreste Caracas

Subscription to OECD periodicals may also be
placed through main subscription agencies.

Les abonnements aux publications périodiques de
l'OCDE peuvent être souscrits auprès des
principales agences d'abonnement.

Orders and inquiries from countries where Distribu-
tors have not yet been appointed should be sent to:
OECD Publications Service, 2 rue André-Pascal,
75775 Paris Cedex 16, France.

Les commandes provenant de pays où l'OCDE n'a
pas encore désigné de distributeur devraient être
adressées à : OCDE, Service des Publications,
2, rue André-Pascal, 75775 Paris Cedex 16, France.

3-1994

OECD PUBLICATIONS, 2 rue André-Pascal, 75775 PARIS CEDEX 16
PRINTED IN FRANCE
(81 94 05 1) ISBN 92-64-14111-1 - No. 46627 1994